SIKH RELIGION

"ਬਿਨੁ ਉਪਮਾ ਜਗਦੀਸ਼ ਕੀ ਬਿਨਸੈ ਨ ਅੰਧਿਆਰਾ ॥"

"Without praise of the Almighty,
Darkness shalt prevail in one's mind."
(Guru Nanak)

**Sikh Missionary Center
P.O. Box 02664
Detroit, Michigan 48202**

ACKNOWLEDGMENT

The Sikh Missionary Center is grateful to all the contributors for their financial assistance and moral support in publication of this book.

ISBN: 0-9625383-0-2

Printed By: Braun-Brumfield, Inc.
Ann Arbor, Michigan U.S.A.

Contents

INTRODUCTION

Sikh religion was founded by Guru Nanak in the form of ten Gurus (1469 - 1708) in India. The tenth Master, Guru Gobind Singh ended the personal Guruship and proclaimed Guru Granth Sahib (Holy Scripture) as the last Guru forever.

Guru Granth Sahib was written and compiled by the Gurus themselves and hence it is authentic. Nobody is allowed to change even a comma or a period in it (1430 pages).

Guru Granth Sahib does not narrate the life story of the Gurus, but it is wholly dedicated to the glory of the Almighty God only. Sikhism is not a blend or a reproduction of earlier religions but it is a new revelation altogether. The teachings that the Gurus gave to this world, came DIRECT to them from God, which the Gurus confirm:

'This Word comes from Him, Who hath created the world.'
(Guru Nanak)

To attain salvation, Sikhism rejects all fasts, rites and rituals. It rejects the claims of Yoga, mortification of body, self-torture, penances and renunciation. Sikhism does not believe in the worship of gods and goddesses, stones, statues, idols, pictures, tombs or crematoriums. Only One God, the Formless, is to be Glorified.

The Gurus preached Sikh religion strictly as monotheistic-requiring belief in none other than One Supreme Being only.

The idealistic approach of Sikhism is that it recognizes the existence of the same heavenly Light in every human being, rich or poor, high or low irrespective of caste, creed, color, race, sex, religion or nationality. Therefore the doors of the Sikh temple called Gurdwara (House of the Guru) are open for all in this world without any prejudice or social discrimination. Every person in this world has equal right to enter and join the services in the Gurdwara.

The institution of Langar (Guru's free Kitchen) was started by the first Guru and strengthened further by the later Gurus. The rules of the Langar require that all should sit in the same row and partake of the same food without any discrimination of being high or low, rich or poor, and prince or the peasant. The institution of Langar, thus, translates the principle of equality into practice. It was the injunction of the third Guru that none would have his audience unless one had eaten in the Langar. Even Akbar, the Emperor of India, had to sit with common people and dine before he could see the Guru.

Before we proceed translating Gurbani (Divine Word) to English, we confess to our limitations since there is no authentic English version of our holy scripture to guide us. This is so because each translation would reflect the translator's ability to understand both the languages. His dedication and involvement with religion would be evident in his work. This will result in diverse translations leaving no standardized version. In the case of our scripture there are numerous difficulties encountered by a translator. For example, "Sidh Gosht" - Guru Nanak's dialogue with the Sidhas, the concept of "NAM", the exhortation - "Nam Japo", concept of "Sehaj Anand" and "Onkar", are highly difficult to translate. The English word 'name' is not at all synonymous for 'NAM'. This is a Herculean task since the English speaking people know no such thing as the 'True Name' nor can they comprehend the practice of 'Nam Japna'. There is no existing vocabulary to help translate these and a lot more abstract thoughts listed in Guru Granth Sahib.

While reading this book it should be remembered that it is completely impossible to justly translate any one language to another. Translation is not an exact science and therefore, literal interpretation of Gurbani is unachievable- there can be no accurate and definitive translation of our scripture. We, the authors, have endeavored to translate Gurbani to English, while preserving the quintessence of its message as ordained by the Guru.

All quotations are from Guru Granth Sahib unless otherwise noted. The English translation of the original verses has been taken from the various authors whichever was found most befitting, and Sikh Missionary Center is most grateful to all those authors.

The purpose of this book is to spread the doctrine of Sikhism as laid down by the Gurus. There is no limit to the praise of the Almighty, but the authors have attempted to express Guru's Divine Message and the Glory of His Kingdom in few and simple terms.

Nam is the central theme in the hymns of Guru Granth Sahib. Power of Nam is glorified and admired in Sikh Scripture. It is the cure of all sufferings. In Guru Granth Sahib, Nam is another name for God. It is Nam that sustains all beings and the universe. He is not a mental abstraction. He is the source of all life- physical as well as spiritual. Nothing is so perfect that it could or would exist apart from and independent of Nam (HIM).

Rebirth in descending order is a punishment and curse for one's deeds. The soul passes through animal lives suffering untold agonies. Human life is a blessing. Human being is the crown of His Creation. Man has the capacity of being conscious of his own being. He has the capability to attain the highest pinnacle of spiritual advancement. Human form is the opportunity for the spiritual and moral progress. No religion and no philosophy can exist without man. Sikh Gurus sing the nobility of human being because he has the awareness of the Divine and it is only through human body that one can get salvation by meditating on Nam. Man cannot find his way to salvation through intellectual acrobatics and speculative ventures or ceaseless trance. It is achieved only through meditation on Nam. When the Gurus and the Bhaktas (saints) sing the Praises of the Lord, they sing them to man. They encourage man to advance to the loftiest peaks of spiritual glory. The exhortation "Nam Japo" by the Gurus is directed towards man because the highest spiritual goal is within the reach of man only. "Nam Japo" aims at spiritual evolution which is the ultimate goal of Guru's Sikh.

"Were there any one Thy equal, O God, I'd praise Thee before him. (Since Thou hast neither equal nor rival) There- fore I will praise Thee before Thyself. Thy Name giveth sight to me, the blind."

(Guru Nanak)

With complete dedication and full humility, we extend our salute to our Lord, the Supreme Monarch.

March, 1990   Sikh Missionary Center

GURU - THE DIVINE LIGHT

The word Guru is so popular in India that in order to understand the fundamental concept of 'guru' in Sikhism, one must first completely drive out of one's mind the prevalent popular notion of a guru. The popular term 'guru' often used for a Brahman, a yogic teacher or a guide or even a school teacher, has made the Guruship so cheap that a scholar describes these gurus as 'wicks which smell foul after the lamps are extinguished.'

The term 'Guru' in Sikhism is not used for a teacher or a guide or an expert or even a human body. The word Guru is composed of two terms-

GU- means darkness and
RU- means Light.

In Sikhism the word 'Guru' is, thus, defined as the Light that dispels all darkness, and that is called JOT (Divine Light). Guru Nanak was, therefore, the EMBODIMENT of Divine Light:

'Gur Nanak Dev Govind roop.'
(Basant Mohalla 5, p-1192,
Guru Granth Sahib)
'Guru Nanak is embodiment of the Light of God.'
(Translation of the above)

The Guru in Sikhism is a perfect Prophet or Messenger of God in whom the Light of God shines fully, visibly and completely. Guru is in union with Divine. Thus he ushers the devotees, the seekers of Truth into a spiritual birth. Through him the Glory of the Lord is transmitted to humanity. On account of his Divine prerogatives, the Guru, though human in form, is Divine in Spirit.

Literally Guru Nanak's body was a platform from which God Himself spoke and delivered His message- Gurbani (Divine Word). God manifested Himself through Guru Nanak:

'Gur meh aap samoai sabad vartaya.'
(Var Malar ki Mohalla 1, p-1279)

'In the true Guru (Nanak) He installed His Own Spirit
Through him, God speaketh Himself.'
                        (Translation of the above)
In another place in Gurbani it is said:

'Gur meh aap rakhaya kartare.'
                    (Maru Mohalla 1(15), p-1024)
'In the body of Guru (Nanak) God revealeth Himself.'
                        (Translation of the above)

God is in the Guru and Guru is in God. Though God is
everywhere and in everybody but His traits are illuminated
through the Guru. The Jot (Divine Light) that enshrined Guru
Nanak's body and the Primal Jot of God are, therefore, one and
the same:
'Gur Nanak Nanak har soai.'
                    (Gaund Mohalla 5, p-865)
'O Nanak, Jot of Nanak and God are one.'
                        (Translation of the above)

Again the Janamsakhis (biographies) reveal that God spoke
to Guru Nanak and said:

'Mei aad parmeshar aur tu gur parmeshar.'

'I am the Primal God and thou art Guru God.'

Guru Nanak never claimed that only his disciples or devotees could get salvation or go to heaven. Since he was the embodiment of Divine Light, and as the Divine Light does not belong to
any particular sect or religion, so he stood guarantee for the entire
humanity, and said,"Whosoever meditates upon One God, the
Formless, will get salvation."

'Jo jo japai so hoi punit Bhagat bhai lavai man hit.'
                    (Gauri Sukhmani Mohalla 5, p-290)

'He shall become pure whosoever repeateth His Name

With devotion, affection and heartfelt love.'
(Translation of the above)

When Guru Nanak conferred Guruship on Bhai Lehna (later called Guru Angad), the JOT was passed on and Guru Angad too became the embodiment of Divine Light. In the same way all the nine Gurus were the embodiments of Gur Nanak Jot[1]. The tenth Master, Guru Gobind Singh then conferred the Guruship on the Adi Granth (Holy Scripture), which too became the embodiment of Divine Light. Gur Nanak JOT is, therefore, enshrined and preserved in Guru Granth Sahib (it is no longer the Adi Granth, but the Guru Granth), and **it is the Living Guru forever. For the Sikhs, the Guru Granth is the manifestation of the Guru's Spirit and through it, Guru Nanak lives on in the Sikh Faith.**

Sikhism endeavors to uplift the human soul from the shackles of Maya (materialism). It aims at a virtuous life which leads to the ultimate realization of a state of Eternal Bliss. The objective of Guru Nanak's Guruship was to give instructions in the True Name, to save humanity from immersing in the ocean of distress and misery arising out of worldly life, and to blend the human souls with their Creator, thus, emancipating them from the cycle of transmigration breaking all barriers and bonds of sufferings. This is the essential character of Sikh faith.

The law of Karma or fatalism is repugnant to Sikh Religion as it does not reconcile with the merciful trait of the Almighty Lord. There is no such thing in Sikhism as eternal damnation or an everlasting pit of fire created by the revengeful God. Guru's grace erases the blot of thousands of evil deeds of the past and the present. It is also the savior of the future. Meditation on Nam burns countless sins. **Singing the glory of the Lord through the Divine Word, can redeem a repentant sinner and, thus, doctrine of Karma ceases to operate. Such is the splendor of Guru Nanak's doctrine of God's Grace and Compassion.**

1: *Gur Nanak Jot is not a human body but the Divine Light.*

INDIA BEFORE GURU NANAK

After its climax, Buddhism started degenerating in India. Statues of Buddha and Budhisattvas became very common and were installed in their temples. Buddhist monks preached lesson of non-violence and non-resistance which made the people non-aggressive even in self defence.

When Buddhism was driven out of India, the Hindu society set up their own gods and goddesses and began to worship their stone images. The Hindu priests who had been for centuries, the self-made custodians of religion and its teachings, had reduced the religion to a mockery performing rites and rituals and superstitious ceremonies devoid of any sense and meaning.

> "The Hindu leaders neglected to teach the spiritual realities to the people at large who were sunk in superstitions and materialism. Religion became confused with caste distinction and taboos about eating and drinking...,"

writes Dr. S. Radhakrishnan, a philosopher and former President of India.

The Hindu society was over-ridden with caste system. The religion became the privilege only of the upper class called the Brahmans. The sacred religious books were neither accessible to the other classes nor could the people understand them because they were written mostly in Sanskrit, a language not spoken by the masses. Religious reading, writing and teaching was strictly the monopoly of the Brahmans. The lowest of the lowest class was called the Untouchables. A touch or even a shadow of these untouchables seemed to pollute the higher classes.

Such was the condition of Hindu India when Muslim invaders from the west began pouring in large numbers one after the other. For the Muslim invaders, from Mahmood of Gazni in the eleventh century to the Moghuls in the sixteenth century (at the time of Guru Nanak), the Punjab was always the gateway of India. All these Muslim invaders massacred men, women and children without mercy, plundered their homes, desecrated and demolished their temples and robbed the wealth of these temples. The Hindus were converted to Islam at the point of the sword. Nobles, scholars, sufies, poets and philosophers who also came along with these invaders, settled in the various parts of India, and they laid the foundation of Indo-Muslim culture in the country.

Many Muslim historians have given account of the happenings of that time. A few examples of the treatment of Hindus by the Mohammadan conquerors of India, are given below:

Shahab-ul-Din, King of Gazni (1170-1206), put Prithwi Raj, King of Ajmer and Delhi, to death in cold blood. He massacred thousands of the inhabitants of Ajmer who opposed him , reserving the remainder for slavery (The Kamiu-t Tawarikh by Asir).

In the Taj-ul-Ma'asir by Hassn Nizam-i-Naishapuri, it is stated that when Qutb-ul-Din Aibak (1194-1210) conquered Meerat, he demolished all the Hindu temples of the city and erected mosques on their sites. In the city of Aligarh, he converted Hindu inhabitants to Islam by the sword and beheaded all those who adhered to their own religion.

Abdulla Wassaf writes in his Tazjiyat-ul-Amsar wa Tajriyat ul Asar that when Ala-ul-Din Khilji (1295-1316) captured the city of Kambayat at the head of the gulf of Cambay, he killed the adult male Hindu inhabitants for the glory of Islam, set flowing rivers of blood, sent the women of the country with all their gold, silver, and jewels, to his own home, and made about twenty thousand maidens his private slaves.

Ala-ul-Din once asked his Qazi[1], what was the Mohammadan law prescribed for the Hindus. The Qazi replied, "Hindus are like the mud; if silver is demanded from them, they must with the greatest humility offer gold. If a Mohammadan desire to spit into a Hindu's mouth, the Hindu should open it wide for the purpose. God created the Hindus to be slaves of the Mohammadans. The Prophet hath ordained that, if the Hindus do not accept Islam, they should be imprisoned, tortured, finally put to death, and their property confiscated."

Sayad Mohammad Latif writes in his history of the Punjab, "Great jealousy and hatred existed those days between the Hindus

---

1: *Qazi- A Mohammadan high priest.*

and Mohammadans and the whole non-Muslim population was subject to persecution by the Mohammadan rulers."

Bhai Gurdas, a Sikh scholar, writes, "My Lord, it is strange that the people of Kalyug (dark age or the age of falsehood) have developed the attitude of a dog and they take pleasure in swallowing ill-gotten things. The rulers commit sins and those who are herdsmen, are killing the sheep themselves. The people being ignorant are not in a position to discriminate between truth and falsehood. Those who pose as benefactors are engaged in amassing wealth by fraudulent means. Love between man and woman is based on money, they meet at pleasure and depart at will. The Qazi who occupies the seat of justice, accepts bribes and then passes unjust orders."

Guru Nanak describes the situation as:

'Kings are butchers Cruelty their knife, and Sense of duty
and responsibility have taken wings and vanished.'
(Slok Mohalla 1, p-145)

It has always been believed that whenever the Righteousness vanishes from this world and the Falsehood takes its place, there has been a call from the Heaven to restore peace and justice on earth. Out of the dark clouds of falsehood, hypocrisy, injustice, cruelty and bigotry, there came a ray of sunshine from the Heaven as described by Bhai Gurdas, a Sikh apostle:
"Heaven at last heard the prayers of the people,
Guru Nanak was sent to the world.
The disciples met and drank the nectar of his Lotus
feet,
And realized the Divine in this age of materialism.

Guru Nanak re-established Dharma,
All castes he merged into one caste of man.
The rich and the poor he brought on one level,
From this Founder of Humanity a new race of love
goes forth;
In humility they bow down to each other.
The Master and the disciple became one,

His song of Nam gives us a new life,
He is the Saviour in this age of materialism.

Nanak came, the world was lighted,
The sun rose, the darkness disappeared.
Wherever the Guru put his foot,
It became the temple of worship.

The far-famed seats of the Sidhas changed their
                                        names,
The Yoga-houses became Guru-houses.
Humanity resounded with his divine hymns;
In every house of the disciple, the Lord was
                                        worshipped.
The Guru went in all directions,
Seeking his own all over the earth.
A river of love and peace Flows in us singing his song."
                    (Bhai Gurdas, Var 1-pauri 23,27)

Heaven at last heard the cries and prayers of the oppressed
and there appeared the Savior of Humanity, Prophet of Peace,
Fountain of Heavenly Love and Ocean of Virtue in the name of
GURU NANAK, the founder of Sikh religion.

GURU NANAK DEV
(1469 - 1539 A.D.)

Guru Nanak was born in 1469[1] at Rai Bhoeki Talwandi now known as Nankana Sahib situated in Punjab province of West Pakistan. This place is about 55 miles north-west of Lahore. His father, Mehta Kalu was a Patwari- an accountant of land revenue in the government. Guru's mother was Mata Tripta and he had one older sister, Bibi Nanki. From the very childhood, Bibi Nanki saw in him the Light of God but she did not reveal this secret to anyone. She is known as the first disciple of Guru Nanak.

GURU'S SCHOOLING:

At the age of seven, Guru Nanak was sent to school, which was run by teacher, Pandit Gopal Das, at his village. As usual the teacher started the lesson with an alphabet but the teacher was wonder-stuck when the Guru asked him to explain the meanings of the letters of the alphabet. However at the helplessness of his teacher, the Guru wrote the meanings of each and every letter of the alphabet. This was the first Divine Message delivered by Guru Nanak[2]. This was an explanation of deeper truth about human beings and God and the way to realize God in terms of the alphabet. The teacher stood abashed before the Divine Master and bowed to him. He then took him back to his father and said, "Mehtaji, your son is an Avtar (prophet) and has come to redeem the victims of Kalyug (the age of Falsehood). He is destined to be a world Teacher, there is nothing that I can teach him."

Many writers believe that Guru Nanak was first sent to different schools belonging to the Hindus and Muslims to learn about Vedas (Hindu Scriptures) and Quran (Muslim Scripture), and only after obtaining the knowledge from those scriptures, he

---

1: *The Puratan Janamsakhi (biography) and Bhai Gurdas give the birthdate as October 20 (Kartik) while others give it as April 15 (Baisakh) in 1469.*

2: *This is called Aad Bani (the first Divine Message). This refers to Rag Asa Mohalla 1- Patti Likhi, page-432 of Guru Granth Sahib.*

started his religion. According to Malcolm, Guru Nanak is said to have learnt all earthly scenes from Khizr -the Prophet Elias. "There is a reason to believe," writes Cunningham, "that in his youth he made himself familiar with the popular creeds both of Mohammedans and the Hindus and that he gained a general knowledge of the Quran and Brahmanical Shastras."

It seems that all these scholars of history have not grasped the basic fundamental fact about the divinity of Guru Nanak. He was born with divine status, thus, his teachings were heavenly. These writers seem to be very much ignorant of the fact that Guru Nanak was an **Embodiment of Divine Light.** He was a celestial being and his divine attributes put him above mankind and its schools. Historians have failed to visualize the splendor in Guru's Jot. Heavenly Spirit does not learn from man-made institutions. He was a heavenly messenger and a born world teacher who taught the mankind the path of righteousness and truth. Guru Nanak's divinity is above all earthly institutions and their teachings. The Message that Guru Nanak gave to this world, came to him direct from God as he confirms himself:

"O Lalo[3] as comes the Divine Word from God to me
So do I narrate it."
(Tilang Mohalla 1, p-722)
"I am saying what He commandeth me to say."
(Wadhans Mohalla 1, p-566)

It is also mentioned in the Janamsakhi (biography) that many times Guru Nanak said to his companion Mardana[4], "Mardana, play the rebec, the Divine Word is coming." This confirms the fact that education from the Hindu and Muslim religious institutions, **had no bearing at all on the Divine Word that Guru Nanak received from God and delivered to this world. To say that Guru went to different institutions to learn, is violating the sanctity of Guruship.**

3: *Lalo was Guru's disciple.*

4: *Mardana was a Muslim minstrel and Guru's disciple and constant companion.*

CEREMONY OF SACRED THREAD:

Guru Nanak was nine years old and according to the custom among the higher castes of Hindus, he was required to invest himself with the sacred thread called 'Janaeu'. Great preparations were made by his father for this ceremony. The family priest named Hardyal, started chanting Mantras (Hindu hymns) and was ready to put the thread around Guru's neck when he refused to wear it. The whole assembly was astonished. They tried to persuade him every way to wear the Janaeu but in vain. Then the Guru uttered the following Sabad[5]:

" Though men commit countless thefts, countless adultries,
    utter countless falsehoods and countless words of abuse
Though they commit countless robberies and villainies night
    and day against their fellow creatures;
Yet the cotton thread is spun, and the Brahman cometh to
    twist it.
For the ceremony they kill a goat and cook and eat it, and
    evreybody then saith 'Put on the Janaeu'
When it becometh old, it is thrown away, and another is put
    on,
Nanak, the string breaketh not if it is strong"
                           (Asa di Var, Mohalla 1, p-471)

The priest in utter despair asked, "What kind of sacred thread O Nanak, would you wear?" The Guru replied,

" Out of the cotton of compassion
Spin the thread of contentment
Tie knots of continence,
Give it twist of truth.
That would make a Janaeu for the soul,
If thou have it, O Brahman, put it on me.

5: *Word 'utter' is used in this book when Sabad is said to have come to Guru direct from God while 'recite' is used when the existing Sabad was repeated.*

Such a thread once worn will never break
Nor get soiled, burnt of lost,
The man who weareth such a thread is blessed."
(Asa di Var, Slok Mohalla 1,p-471)

COBRA SERVES THE DIVINE MASTER:

As usually is the case in villages, the father sent his son to graze the buffaloes in the pastures. One day while the Guru was grazing the buffaloes, he fell asleep under a tree and the herd destroyed the crops in the neighboring fields. When the owner saw his crops damaged, he became furious and lodged a complaint with Rai Bular, an officer-in-charge of that area. Rai Bular sent for the son and his father to adjust the quarrel. The Guru told them that no damage was done to the crops; rather it was blessed by God. Rai Bular sent his messengers to inspect the fields. But to everybody's surprise the investigators could not find any damage in the fields rather the crops were doubly blossoming. The field where this miracle happened is now known as Kiara Sahib.

On another day the Guru was sent to graze the buffaloes in the pastures and he fell asleep under the shade of a tree. As the sun rose higher, the shadow moved away. A big cobra came out of its den and provided shadow with its hood over the face of the Divine Master. Rai Bular happened to pass by that side with his attendants. When he saw this strange scene, he was convinced that the boy was a man of God. Upon seeing the people, the cobra retreated to its den and Rai Bular touched Guru's feet in great reverence and thus became Guru's disciple.

GURU SITS IN SECLUSION:

As he grew a little older, he avoided company and sought seclusion. For days he would sit silent in solitude and spent his time in meditation. Parents became anxious about his health and to them his unworldliness appeared insane. One day they sent for their physician Hari Das. The physician came and began to feel

Guru's pulse. He withdrew his arm and asked, "O physician, what
art thou doing?" The physician replied that he was diagnosing his
disease. Upon this the Guru laughed and then uttered the following Sabad:

> "They have sent for the physician for me!
> He taketh my hand and feeleth my pulse.
> What can a pulse disclose?
> The pain lies deep in the heart.
> Physician, go back and heal thyself,
> Diagnose thy own disease,
> Then thou mayst diagnose the diseaseof others
> And call thyself a physician."
>   (Malar ki Var, Mohalla 1 p-1279)

Hari Das was familiar with such cases of deranged mind
and thus asked, "So you think that I am sick too and need a cure."
The Guru replied, "You suffer from the sickness of your soul.
Egoism is the disease. It separates us from the source of life, God
Himself." Hari Das asked if there was any remedy. The Guru
replied,

> "When man shall possess the Name of the Bright One,
> His body shall become like gold and his soul be made pure;
> All his pain and disease shall be dispelled,
> And he shall be saved, Nanak, by the true Name."
>   (Malar Mohalla 1, p-1256)

After a good deal of discussion, Hari Das bowed before the Divine
Master and told his parents to leave anxiety about their son as he
was born **'A healer of the world's sickened souls.'**

TRUE BARGAIN:

In spite of the accumulating evidence about the spiritual greatness
of the Guru, Mehta Kalu was not convinced and thought that his
son was wasting time in profitless contemplation. So he wanted to
put him to trade. He gave the Guru twenty rupees (Indian cur-

rency) and sent him to the nearest town- Chuharkana, to buy goods of common use and then sell them at a profit. The family servant Bala was also sent with him.

On his way the Guru met a group of faqirs (ascetics) who were hungry for several days. The Guru spent all the money in feeding the faqirs and called it a true bargain. He realized the nature of his act and did not go home but sat under a tree outside his village. Bala went home and he narrated the whole story to his father. The father became very angry but the Guru explained to him that he could not think of a more profitable bargain. The aged tree under which he sat is still preserved. It is called Thumb Sahib or the holy tree in memory of the Guru.

All this failed to have any effect on Guru's disinclination towards ordinary world affairs and he remained deeply immersed in meditation.

GURU'S MARRIAGE:

In order to bring him around the worldly affairs, the next step came the marriage. The marriage date is given different in different Janamsakhis (birth stories), and it is presumed that he was between 14 to 18 years of age when he got married. His wife, Sulakhni, was the daughter of Bhai Mula, a resident of Batala in Gurdaspur district. She gave birth to two sons, Sri Chand and Lakhmi Das.

His father soon found out that even the married life did not divest him of his pre-occupation with matters pertaining to his Divine mission. As a matter of fact, his concept of duty was not to serve himself and his family rather to transcend it so that the self might participate in the divine scheme of things and spiritualize the world around him. Humanity was his family and serving the humanity was the service of the Lord. Bhai Gurdas writes that the Guru saw the whole world in flames; flames of falsehood, tyranny, hypocrisy and bigotry. He had to go and extinguish that fire with eternal love, truth and dedication. He had the divine mission to teach to humanity, the lesson of the brotherhood of mankind and the fatherhood of God. "The Primal Being created the Light; all men are the creation of Providence: all human beings have sprung from one Light. Who, then, is bad and who is good?"

GURU NANAK COMES TO SULTANPUR:

Jai Ram, Guru's brother-in-law was serving as Dewan (steward) to the governor, Nawab Daulat Khan Lodhi of Sultanpur. It is said that both Jai Ram and Rai Bular were of the opinion that Nanak was a saint ill-treated by his father; and thus Jai Ram promised to find a job for him in Sultanpur. Guru's sister was deeply devoted to her younger brother. On their annual visit to Talwandi, when she noticed her father's impatience at her brother's indifference towards worldly activities, she decided to take him to Sultanpur. Her father gave his consent.

Jai Ram got the Guru the post of a store-keeper of Nawab's state granary where the grain was collected as a part of land revenue and later sold. The Guru carried out the duties of the store-keeper very efficiently. The minstrel Mardana subsequently joined the Guru and other friends too followed. Guru Nanak introduced them to the Khan, who provided them suitable jobs in his administration. Every night there was a Sabad-Kirtan (singing divine hymns).

One day he was weighing provisions and was counting each weighing as 'one, two, three.........ten, eleven, twelve, thirteen'. When he reached the number thirteen (13)- 'Tera' (in Punjabi language Tera means number 13, and Tera also means 'thine', that is 'I am Thine, O Lord'), he went into ecstasy. He went on weighing by saying,"Tera, tera, tera,......." The customers did not know how to carry the bountiful gifts of this store-keeper. They could not understand the bounties of the Lord.

Ultimately the situation reached its climax when a charge was levied against the Guru that he was recklessly giving away the grain. The Nawab ordered an inquiry which was conducted very carefully. The Guru's detractors were surprised when the stores were found full and the accounts showed a balance in favor of the Guru. After that the Guru sent in his resignation to the employer to embark on his divine mission.

GURU'S DISAPPEARANCE:

The Janamsakhis narrate that one morning, Guru Nanak went to bathe in the neighboring river called Baeen. While bathing he disappeared in water and remained as such for three days[6]. During that period he had a vision of God's presence where he was entrusted by the Almighty with the task of preaching the Divine Name (NAM) to the world. The Almighty gave him a goblet brimming with nectar of 'NAM' which Master Nanak drank and then Almighty commanded:

"Thou art welcome, O Nanak, that hath absorbed thyself in
Nam
Do go hence and do the work for which thou wast born
People of Kalyug have adopted horrible practices and are
extremely degraded in mind.
They worship a variety of gods, have forsaken the Name and
are immersed in sin.
Go thou, spread Love and Devotion to the Name, and lighten
the burden of the earth.
Go thou, and glorify the name of God and destroy
hypocrisy."

The Guru then sang the following Sabad:

Were I to live for millions of years and drink the air for
my nourishment;
Were I to dwell in a cave where I beheld not sun or moon, and
could not even dream of sleeping;
I should still not be able to express Thy worth; how great
shall I call Thy Name?
O true Formless One, Thou art in Thine Own place-
As I have often heard I tell my tale- if it please Thee, show
Thy favor unto me.
Were I to be felled and cut in pieces, were I to be grounded
in a mill;
Were I to be burned in a fire, and blended with its ashes,
I should still not be able to express Thy worth; how great
shall I call Thy Name?

6: *Some writers say that after taking bath in the river, he went to the nearby forest.*

Were I to become a bird and fly to a hundred heavens;
Were I to vanish from human gaze and neither eat nor drink,
I should still not be able to express Thy worth; how great
                    shall I call Thy Name?
Nanak, had I hundreds of thousands of tons of paper and a
        desire to write on it all after the deepest research;
Were ink never to fail me, and could I move my pen like the
        wind,
I should still not be able to express Thy worth; how great
        shall I call Thy Name?
                              (Sri Rag Mohalla 1, p-14)

Then a voice was heard,"O Nanak, to him upon whom My look of kindness resteth, be thou merciful, as I too shall be merciful. My name is God, the Primal Brahm, and thou art the Divine Guru (Mei aad Parmeshar aur tu Gur Parmeshar)."
    This has been the revelation of the Puratan Janamsakhi. The Guru himself confirms that the Almighty asked him to go to the world and sing His praises. The Guru says that after he had done his duty in this world, the Almighty called him again:

"Me, a minstrel out of work, God applieth to His work;
Thus spake the Almighty unto me
Night and day, go and sing My praises.
The Almighty again did summon this minstrel to His most
                    Exalted Court.
On me He bestowed the robe of Honor of His praise and
                    prayer,
On me He bestowed the goblet brimming with Nectar of His
                    Holy Name,
Those who at the bidding of the Guru
Feast and take their fill of the Lord's Holiness attain Peace
                    and Joy.
Thy minstrel spreadeth Thy Glory by singing Thy Word;
Nanak, he who uttereth true praises obtaineth the Perfect
                    One."
                              (Majh di Var-pauri 27, p-150)

It is said that after three days when he reappeared, some

people saw hallow around his head. Some people say that Guru Nanak's Guruship started with his reappearance from the water. It should be pointed here in this respect that there are Three Entities in Sikhism- God, Guru, and Gurbani (Divine Word). According to Sikhism there is One but One God; He sends His emissary called Guru, who is embodiment of Divine Light. God then delivers His message (Gurbani) through His emissary, the Guru.

Without the Guru, there can be no Gurbani. Guru is a channel through whom Gurbani is delivered. Therefore, when at the **age of seven,** Guru Nanak delivered the first Divine message to his teacher (Rag Asa Mohalla 1, Patti Likhi, p-432), he had to be and **he was the Guru.** Before disappearing in the river, a lot of Gurbani was already delivered by the Guru. **He was, thus, born as Guru** and his Guruship started from the very birth.

Bhai Gurdas, a Sikh apostle writes that first the Almighty bestowed His blessings on Baba (Guru Nanak) and then He sent him to this world to spread the Divine Word:

> "Pehlan babei paya bakhash dar, pichhon dei phir ghal ka maee." (Bhai Gurdas- Var 1, pauri 24)

Who was Guru Nanak's Guru? When he was asked, who his Guru was, Guru Nanak replied that God Himself was his Guru:

> "Unfathomable and Infinite is God Who acted as Guru of Nanak." (Sorath Mohalla 1, p-599)

The Guru remained silent for a day after the reappearance and then he made this announcement, "There is no Hindu and no Musalman." This meant that there was no difference between man and man. (But some interpret that both Hindus and Muslims had forgotten the precepts of their religions). This declaration made Nawab Daulat Khan and his Qazi very mad. The Nawab asked the Guru to explain whether his Qazi was not a true Muslim. The Guru described the traits of a true Muslim:

> "He who is firm in his faith,
> Has a right to be called a Muslim.
> His acts must be in accord with his faith in Prophet,

He must clean his heart of his pride and greed,
 Not troubled by the two impostors- life and death,
Resigned to the Will of God;
Knowing Him as the Doer,
Free himself from the self, and
Be compassionate towards all beings, O Nanak,
Such a one may call himself a Muslim."
                        (Majh ki Var Mohalla 1, p-141)

The Nawab then asked the Guru, "If there is no difference
between the Hindus and the Muslims, why don't you join us in our
Namaz (Muslim prayer)?" The Guru agreed to join them to take
part in their prayer in the mosque where Qazi led the Namaz.
When Namaz was offered, the Qazi and the Nawab both stood,
kneeled and bowed in their prayer but the Guru remained standing. After the Namaz was over, the Qazi said,"Why did you not
take part in the prayer?" The Guru replied,"I did take part in the
prayer but both of you did not." Then he explained,"While the
Qazi performed the service, he remembered that there was a well
in his courtyard, and his mind was filled with apprehension lest his
newly-born filly should fall in the well. The Qazi's mind was,
therefore, not present in the prayer. Also while the Nawab was
pretending to pray, his mind was set on purchasing horses in
Kabul."
    Both admitted the truth of Guru's statements and the Nawab
cried aloud to the Qazi,"Thou seest not Khuda (God) speaking to
us through Nanak?" The Muslims perform five Namaz at five
different times a day. The Guru addressed the meaning and virtue
of Namaz:

"Five prayers thou sayest five times a day,
With five different names;
But if Truth be thy first prayer,
The second to honestly earn your daily living,
The third to give in God's name,
Purity of mind be thy fourth prayer,
And praise and prayer to God thy fifth;
If thou practiseth these five virtues,
And good deeds be thine Kalma- the article of faith,

Then thy can call thyself a true Muslim.
By mere hypocrisy, O Nanak,
A man is deemed false through and through."

(Majh ki Var Mohalla 1, p-141)

Guru Nanak never asked a Muslim or a Hindu to become his disciple to get a place in heaven after death. He told the Muslim to become a true Muslim and to a Hindu to become a true Hindu in order to get salvation.

TRAVELS OF GURU NANAK:

Guru Nanak Dev saw the world suffering out of hatred, fanaticism, falsehood and hypocrisy. The world had sunk in wickedness and sin. So he set out for the regeneration of humanity on this earth. He carried the torch of truth, heavenly love, peace and joy for mankind. He embarked on his Divine Mission and went towards east, west, north and south and visited various centers of Hindus, Muslims, Buddhists, Jainis, Sufis, Yogis and Sidhas. He met people of different religions, tribes, cultures and races. He travelled on foot with his Muslim companion named Mardana, a minstrel. His travels are called Udasis[7].

In his first Udasi (travel),[8] Guru Nanak covered east and south of India and returned home after spending a little more than eight years. He started from Sultanpur in August, 1507 and went to his village Talwandi to meet and inform his parents about his long journey. The old parents wanted comfort and protection from their young son in their old age and so they asked him not to go. But there were thousands and thousands others waiting for the Divine Master for comfort, love and salvation. The Guru, therefore, told his parents,"There is a call from Heaven, I must go whither He directs me to go."

7: *The Janamsakhis use the word 'Udasi' for the Guru's travels. Udasi ordinarily means withdrawal from the world but the Guru never withdrew from the world.*

8: *Some writers say that the Guru came back home after covering the east (after Puri) and then took second Udasi towards the south.*

FIRST STOP AT EMINABAD:

Accompanied by Mardana, the Guru embarked on his mission and left his family behind. He made his first stop at Saidpur, now known as Eminabad, and there he met a poor carpenter named Lalo. The Master looked at poor Lalo graciously and he was blessed with Divine love and lo, he was a blessed man. The Guru chose to stay with Lalo for sometimes as a guest. The news reached Malik Bhago, the chief of the town, that a holy person was staying with Lalo. Malik Bhago was a corrupt man and he had amassed wealth through unfair means. He held a big gathering and invited all holy men including the Guru. The Guru, however, did not accept his invitation. The Malik then made a special arrangement for the Guru and requested him to come and eat at his residence. At last the Guru went there and Malik Bhago said,"O holy man, I have prepared so many dishes for you, but you are staying with a poor carpenter and eating his dry bread. Please stay with me." The Guru replied,"I cannot eat your food because your bread is ill-begotten and has been made with money sucked from the poor through unfair means, while Lalo's bread is made from the hard-earned money." This made Malik Bhago very mad and he asked the Guru to prove his point. The Guru then sent for a loaf of bread from Lalo's house. In one hand the Guru held Lalo's bread and in the other that of Malik Bhago's, and when he squeezed both, milk came out from Lalo's bread and blood dripped from Malik Bhago's bread.   Malik Bhago was completely shaken by his guilt and asked for forgiveness. The Guru asked him to distribute his ill-gotten wealth among the poor and henceforth live an honest life. Malik Bhago was re-born with the Guru's blessing.

SUJJAN THUG:

According to Puratan Janamsakhi, before Guru Nanak turned towards east, he went to Tolumba (now known as Makadampur in west Pakistan) and met Sajjan Thug[9]. Sajjan always wore a white dress, displayed his rosary and thus posed to be a

9: *Sajjan means friend and Thug means robber.*

holyman. He had built a Hindu temple and a Muslim mosque at the courtyard of his residence. He would invite wayfarers to his residence to rest for the night. But at night, he would take away their goods and money and sometimes kill them. The Guru went and stayed with him for the night. At night the Guru did not go to bed early which made Sajjan a bit too nervous to perform his nefarious act of robbing. Sajjan asked the Guru to take rest and sleep but the Guru replied,"God's minstrel does not go to sleep, till God sends word that he should retire." The Guru then asked Mardana to play the rebec and he sang the following Sabad:

"Bronze is bright and shining, but, by rubbing, its sable
blackness appeareth,
Which cannot be removed even by washing a hundred times.
They are friends who travel with me   as I go along,
And who are found standing ready whenever their accounts
are called for.
Houses, mansions, palaces painted on all sides,
When hollow within, are as it were crumbled and useless.
Herons arrayed in white dwell at places of pilgrimage;
Yet they rend and devour living things, and therefore should
not be called white.
My body is like the simmal tree; men beholding me mistake
me. Its fruit is useless: such qualities my body possesseth.
I am a blind man carrying a burden while the mountainous
way is long.
I want eyes which I cannot get; how can I ascend and traverse
the journey?
Of what avail are services, virtues, and cleverness?
Nanak, remember the Name, so mayest thou be released
from thy shackles."
(Suhi Mohalla 1, p-729)

When Sajjan listened the Divine melody, he realized that the Guru's words were actually addressed to him. Upon this he made his obeisance and fell at the Guru's feet, and prayed to him to pardon his sins. The Guru said," Sajjan, in the Sovereignty of God, grace is obtained by two things, open confession and repara-

tion for wrong." Sajjan stood in submission. The Guru asked him
to give all his ill-gotten wealth to the poor. He obeyed the mandate
and became a follower of the Guru after receiving Charanpauhal[10].
It is said that the first historical Sikh temple was constructed on the
spot where this conversation was held.

GURU NANAK AT HARDWAR:

Hardwar is one of the Hindu pilgrimage places on the bank
of river Ganges. It was a Baisakhi day and the pilgrims got up early
in the morning and bathed in the river. As the sun came out, they
started throwing water towards the sun. When Guru Nanak asked
them as to what they were doing, one priest replied,"We are
offering water to our dead ancestors in the region of Sun to quench
their thirst."

Upon this the Guru started throwing water towards the
west. The pilgrims laughed and asked what he was doing. The
Guru replied,"I am watering my fields in my village in the Punjab."
The priest asked,"How can your water reach such a distance?" The
Guru retorted,"How far your ancestors are from here?" One of
them replied,"in the other world."

The Guru stated,"If the water cannot reach my fields which
are about four hundred miles away from here, how can your water
reach your ancestors who are not even on this earth?" The crowd
stood in dumb realization. The Guru preached against superstitions and false rituals, worship of gods and goddesses, penances
and renunciation. He stressed that only One God, the Formless,
was to be glorified. In this way he showed the path of truth and enlightenment. There is a Gurdwara called Nanakwara in Hardwar
on the bank of the river Ganges where the Guru had stayed.

GURU AT GORAKHMATA:

After Hardwar, the Guru took his route towards Gorakhmata, about twenty miles north of Pilibhit, and reached there via

---

10: *Also called Charanamrit. This was a form of initiation by drinking the water in which the Guru's
feet had been washed. The preamble of the Japji was read at the same time. The ceremony was inaugurated
by the Guru.*

Joshi Math and Almora. Almora was ruled by the rulers of Chand family and they used to do their offerings of human beings to please their goddess Chandi. The Guru showed them the path of truth and thus stopped them from massacring innocent people to please their goddess.

From there he reached Gorakhmata which was the abode of Jogis of Gorakhnath clan. These Jogis had powers of Ridhi-Sidhi (supernatural powers). Their blessings were eagerly sought by the family men. People avoided their curses at all costs. Public from far and near had heard about these Jogis and their popularity was widespread. It is said that these Jogis (Yogis) had also heard about the Guru. When he reached there, they received him with great courtesy and invited him to adopt their cult, wear their garb and join them as a Yogi. The Guru explained to them that the life of seclusion which was not in the service of their fellow beings, was worthless. The Guru uttered the following Sabad:

"Religion consisteth not in a patched coat, or in a Jogi's
staff, or in ashes smeared over the body;
Religion consisteth not in earrings worn, or a shaven head,
or in the blowing of horns.
Abide pure amid the impurities of the world; thus shalt thou
find the way of religion.

Religion consisteth not in mere words;
He who looketh on all men as equal is religious.
Religion consisteth not in wandering to tombs or places of
cremation, or sitting in attitudes of contemplation;
Religion consisteth not in wandering in foreign countries,
or in bathing at places of pilgrimages.
Abide pure amid the impurities of the world; thus shalt thou
find the way of religion.

On meeting a true Guru doubt is dispelled and the
wanderings of the mind restrained.
It raineth nectar, slow ecstatic music is heard, and man is
happy within himself.
Abide pure amid the impurities of the world; thus shalt thou
find the way of religion.

Nanak, in the midst of life be in death; practice such
religion.
When thy horn soundeth without being blown, thou shalt
obtain the fearless dignity-
Abide pure amid the impurities of the world, thus shalt thou
find the way of religion."
(Suhi Mohalla 1, p-730)

On hearing this, the Yogis made Guru Nanak obeisance.
The Guru's teaching became so effective that Gorakhmata became
Nanakmata.

REETHA SAHIB:

There were forests around Gorakhmata. About forty miles
from there, the Guru met another group of Yogis. He sat under a
soapnut tree and told them that by discarding family life and living
in the forests away from worldly life, could not bring salvation. The
inner change for attainment of peace and everlasting joy and happiness, could be obtained anywhere by contemplating on God's
name. The Yogis asked,"Master, the fire of desire is not quenched
even by endless subjection of the body to discipline. Pray tell us a
way to quench it." The Guru replied,

"Destroy the feeling of egoism
Destroy the sense of duality and attain oneness with Lord,
The path is hard for ignorant and egoistic;
But those who take shelter in the Word and absorbed in it,
And he who realizes that He is both within and without,
His fire of desire is destroyed by the Grace of the Guru,
says Nanak."
(Ramkali Mohalla 1, Sidh Gosht-46, p-943)

The shrewd mind of the Yogis wanted to test the Guru still
further. Knowing that the Guru did not have anything to offer, they
asked him to give them something to eat. The Guru was sitting
under the soapnut tree and soapnuts are always bitter. He gave
them soapnuts to eat. To the utter surprise of the Yogis, the

soapnuts were very sweet. By the Grace of God, the soapnuts of half-side of the tree where the Guru was sitting, became sweet and the other half of the same tree had bitter soapnuts. The same is true even to-day. That place is called Reetha Sahib and there is a Gurdwara in the memory of the Guru.

GURU AT BANARAS:

After Gorakhmata, the Guru took southernly route and passing through Gola, Ayudhya and Prayag (Allahabad), reached Banaras, also called Varanasi- which was said to be the seat of Hindu religious learning and abode of Lord Shiva. The Guru and his companion Mardana encamped in a public square of the city. Pandit Chatur Das was the chief Brahman of the city. Guru's dress was neither of a family man nor of a Sanyasi (ascetic). Seeing this Pandit Chatur Das held a long discussion with the Guru. The Guru asked the Pandit what did he read, what did he teach to the people and what type of knowledge did he impart to his disciples? The Pandit replied,"By the will of God I teach the people the fourteen sciences- reading, swimming, medicine, alchemy,astrology, singing the six rags and their raginis, the science of sexual enjoyment, grammar, music, horsemanship, dancing, archery, theology, and statesmanship." The Guru explained that better than all these was the knowledge of God. Upon this the Guru uttered the fifty-four stanzas of Ramkali Mohalla 1- Dakhni Omkar. The true God is superior to all other gods. The first two stanzas are as follows:

"It is the one God who created Brahma;
It is the one God who created our understanding;
It is from the one God the mountains and the ages of the
                world emanated;
It is the one God who bestowed knowledge.
It is by the Word of God man is saved.
It is by the name of the one God the pious are saved.
Hear an account of the letter O-[11]
O is the best letter in the three worlds.
Hear, O Pandit, why writest thou puzzles?

---

11 *The symbol of the eternal God. Here it is used instead of the name.*

Write under the instruction of the Guru the name of God, the
Cherisher of the world.
He created the world with ease; in the three worlds there is
one Lord of Light.
Under the Guru's instruction select gems and pearls, and
thou shalt obtain God the real thing.
If man understand, reflect, and comprehend what he readeth,
he shall know at last the True One is everywhere.
The pious man knoweth and remembereth the truth- that
without the True One the world is unreal."
(Ramkali Mohalla 1- Dakhni Omkar, p-929)

On hearing the Sabad of Ramkali, Pandit Chatur Das fell
at the feet of the Guru, and became a Sikh, and did much to spread
Sikh religion in that area. The place where the Guru stayed, is now
called as Guru ka Bagh Gurdwara.

GURU AT GAYA:

After Banaras he reached Gaya which is a famous Hindu
pilgrimage place situated at the river   Phalgu (Sarju). The Hindu
priests had declared that any offerings made at Gaya especially at
the time of Baisakhi would secure salvation for seven generations
of those who had departed from this world. The simple minded
people made huge offerings and the priests fed the piters (ancestors) by offering rice balls, lighted up little lamps to illuminate their
paths in the high heavens. The Guru started laughing which made
the priests very angry. At that point the Guru explained that those
who left their bodies on earth, did not need any food nor a glow of
lamp to see. If this body could not go to the other world, obviously
it was not possible for any material substance of this world to reach
the other side. So the Guru enlightened the people and asked them
to worship One God, the Formless.

GURU TO KAMRUP:

After Gaya he passed through the area where modern city
of Patna stands and reached Hajipur. Thence passing through

Kantnagar he reached Malda. The town of Malda was situated at the confluence of rivers Ganges and Mahanadi. It is reported that a local merchant of Malda did a great service to the Guru for which he received Guru's blessings. The next stop was Dhubri in Assam. After Dhubri he proceeded along the Brahmputra river on to Kamrup, a place near the modern city of Gauhati. This whole route is marked by many old historical Gurdwaras bearing association with the Guru.

The city of Kamrup was ruled by a woman of black magic. She had assumed the name of Nurshah, the name of one from whom she had learnt this art. She and her female companions practiced black magic and exorcised strange powers in that locality. She owned the whole country around and many a mystic, yogi etc. fell prey to her magical schemes.

The Guru stayed under a tree outside the city while Mardana went into the city to get something to eat. On his way he met some women and fell victim to their machination, who made a lamb of him. Under mesmeric influence Mardana did all what they commanded him to do. He was thus imprisoned by the witchcraft of Nurshah and could not return to the Guru. The Guru knew what had happened to his minstrel and he started to rescue him from his captors. Nurshah saw the Guru coming and tried to captivate him with her charms but her art of magic failed. She found out that her spells were of no avail. On their fruitless efforts, the Guru uttered the following Sabad on Kuchaji or the woman of bad character:

"I am a worthless woman; in me are faults; how can I go to enjoy my spouse?
My spouse's wives are one better than the other; O my life, who careth for me?
My female friends who have enjoyed their Spouse are in the shade of the mango.[12]
I do not possess their virtues; to whom can I attribute blame?
What attributes of Thine, O Lord, shall I blazon abroad?
What names of Thine shall I repeat?
I cannot even attain one of Thy many excellences: I am ever

12: *That is, they are fortunate. The mango is an evergreen, and its leaves always afford shelter.*

a sacrifice unto Thee.
Gold, silver, pearls, and rubies which gladden the heart-
These things the Bridegroom hath given me, and I have fixed
my heart on them.
I had palaces of brick fashioned with marble.
In these luxuries I forgot the Bridegroom and sat not near
Him.
The Kulangs cry in the heavens, and the cranes have come to
roost.
The woman goeth to her father-in-law's; how shall she show
her face as she proceedeth?
As morning dawned she soundly slept, and forgot her
journey.
She separated from Thee, O Spouse, and therefore stored up
grief for herself.
In Thee, O Lord, are merits; in me all demerits: Nanak hath
this one representation to make,
Every night is for the virtuous woman; may I though
unchaste obtain a night also."
(Rag Suhi Mohalla 1, p-762)

The Guru also uttered the following Sabad on this occasion:

"In words we are good, but in acts bad.
We are impure-minded and black-hearted, yet we wear the
white robes of innocence.
We envy those who stand and serve at His gate.
They who love the Bridegroom and enjoy the pleasure of His
embraces,
Are lowly even in their strength, and remain humble.
Nanak, our lives shall be profitable if we meet such women."
(Sri Rag ki Var Mohalla 1,2-7,p-85)

After the Guru uttered these Sabads, Nurshah thought that
she would tempt him with wealth. Her attendants brought pearls,
diamonds, gold, silver and laid down before him. She then
prayed,"O great magician, accept me as thy disciple and teach me
thy magic." The Guru rejected all the presents and uttered the
following Sabad:

"O silly woman, why art thou proud?
Why enjoyest thou not the love of God in thine own home?
The Spouse is near; O foolish woman, why searchest thou
                              abroad?
Put surma needles of God's fear into thine eyes, and wear the
                    decoration of love.
Thou shalt be known as a devoted happy wife if thou love
                    the Bridegroom.
What shall a silly woman do if she please not her Spouse?
However much she implore, she may not enter His chamber.
Without God's grace she obtaineth nothing, howsoever she
                        may strive.
Intoxicated with avarice, covetousness, and pride, she
                    is absorbed in mammon.
It is not by these means the Bridegroom is obtained; silly
                is the woman who thinketh so.
Go and ask the happy wives by what means they obtained
                        their Spouse-
'Whatever He doeth accept as good; have done with
                    cleverness and orders,
Apply thy mind to the worship of His feet by whose love
            what is most valued is obtained.
Do whatever the Bridegroom biddeth thee; give Him the
            body and soul; such perfumes apply.'
Thus speak the happy wives: 'O sister, by these means the
                    Spouse is obtained.
Efface thyself, so shalt thou obtain the Bridegroom; what
                    other art is there?'
Only that day is of account when the Bridegroom looketh
    with favor; the wife hath then obtained the wealth of
                        the world.

So who pleaseth her Spouse is the happy wife; Nanak, she is
                    the queen of them all.
She is saturated with pleasure, intoxicated with happiness,
            and day and night absorbed in His love.
She is beautiful and fair to view, accomplished, and it is
                she alone who is wise."

(Tilang Mohalla 1, p-722)

On hearing this Sabad, Nurshah and her companions fell at the feet of the Guru and asked for forgiveness and blessing to obtain salvation. The Guru told them to repeat God's Name conscientiously, perform their domestic duties, renounce magic and thus they would secure salvation. It is said that they became Guru's followers. After a short stay he departed leaving behind the awakened souls,to carry on his Divine mission.

KAUDA RAKHSHASH:

The Guru travelled many miles in the wilderness of Assam. His minstrel Mardana was very hungry and tired, so they sat under a tree. After sometimes Mardana went to get something to eat. On his way he met Kauda, the cannibal. Kauda took Mardana by surprise and bound him hand and foot by a rope and then carried him to the spot where he had kept a big pan full of oil for frying the flesh of his victims. Kauda started to lighten fire under the pan. When Mardana saw that, he was very frightened and prayed to the Guru to come to his rescue. The Guru already knew and was on his way to get him released.

Kauda was trying to light the fire when the Guru appeared. This bewildered Kauda completely. The Guru looked at him compassionately and graciously and said,"Kauda! See-est thou not what thou dost, wilt thou cast thyself in the burning fire of hell?" The very gracious and holy sight of the Divine Master made such people realize their guilt and they fell on his feet and begged for mercy. Kauda whose conscience was dead with heinous crimes, suddenly came to realization and was overwhelmed with repentance. He fell on the feet of the Master and prayed for mercy. The gracious Master blessed him with the Name. Kauda was completely a changed man and thereafter lived as a devout disciple of the Guru.

GURU AT JAGAN NATH PURI:

After Golaghat Nagar and Dhanasri valley where cannibals inhabited in large numbers, the Guru went back to Gauhati. From there he proceeded to Shillong and thence to Silhet where an old Gurdwara stands in his memory. He then went to Dacca and on the way he passed through Calcutta and Cuttack and finally reached Puri.

The temple of Jagan Nath, the Lord of the East, was one of the four most revered temples of the Hindus- the other three being Som Nath, Badri Nath and Vishwa Nath. It is said that Jagan Nath's idol was sculptured by the architect of the gods and it was installed at the temple by Lord Brahma himself. It was the anniversary of installation of the idol when Guru Nanak reached the temple. The Guru visited the temple not to adore their Lord but to teach the people **that the worship of God was superior to the worship of the deity.** It was the evening time and the priests brought a salver full of many lighted lamps, flowers, incense and pearls and then all stood to offer the salver to their enshrined idol-god. The ceremony was called 'Arti', a song of dedication. The high-priest invited the Guru to join in the god's worship. The Guru did not join their service which enraged the priests. On being asked the reason the Guru explained that a wonderful serenade was being sung by nature before the invisible altar of God. The sun and the moon were the lamps, placed in the salver of the firmament and the fragrance wafted from the Malayan mountains was serving as incense. The Guru, therefore, instead of accepting the invitation of the high-priest to adore the idol, raised his eyes to the heaven and uttered the following Sabad of Arti:

"The sun and moon, O Lord, are thy lamps; the firmament
Thy salver; the orbs of the stars, the pearls enchased in it.
The perfume of the sandal[13] is Thine incense; the wind is
Thy fan; all the forests are Thy flowers, O Lord of light.
What worship is this, O Thou Destroyer of birth?
Unbeaten strains of ecstasy are the trumpets of Thy worship.
Thou hast a thousand eyes and yet not one[14] eye;
Thou hast a thousand forms and yet not one form;
Thou hast a thousand pure feet and yet not one foot;

13: *Malianlo- wind from Malay tree- sandlewood tree.*

14: *All the eyes of the world are Yours but Thou has no material eye as being Formless.*

Thou hast a thousand organs of smell and yet not one organ-
I am fascinated by this play of Thine.
The Light which is in everything is Thine, O Lord of Light.
From its brilliancy everything is brilliant;
By the Guru's teaching the light becometh manifest.
What pleaseth Thee is the real Arti.
O God, my mind is fascinated with Thy lotus feet as the
bumble-bee with the flower: night and day I thirst for them
Give the water of Thy grace to the sarang[15] Nanak, so that he
may dwell in Thy name."
(Dhanasri Mohalla 1, Arti, p-663)

According to the Puratan Janamsakhi, the Guru ended his
first Udasi with the visit to Puri and returned to Punjab. After some
time he took his second Udasi to cover the south. If the Guru had
returned from Puri, he must have visited some important places
on his way back, but there is no mention of it in the Janamsakhi.
However, the Meharban version of the Janamsakhi treats the
eastern and the southern journeys as a single Udasi. Others argue
that the geographical location of Puri is as such that a visitor
planning to visit south India, would not return to Punjab and then
start for the southern journey. Many writers therefore, believe that
the Guru continued his southward journey from Puri.

GURU TO SANGLADEEP (CEYLON):

From Puri the Guru went to Gantur of present Andhra
Pradesh district, Kanchipuram, Tiruvannamalai and Tiruchchirupalli. All these places have Gurdwaras to mark the visit of the
Guru. From Tiruchchirupalli he sailed down to Kaveri river and
reached Nagapatnam, a very old port of south India. From there he
proceeded to Sangladeep (Ceylon) and Betticola was the first place
of his stay in the island. Thence he went to Matiakalam (now
known as Matalai) which was the capital of Sangladeep under Raja
Shiv Nabh.
Bhai Mansukh, a trader from Punjab and a disciple of the

15: *The sarang is a bird which is also known as Chatrik or Papiha. It is supposed to drink water only
when moon is in the mansion of Arcturus, so when its time comes to drink it is naturally thirsty.*

Guru, had been to Sangladeep in connection with his business long before the Guru's visit to the island. By reason of his trade, Bhai Mansukh had access to Raja Shiv Nabh and thus he had told the Raja all about Guru Nanak. The Raja inquired how he could meet the Guru. Mansukh told him,"Rise early in the morning and recite Moolmantar. If you earnestly pray, the Guru will respond to your prayers."

Every morning Raja Shiv Nabh meditated and prayed for the holy sight (darshan) of the Guru. Time passed on but the Guru did not appear. Many persons came and claimed to be the Guru but all were found to be the fake claimants. One day news was brought to the Raja that a holy man, with a rare glory beaming on his face (spiritual aura), had arrived in the old neglected garden, and as soon as he set his foot in the garden, the withered trees sprouted into green foliage.

Due to the previous fake claimants, the Raja devised a plan to test the visitors before he could bow his head to any one of them. The Raja, therefore, sent beautiful girls to seduce the new-comer with their beauty and charm. The report was sent to the Raja that the girls not only failed to seduce the visitor, but they themselves had been transformed under his spell. Hearing this, the Raja hurriedly came to see the holy Master. Spontaneously he fell at the feet of the Guru. The Guru placed his hand on his head and blessed him. Who could describe the ecstatic joy that had dawned upon Raja.

The whole city rushed to the garden to have holy sight of the Master. A dharamsala, a religious common place, was built where the Guru held daily religious congregations and preached his divine doctrine. People were enlightened with God's Name and they became Guru's followers.

After staying there for some time the Guru started in the southerly direction and reached Katargama. Thence he reached Sita Eliya, a place where Sita spent her period of captivity. At the time of Guru Nanak's visit, this place was in the Kotte kingdom of Raja Dharma Prakarma. The inscription discovered by Dr. Karuna Ratna and Parana Vitana in the famous museum of Anurodh Pura, furnishes a brief account of the encounter of Jnanakacharya (Nanak) with the Buddhist Bhikshu, Dharma Kirt-sthavira. This inscription also informs that the Raja Dharma Prkramabahu had promised to embrace Guru Nanak's creed if he won in the debate. Guru Nanak won. But before he could embrace the Guru's creed, the Brahmans very cleverly arranged another public debate, this time between the Guru and Dharma Dvajapandita and maneuvered the result in favor of the latter. In this way they did not let the ruler fall under the influence of the Guru.

RETURN FROM SANGLADEEP:

Worship of Shiv's idol was very common in southern India at that time. There were twelve Shivling temples and six of them were situated in the south. Southern India was also ridden with caste system. Guru Nanak had to visit all such places to show the people the path of Eternal Truth i.e. the worship of Almighty, the Formless. This was superior and fruitful than the worship of the idols.

After staying for some time (may be a year) in Sangladeep, the Guru reached Cochin on his wayback journey. There is a Gurdwara at this place to mark the memory of the Guru. Delivering his divine doctrine he passed through Palghat, Nilgiri Hills, Rangapatan and then reached Pandharpur. Saint Nam Dev whose Bani is included in Guru Granth Sahib, passed most of his life at this place. From there he reached Barsi which was the native place of Saint Trilochan whose two Sabads are included in Guru Granth Sahib. From there he passed through Poona, Amarnath, Nasik, Aurangabad and reached Amreshwar where there was famous temple called Onkar Mandir. Here the worship of Shivling (Shiv's idol) was considered as a worship of God. The people considered Sanskrit as the language of the gods and learning of Sanskrit language was considered as act of holiness.

The Guru preached against the idol worship and stressed that one should only worship One but One God, the Formless. The gospel preached by the Guru at the Onkar Mandir, is included in Guru Granth Sahib as Ramkali Mohalla 1- Dakhni Onkar, page 929.

Then he proceeded to Indaur, Ujjain, Baroda and finally reached Palitana where there was a famous Jain temple. Jaini Sadhus would not take bath for many days thinking bathing killed some life in the water. Here he had discussion with a Jain Sadhu named Ambhi. He explained to the Sadhu that running away from water would not do any religious good but the worship of the Almighty was the only answer.

The Guru went through almost all the famous Hindu pilgrimage places in the area and delivered his message of Oneness of God and to have belief in none other than One Supreme Being only. He visited Somnath, Sudhana, Puri and Dwarka. From Kathiawar through Kachh and Chataur, he reached Ajmer. There was a famous Muslim saint, Khawaza Mai-u-din Chisti, who propagated Islam for about seventy years at Ajmer. It was an annual Muslim gathering to celebrate Khawaza's day when the Guru reached there. He forbade the Muslims from worshipping the Makbras (the tombs of their saints), but asked them to worship only One God.

Passing through Pushker, he reached Gokal Mathura-Bindraban. People were in full preparation for celebrating Lord Krishna's birthday. The Hindus placed Krishna's idol (which they call Thakur) in a small cradle.They were swinging it and were putting all their offerings before the idol. The Guru exposed the futility of idol worship and preached them to worship God, the Formless.

After that he arrived at Delhi and stayed at Majnu da Tilla. There is a Gurdwara at this place at the bank of river Jamna. A Gurpurb of Baisakhi is celebrated at this place every year in April. Thence he went to Panipat where he met a Muslim saint Sheikh Sharf or Taher and urged him to worship only one God, the All-Pervading Divine Spirit instead of worshiping the tombs of the saints.

Passing through Pehwa, he reached Kurukshetra[16], a place where the famous battle of Mahabharat was fought between the Kauravs and the Pandavs. It was an occasion of solar eclipse when the Guru visited Kurukshetra. Thousands of people including a large number of Brahmans and saints had gathered there. Hindus consider it sacred to go to Kurukshetra at the time of solar eclipse, bathe in the holy tank and give alms to Brahman priests. According to Hindu belief, solar eclipse occurs when sun, the god, is harassed by its enemies, the demons. None is required to eat anything during the eclipse.

16: *Some writers believe that the Guru went to Kurukshetra in the beginning of the first Udasi.*

The Guru went there to draw attention of the erring Hindu community towards the fact that eclipse was nothing but only a natural phenomenon. The Guru took his seat near the sacred tank and when the sun was eclipsed he began to cook deer which was presented to him by Prince Rai Singh[17]. A big crowd gathered around the Guru, for it was a sacrilege to cook meat. The Brahmans led by Nanu besieged the Guru and were ready to club him to death. The Guru stood up and spoke. His words worked like a magic and the crowd stood spell-bound. The Guru uttered the following two Sabads on this occasion:

"Man is first conceived in flesh, he dwelleth in flesh,
When he quickeneth, he obtaineth a mouth of flesh; his bone,
                    skin, and body are made of flesh.
When he is taken out of the womb, he seizeth teats of flesh.
His mouth is of flesh, his tongue is of flesh, his breath is
                    in flesh.
When he groweth up he marrieth, and bringeth flesh home
                    with him.
Flesh is produced from flesh; all man's relations are made
                    from flesh.
By meeting the true Guru and obeying God's order,
                    everybody shall go right.
If thou suppose that man shall be saved by himself, he shall
                    not: Nanak, it is idle to say so."
        (Var Malar ki- Slok Mohalla 1- 25.1, p-1289)

The Guru continued:

"Fools wrangle about flesh (meat), but know not divine
                    knowledge or meditation on God.
They know not what is meat, or what is vegetable, or in what
                    sin consisteth.
It was the custom of the gods to kill rhinoceroses, roast
                    them and feast.
They who forswear flesh and hold their noses when near it,

17: *Bhai Mani Singh Janamsakhi.*

devour men at night.
They make pretenses to the world, but they know not divine
knowledge or meditation on God.
Nanak, why talk to a fool? He cannot reply or understand
what is said to him.
He who acteth blindly is blind; he hath no mental eyes.
Ye were produced from the blood of your parents, yet ye eat
not fish or meat.
When man and woman meet at night and cohabit,
A foetus is conceived from flesh; we are vessels of flesh.
O Brahman, thou knowest not divine knowledge or
meditation on God, yet thou callest thyself clever.
Thou considereth the flesh that cometh from abroad[18] bad,
O my Lord, and the flesh of thine own home good.
All animals have sprung from flesh, and the soul taketh its
abode in flesh.
They whose Guru is blind, eat things that ought not to be
eaten, and abstain from what ought to be eaten.
In flesh we are conceived, from flesh we are born; we are
vessels of flesh.
O Brahman, thou knowest not divine knowledge or
meditation on God, yet thou callest thyself clever.
Meat is allowed in the Purans, meat is allowed in the books
of Musalmans, meat hath been used in the four ages.
Meat adorneth sacrifice and marriage functions; meat hath
always been associated with them.
Women, men, kings, and emperors spring from flesh.
If they appear to you to be going to hell, then accept not
their offerings.
See how wrong it would be that givers should go to hell and
receivers to heaven.
Thou understandest not thyself, yet thou instructest others;
O Pandit, thou art very wise!
O Pandit, thou knowest not from what flesh hath sprung.
Corn, sugar-cane, and cotton are produced from water[19];
from water the three worlds are deemed to have sprung.

18: *The meat of animals*

19: *Water assists the growth of vegetables, and on vegetables andimals are fed.*

Water saith,'I am good in many ways'; many are the
modifications of water.
If thou abandon the relish of such things, thou shalt be
superhuman, saith Nanak deliberately."
(Ibid, 25-2, p-1289)

GURU TO SARSA:

From Kurukshetra the Guru passed through Jind where
there is Gurdwara in his memory and then reached Sarsa. Here he
met a Muslim saint. The Muslim Pir had great influence over his
disciples and he had given them the guarantee of securing a place
in heaven for them. In return of such a guarantee, the disciples
would bring big offerings in cash and kind to the Pir. The Guru
explained to them that in order to get salvation, they should
worship One God, the mere offerings would lead them no where.

TO SULTANPUR:

Sultanpur was about 135 miles north east of Sarsa and after
eight years and covering more than six thousand miles on foot, the
Guru reached Sultanpur. The elder sister, Bibi Nanki and her husband, and other acquaintances were overjoyed to see him back.

HOME COMING:

After staying sometimes at Sultanpur, the Guru started towards Talwandi. His father was about 75 years old. There was no
postal service in those days. The old parents were waiting for their
son to return. At last their son reached home and their joy knew no
bounds. People from far and near came to have holy sight of the
Guru. They started rejoicing his company again. At that time the
Guru's children and his wife were with his in-laws at Pakhokey, a
place about 110 miles towards Lahore. So he proceeded to see his
wife and children.

Ajita was the Chaudhry (chief) of that village. He had heard
about the Guru but he had never met him before. Ajita was so
much impressed with the first holy sight of the Guru that he

immediately became his disciple.

FOUNDATION OF KARTARPUR:

Some writers say that the Guru founded Kartarpur (city of the Creator) after his third Udasi. Others believe that he started the habitation of Kartarpur in 1516 right after he came back from his first travel in 1515. Although wherever he went, he set up the missionary centers, yet he wanted to set up a central place to co-ordinate the efforts and activities of his mission. Therefore he chose this place near Pakhokey along the bank of the river Ravi. When he broke this news to Chaudhry Ajita, he immediately agreed with him. The Chaudhry and many other people of that village denoted their land for the new town. The foundation of Kartarpur was started immediately. The Guru brought his parents to Kartarpur and so did Mardana. Morning and evening religious congregations were started.

SECOND UDASI:

After starting the habitation of Kartarpur, the Guru started his second travel towards north. He made his first stop at Sialkot[20], a city about 50 miles east of Kartarpur. After the Muslim invaders established their rule in India, many Muslim faqirs (saints and preachers) also came along with them and these faqirs set up their own centers at different places to preach Islam. Through their missionary work most of the Hindus were converted to Islam. Pir Hamza Ghons was one of those faqirs who set up his center at Sialkot. There lived a Hindu family in that city who did not have any children. Thinking that the Pir had miraculous powers, the

---

20: *Some writers describe a different route of the second Udasi. They believe that it started from Talwandi to Lahore, Sultanpur and passing through Jullundhur and Hoshiarpur, the Guru reached the abode of Pir Budhan Shah, where later on, the sixth Guru founded the city of Kiratpur. From there the Guru proceeded to Bilaspur and then visited Mandi, Rawalsar, Jawalaji, and Kangra. Thence he marched to Baijnath, Kulu and Sapiti Valley and stayed in a village called Mulani. Some relics of the Guru are reported to have been preserved and worshipped by the people of this village. Then passing through Prang Passes, the Guru reached Tibet and thence proceeded to Mansarovar Lake and Kailash Parbat (Sumer Parbat). Through the Chasul Pass, he entered Ladakh and then through Skardu and Kargal, he reached Amarnath. After passing through Pehlgam, Anant Nagar, he reached Srinagar and Bara Mula, and then wending his way to Hasan Abdal, Tilla Bal Gudai and Sialkot, he returned to Talwandi.*

head of this Hindu family begged the Pir to bless him with a son. He promised that if a son was born, he would offer him to the Pir. By the grace of God, a son was born, but the man shied away to keep his promise and did not offer his son to the Pir. This enraged the Pir so much that he branded the whole city as full of liars and wanted to destroy it in revenge. In order to accomplish the destruction of the city, he sat in seclusion and undertook a fast of forty days. The people became very frightened and his disciples would not allow any one to come near him.

The Guru sat nearby and asked Mardana to play his rebec and started the Divine Sabad. Upon this the Pir was so much shaken up that he was forced to break his fast. As he listened to the Divine praise and prayer, he calmed down and sat before the Guru. The Guru made the Pir understand that for the mistake of one person, there was no justification of destroying the whole city. Pir Hamza Ghons was touched with the reality and truth.Thus he abandoned his revengeful act of destruction. There is a Gurdwara in honor of the Guru in Sialkot.

From there the Guru proceeded to Jammu and the temple of Vaishnu Devi goddess. Preaching his doctrine of Truth, he passed through Vairi Nag, Kukar Nag and Anant Nag springs and reached Pehalgam and then Amarnath, a place about 90 miles east of Srinagar. The Hindus worshiped Shivling at Amarnath, but the Guru discussed the uselessness of idol worship and asked them to worship one and only one God. A few miles before Amarnath there is a Gurdwara called Matan Sahib.

There lived at Srinagar a very learned Pandit called Brahm Das who always had some camels following him, loaded with volumes of ancient wisdom. This meant that he had the mastery over the knowledge contained in that load of religious books. He learnt that a holy man and a great Teacher had arrived in the valley and that many people had gone to him for his blessing. He first decided to go to him (Guru), but then his pride of knowledge kept him away. One day however, he went to see his friend, Kamal and mentioned to him about a strange visitor (Guru Nanak) in the valley.

Kamal was a devout Muslim and a seeker of Truth. He went to see the Guru without any hesitation. When Kamal got the glimpse of the Guru, he fell on Guru's feet and fainted with joy. As he regained consciousness, he found in his own heart the Light he had been yearning for years. Kamal got the blessing and became Guru's follower. The Guru asked him to settle in the valley of Kurram from where he spread Guru's doctrine to Kabul, Qandhar and Tirah.

After that Brahm Das also came to see the Master. He entered into discussion with the Guru and boasted of his knowledge of ancient wisdom. Seeing his camels loaded with books, the Guru uttered the following Sabad:

"One may read cartloads of books,
One may read caravan-loads of books,
One may study boatloads of books
Or fill cellars with volumes of his study;
One may read for years and years
And spend every month in the year in study only;
And one may study all one's life Right up to his last breath;
O Nanak, only One word, God's name, would be of account,
All else would be senseless discussion of pride."
(Asa Mohalla 1- Slok Mohalla 1, 1.9, p-467)

On hearing this Brahm Das begged,"Forgive me, O holy Guru! I have read sacred books and have acquired academic knowledge of all the six schools of philosophy, but I must confess that I have attained no peace of mind. Pray tell me, how can I get it?"

The Guru explained,"Academic knowledge breeds pride and pride darkens man's vision. Ego is the greatest barrier and unless a man gets rid of it, he cannot grasp the Truth, and there can be no peace of mind." Brahm Das fell at the feet of the Guru and begged,"Save me O Lord! I was in the dark and I am a sinner; bless me with peace." Brahm Das got the blessing and became Guru's disciple. He was entrusted with the task of preaching Sikh faith amongst the people of Kashmir valley.

GURU TO KAILASH PARBAT:

From Amarnath the Guru entered into Tibet and then proceeded to the Mansarovar Lake and Kailash Parbat (also called Sumer Parbat). There he met many renowned Sidhas. They inquired of the Guru about the conditions prevailing in India. The Guru told them that falsehood overshadowed the land and the moon of truth was completely enshrouded in the darkness of ignorance. The kings were butchers and justice had taken wings and flown away. Then he further said,"Nathji, when the Sidhas (Yogis) are hiding themselves in mountain enclaves, who is left over there to lead the people in the right direction?"

The Sidhas wanted the Guru to wear their garb and become a yogi, but they could not succeed. They had the supernatural powers which they tried upon the Guru. They asked him to bring water from the nearby spring. The Guru took a bowl and went to bring water. By their miraculous powers, the Sidhas turned the water into jewels and diamonds. They had thought that the Guru would be overwhelmed with the wealth. He did not care about the jewels and came back with empty bowl. They still tried many more tricks but failed to succeed. At last they acknowledged the superpowers of the Guru and sat around him in submission and the discussion ensued[21]. The Guru convinced them that instead of wearing empty forms and doing hard penances, they should exert themselves in the service of mankind. A Sidh called Charpat asked the Guru,

"The world is an ocean, and is said to be difficult to cross;
how shall man traverse it?
Saith Charpat, O Audhut Nanak, give a true reply."
(Ramkali Mohalla 1, Sidh Gosht-4, p-938)

The Guru replied,

"As the lotus floats in water, but remain unaffected by its
waves;
As the swan swims in it and is not drenched by water;
So by meditating on the Word and repeating God's name,
Shalt thou be able to cross safely ocean of the world.

21: *This discussion with the Sidhas is given in Ramkali Mohalla 1- Sidh Gosht, page 938 of the Guru Granth Sahib.*

Nanak is a servant to those who remain unattached in the
world, in whose hearts the one God abideth, who live
without desires in the midst of desires,
And who see and show to others the Inaccessible and
Incomprehensible God."
(Ibid, Sidh Gosht-5, p-938)

Another Yogi asked:

"What is the source of thy system
And when did it start?
Who is thy Guru, of whom thou art the disciple?"
(Ibid.43, p-942) The

Guru replied:

"My system began
With the beginning of the breath of life.
Its source is the wisdom of the True Guru,
The True Guru is the Word,
And intentive consciousness is the disciple."
(Ibid.44, p-943)

Images of Guru Nanak are said to be present in some of the
temples of this area. From Kailash Parbat, the Guru turned north-
west and entered Ladakh area through the Chasul Pass and then
reached Karunagar. A remarkable point of this place is that there
are a few villages in the neighborhood where none except Guru
Nanak is worshipped. At a short distance from Karunagar, there is
a place called Gumpha Hemus which keeps the memory of Guru
Nanak's visit alive. The people here have preserved the stone on
which the Guru is believed to have seated himself during his visit.
Thence he came to Skardu where there is a Gurdwara named after
the Guru. From there he proceeded to Kargal, Pehalgam, Anant
Nagar, Srinagar and Bara Mula and thence came back to Kartarpur.

Kashmir had been the center of the learned Pandits (Brahmans). In view of that, this area was deeply involved in idol-
worship and other related rites and rituals. The Guru professed the
qualities of God emphasizing that one should worship none other
than One Supreme Being. He further stressed that other rites and
rituals were of no avail. Pandit Brahm Das who became Guru's

disciple, did great service in preaching the Guru's doctrine in the valley of Kashmir.

THIRD UDASI:

The third Udasi was undertaken towards the west. Guru Nanak reached Pakpatan (Ajodhan) where he met Sheikh Brahm who was the eleventh in succession to Baba Farid, whose Bani is also included in Guru Granth Sahib. The Guru had wide range of discussion with Sheikh Brahm. The Guru stated,

> "Thou art the tablet, O Lord, Thou art the pen, and Thou art
> also the writing,
> Speak of the one God; O Nanak, why should there be
> second."
> (Var Malar ki Mohalla 1, 28-2, p-1291)

The Sheikh asked the Guru to explain,"You say ,'There is only one God, why should there be a second?', and I (Sheikh) say:

> There is one Lord and two ways;
> Which shall I adopt, and which reject?"

The Guru replied:

> "There is one Lord and one way;
> Adopt one and reject the other."

In a Var (like Asa di Var) there has to be two beings; and the Sheikh asked the Guru to let him hear a strain in praise of the One God. "My idea is", said the Sheikh,"that adoration cannot be performed without two beings, that is, God and the Prophet. Let me see whom thou makest man's intercessor." Upon this the Guru asked Mardana to play the rebec and he uttered the first Slok and Pauri of Asa di Var:

> "I am a sacrifice, Nanak, to my Guru a hundred times a day,
> Who without any delay made demigods out of man.
> Nanak, they who, very clever in their own estimation, think

not of the Guru,
Shall be left like spurious sesames in a reaped field-
They shall be left in the field, saith Nanak, without an owner.
The wretches may even bear fruit and flower, but shall
contain ashes within their bodies.

Pauri:
God Himself created the world, and formed Himself into
Name,
He created Nature by His power; seated He beheld His
work with delight.
O Creator, Thou art the Giver; being pleased Thou bestowest
and practisest kindness.
Thou knowest all things; Thou givest and takest life with a
word.
Seated Thou beholdest Thy work with delight."
(Asa Mohalla 1, p-462-63)

The Sheikh then wanted a knife,"Give me such a knife that
those who are killed with it, shall be acceptable to God. With the
ordinary knife the lower animals are killed. If a man's throat be cut
with this knife, it becomes carrion."

The Guru replied in affirmative:

"Truth is the knife, truth is pure steel;
Its fashion is altogether incomparable.
Put it on the hone of the Word,
And fit it into the scabbard of merit;
If any one be bled with that, O Sheikh,
The blood of avarice will be seen to issue forth.
If man be slaughtered with it, he shall go to meet God,
O Nanak, and be absorbed in the sight of Him."
(Ramkali ki Var, Mohalla 1, 19.2, p-956)

On hearing this the Sheikh raised his head in amazement
and said,"Well done. O Nanak, there is no difference between God
and thee. Kindly bless me so that I too may be on good terms with
Him." The Guru replied,"Sheikh Brahm, God will cause thy ship to

arrive safe." The Sheikh requested the Guru to give him the firm promise of this. The Guru complied and blessed him with salvation.

According to Puratan Janamsakhi, the first nine pauries (stanzas) of Asa di Var, were uttered by the Guru during the discussion with Sheikh Brahm and other fifteen pauries of Asa di Var were uttered for Duni Chand Dhuper of Lahore. The Guru then proceeded to Multan, Uch, Sakhar and reached Lakhpat, where a Gurdwara stands marking the memory of the Guru. Thence he reached Kuriani where a tank is called after Guru's name. Then he visited Miani, about fifty miles west of city of Karachi. He visited the temples of Hindus and the Muslims in the area. Near Hinglaj, there is a Dharmsala preserving the memory of the Guru's visit to this place. From there the Guru boarded a ship for Arabia.

GURU NANAK AT MECCA:

He disguised himself in the blue dress of a Mohammadan pilgrim, took a faqir's staff in his hand and a collection of his hymns called 'Pothi' under his arm. He also carried with him like a Muslim devotee, a cup for his ablutions and a rug whereon to pray. Like a pilgrim he went inside the great mosque where the pilgrims were engaged in their devotions. When he lay down to sleep at night, he turned his feet towards the Kaaba. A priest, Jiwan[22] kicked him and said,"Who is this infidel sleeping with his feet towards the House of God?" The Guru replied,"Turn my feet in the direction in which God is not." Upon this Jiwan seized the Guru's feet and dragged them in the opposite direction. Whereupon, it is said, the Kaaba (temple) turned around, and followed the revolution of Guru's body. Some say that when the Guru asked the priest to turn his feet in the direction where God was not, the priest came to realization that God was everywhere. But those who witnessed this miracle were astonished and saluted the Guru as a supernatural being.

Then the Qazis and the Mullas crowded round the Guru and asked whether he was a Muslim or a Hindu? The Guru replied

---

22: *Bhai Gurdas, Var-1, pauri-32.*

that he was neither of the two. Then they asked,"Who is the superior of the two, the Hindu or the Muslim?" The Guru replied,"Without good deeds, both will repent. The superiority lies in deeds and not in mere creeds." The chief priest was a seeker of the Truth and he asked for Guru's blessings. The Guru preached the doctrine of Nam. He then gave instructions to the priest in the art of true living, to practice to live in His presence day and night and to glorify the Lord and thereby to rub out the dirt of sins from the tablet of the mind.

.GURU AT MEDINA:

In due time the Guru proceeded to Medina, another holy city of the Muslims where their Prophet Mohammad lived for many years and breathed his last. The Guru reached at nightfall and stopped outside the town. It happened to be a place where lepers were segregated and no provision was made for their comfort or treatment. History states that the Guru healed them all and as a result, the people came in crowds to have holy glimpse of the Guru. Thence he journeyed to Bagdad through Basra.

GURU AT BAGDAD:

There lived a very famous Muslim saint, Pir Abdul Kadar who died in Bagdad in 1166 A.D. He was also known as Dastgir and his successors were called Dastgirs too. The Muslim high priests did not like unethical and immoral musical verses. Instead of condemning the demoralizing poetry, they outrightly rejected the music ('Rag') itself. So according to Muslim Shariat (code of law), music was forbidden. The whole of Sikh scripture is in verse and in various different forms of Rags and Raginis. In the morning the Guru shouted the call for prayer, on which the whole population became rapt in silent astonishment. May be he did it differently than the Muslims. Then Mardana played the rebec and the Guru started the Sabad Kirtan (musical recitation of Gurbani). Whosoever heard was in ecstasy. The news spread in the city. The high priest Pir Dastgir, another holy man, Bahlol and others came to see the Guru.

According to the Mohammadans there are seven skies

above the earth and seven nethers including earth itself. The Guru began to recite the Japji. When he repeated the twenty-second pauri (stanza) of Japji, the Pir got wonder-stuck hearing something contrary to the authority of the holy Quran, that there were hundreds of thousands of nethers and upper regions, and that at last men grew weary of searching for them. The Pir then called upon the Guru to give a manifestation of what he said. Upon this it is said[23], the Guru laid his hand on the priest's son and showed him upper and lower regions described in Japji- pauri 22. To prove whether the boy actually saw those regions, he brought Parshad (sacred food) from one of those regions and gave it to his father. Both the Pir and Bahlol bowed before the Guru and asked for his blessings.

Bahlol became Guru's follower. It is said that he spent sixty years at the foot of the slab, where the sacred feet of the Guru had rested during their discussion. Later on a shrine was built there in the memory of the Guru. The English translation of the inscription on the slab inside the shrine is:

> "In memory of the Guru, that is the Divine Master, Baba Nanak, Faqir Aulia, this building has been raised with the help of seven saints, and the chronogram reads. The blessed disciple has produced a spring of Grace year 917" (Muslim year).

Swami Anand Acharya of Sweden mentions in his book 'Snow Bird', published by Macmillan & Sons, London, that during his visit to Bagdad, he found another inscription on the slab, dated 917 Hijri. The inscription reads:

> "Here spoke the Hindi Guru Nanak to Faqir Bahlol, and for these sixty years since the Guru left Iraq, the soul of Bahlol has rested on the Master's word like a bee poised on a dawn-lit honey rose."

RETURN FROM BAGDAD:

23: *Bahai Gurdas - Var 1, pauri 35-36*

From Bagdad the Guru passed through Iran, Turkstan and Afghanistan and then reached Kabul. Some writers believe that the Guru took the popular route from Bagdad towards Tehran, Kandhar and reached Kabul. On his way he passed through Mehds. Bhai Mani Singh's Janamsakhi makes a reference of his visit to this place. Since the visit of Guru Nanak to Kabul, the Sikh contacts had been carefully maintained. Sikh preachers were stationed there to disseminate the teachings of the Guru. At one time Bhai Gurdas also served as one of the Sikh missionaries at Kabul.

From Kabul the Guru proceeded to Jalalabad, Sultanpur and passed through Khyber Pass to reach Peshawar. There are Gurdwaras at Jalalabad and Sultanpur to mark the visit of the Guru. There are springs of water associated with his visit. The Guru paid a visit to the Gorakh Hatri and had discourse with Jogis. Thence he reached Hassan Abdal, now known as Panja Sahib, and sat at the foot of the hill.

GURU NANAK AND VALI KANDHARI:

On the top of a small hill, there lived a Muslim Faqir called Vali Kandhari who was well-known in the area for possessing miraculous powers. Mardana needed water which could only be obtained from Vali. Mardana told Vali that Guru Nanak had arrived and he advised him to see the Guru, who was a great saint of God. Vali who claimed holiness exclusively for himself, became offended on hearing the Guru's praises. He refused to give water saying that if the Guru were such a holy man, he could provide water to Mardana. When this reply was communicated to the Guru, he sent Mardana back to the Vali with a message that he (Guru) was a poor creature of God, and laid no claims to be a saint. The Vali paid no heed to this protestation and still refused to provide water.

Upon this the Guru picked up one stone and a stream of water immediately issued forth. In fact this water came out from the Vali's tank which dried up. This naturally increased Vali's rage and it is said that through his miraculous powers he hurled a small hillock upon Guru Nanak's unoffending head. The Guru, on seeing the descending hillock, held up his right hand, and as it touched the hand of the Divine Master, the hillock came to a standstill. With the divine touch, the stone melted and softened like wax and left the mark of the Master's palm indelibly deep into it. Vali Kandhari was very much astonished and at last fell at the feet of the Guru and begged for forgiveness. The Guru expressed,"O friend, those who live so high, should not be hard at heart like a stone." Vali was blessed by the Master.

The imprint of the Guru's hand (Punja) is still visible on the stone and the pool of crystal clear water still flows from there. There stands a Gurdwara which is known as 'Punja Sahib'. It is now situated in west Pakistan.

GURU AT SAIDPUR:

Thence the Guru proceeded a second time to Saiyidpur or Saidpur, now known as Eminabad, where he again visited Bhai Lalo. Lalo complained to him of the oppression of the Pathans, who were leading a luxurious life caring little for others. The Guru replied that their dominion should be brief, as Baber was on his way for the conquest of India. Baber invaded the Punjab for the third time and it was the year 1521. He sacked the town of Eminabad and subjected it to massacre, loot and rape. It was a horrible scene, which Guru Nanak himself describes that there laid in the dust, the fairy heads of the damsels and beautiful women.

Most of the writers including many Sikhs say that seeing this horrible scene, the Guru appealed in anguish to the   Almighty when he said:

'Eti mar pai kurlane tai ki dard na aaya.'

(Asa Mohalla 1, p-360)

And they translate the above verse as:

'When there was such slaughter and lamentation,
didst not Thou, O God, feel pain?'

Let us examine if these writers are correct. Did the Guru make such an anguished appeal to God or not?

A. In the very first stanza (pauri) of Japji on the very first page of Guru Granth Sahib, Guru Nanak says:

'Hukam rajai chalna Nanak likhia nal.'

Translation:
    'O Nanak thus runneth the Writ Divine,
    The righteous path, let it be thine.'

Again in Asa Mohalla 5, page 394, it is stated:
    'Tera kia meetha lagei
    Har nam padarth Nanak mangei.'

Translation:
    'Sweet be Thy Will,
    My Lord Nanak beseecheth the gift of nam.'

The above quotations mean that whatever happens in life, should be willfully accepted. In the house of Guru Nanak there is no room for tears or cries.There is no place for appeal before the Divine Writ. One must embrace God's Will as the sweetest gift of life. This is the first lesson preached by Guru Nanak to the humanity in Japji. How could then the Guru go into anguish? Does the Divine Jot also feel anguish?

B. The Guru assures that a true devotee's prayers are always answered by the Almighty and are accepted by Him:

    'Nanak das mukh te jo bolai eeha uha sach howai.'
    (Dhanasri Mohalla 5, p-681)

Translation:
    'Whatever God's servant, Nanak, uttereth shall prove
    to be true both in this world and the next.'

Being embodiment of Divine Light, if the Guru had appealed to the Almighty, He should have accepted his appeal and should have punished Baber. History reminds us that Baber's dynasty was rather blessed with a rule for seven generations.

C. The Guru had reached Eminabad before Baber's attack on
    the city, and he uttered the Sabad given below in which
he told Lalo about the oncoming massacre. He had
warned some people to leave the city and they actually did:

> 'As the word of the Lord cometh to me, so do I
>   narrate it, O Lalo,
> Bringing a bridal procession of sin, Baber has
>   hasted from Kabul and demandeth wealth
>   as his bride, O Lalo;
> Modesty and religion have vanished, falsehood
>   marcheth in van, O Lalo;
> They sing the paean of murder, O Nanak, and smear
>   themselves with the saffron of blood.
> Nanak singeth the praises of the Lord in the city
>   of corpses and uttereth this commonplace-
> He who made men, assigned them different
>   positions,
>
> He sitteth apart alone and regardeth them.
> True is the Lord, true His decision, true the
>   justice He meteth out as an example.
> Bodies shall be cut like shreds of cloth;
>   Hindustan will remember what I say.
>   (Tilang Mohalla 1, p-722)

In view of the above analysis, it seems quite evident that the
Guru did not appeal to God, but the dauntless Gur Nanak Jot
addressed that Sabad to Baber, who then fell on the feet of the
Guru and asked for forgiveness.

Baber wrote in his memoirs,"The inhabitants of
Saidpur were put to sword, their wives and children carried
into captivity and all their property plundered."

Many people were killed and most of the rest were
taken as prisoners by the Baber's army. It is said that the

Guru along with his minstrel Mardana, were also taken to the concentration camp. The prisoners were given handmills to grind the corn. The Guru asked Mardana to play on his rebec and he then started kirtan. As the Divine Sabad was sung-all the prisoners came and sat around the Guru, every grinding mill started working automatically. On seeing this supernatural phenomenon, the guards stood spell-bound and they sent the word to Baber, who came and witnessed the whole scene with his own eyes. Baber was wonder-stuck and asked the Guru if he could offer him anything. Boldly replied the Guru:

> 'Hear, O Baber Mir
> Foolish is the Faqir
> Who begs anything of thee
> Whose own hunger has not appeased.'

Baber said,"O holy man, I see God in thy face. I will do anything you ask for."
The Guru then uttered the following Sabad and put most of the blame of killings on Baber:

> 'Thou ruled over Khurasan,
> Now thou terrified Hindustan (India),
> He has sent you the Moghal as a messenger of death,
> Has slaughter and lamentations
> Awakened no compassion in thee?
> The Creator is the Supreme Lord,
> If a strong man beats another strong man
> No feelings of resentment arise;
> But if a ravening lion falls on a herd, its master should
> show his manliness.
> (Asa Mohalla 1, page 360)

This is the Sabad which other writers have attributed to as Guru's appeal to God. In actuality, this was Guru placing the blame on Baber.

The Guru asked Baber, when his army fell like a lion on

these innocent men, women and children, did he feel any pain for them?

Baber was overtaken by remorse. A new moral and spiritual consciousness was awakened in him, and he fell on the feet of the Guru. He asked the Guru to be gracious unto him. (Historyhas revealed that kings were always afraid of the curses of the holy men).

The Guru replied,"If thou, O Emperor, desireth kind ness, set all thy captives free." Baber agreed on the condition that his empire should be blessed by the Guru and should be allowed to continue for generations. The Guru promised," Thine empire shall remain for a long time." Upon this the Emperor ordered all the prisoners be set free. Baber then asked the Guru for instructions to rule. The Guru explained, "Deliver just judgement, reverence for holy men, forswear wine and gambling. The monarch who indulgeth in these vices shall, if he survives, bewail his misdeeds. Be merciful to the vanquished, and worship God in spirit and in truth."

Now the question is why was Baber blessed with kingdoms instead of being punished? The Gurbani (Divine Word) says:

'Jo saran awai tis kanth lawai eho birdh swamy sanda.'
                              (Bihagra Mohalla 5,p-544)
Translation:
'God embraces him who seeketh His protection; This
          is the characteristic of the Lord.'

The Guru tells us that the characteristic of his Master (God) is such that whosoever begs His pardon, falls on His feet for forgiveness, He embraces him. Since Guru Nanak himself was the embodiment of Divine Spirit, he pardoned Baber when he sought for forgiveness, and he blessed him with a boon of Moghal dynasty which continued for a long time.

GURU AT KARTARPUR:

After the third and the last Udasi the Guru returned to Kartarpur. He travelled all over to preach the gospel of Nam and communicating new awakening in the people's mind to realize Truth. In order that his work should last, he established a network of centers which were called Manjis, side by side with the centers of all other faiths. When he finished his long travels, he settled down at Kartarpur for the rest of about twenty years of his life. He knew that unless he centralized the activities of his new faith, he could not expect it to survive. There were now Sikh centers all over India, Ceylon, Tibet and the Middle East. No founder of any religion had built such a vast organization, breaking all provincial, national, international and cultural barriers, during his life time. When he went abroad on his missionary tours, he put up the robes of religious orders of the holy places he visited. Holiness in those places was inseparable from the holy garbs. When he came back to Kartarpur, he doffed his pilgrim's dress, and wore worldly garments in order to show that he did not desire his followers to devote themselves to an ascetic life. At the same time he sat on his religious throne, and started preaching to the people.

FORMATION OF SANGAT:

First he formed the holy communion which was called Sangat, and the place where the holy communion was held called Gurdwara (House of the Guru). Emphasis were laid on religious instructions and strict discipline. The Japji was recited at the ambrosial hour of the morning, the Sodar (Rehras) in the evening and Kirtan Sohila at night before going to bed. Divine measures (Kirtan) were sung in his presence in the morning as well as in the evening. Regular religious instructions were imparted by the Guru. Such instructions could be given to the individual followers and also in the regular gathering. In order to be the Sikhs of the Guru, the followers were baptized by receiving Charanpauhal (also called Charanamrit). This was the form of initiation administered by drinking the water in which the Guru's feet (generally toe) had been washed, the preamble of Japji was read at the same time, and the ceremony was inaugurated by the Guru himself. The emphasis was laid on the greatness of God, upon His gracious self-revelation, upon the perils of human condition, and upon the paramount necessity of meditation on Divine Name. Those who took pride in their status of caste or wealth, would be sternly admonished, and any one who depended on religious hypocrisy would be soundly condemned. The Guru enunciated an integral view of the spiritual and moral life and those who imbibed it, tried to realize its essence in their own daily conduct. The Guru's teachings emphasized on two things in particular; against limiting of the spiritual and moral conduct to ritual actions, and against confining the moral action to the individual self, or to such narrow confines as one's tribe, race or denomination. His teaching had great effect on the people and many of them embraced his religion. Bhai Buddha, Bhai Lehna (later Guru Angad), Taru Poput, Prithi, Kheda, Ajita Randhawa, Sheikh Mallo and Ubre Khan are some of the examples of conversions at first sight to the faith of the Guru.

LIVING BY HONEST MEANS:

Emphasis were laid on honest hard labor for living. Asceticism was explicitly rejected and instead a disciplined worldliness and family life was set forth as the proper course for the believer. Earnest living through honest hard labor and then out of that hard earned money, giving in the name of the Lord, was the moral way to bring up the family. The Guru himself set up this example by working with his hands in the fields for the remaining about 18 to 20 years of his life at Kartarpur. The Guru emphasized this course in the following Sabad:

"Men without divine knowledge sing hymns.
The Hungry Mulla maketh a home of his mosque.[24]

One who earneth nothing slitteth his ears[25];
Another becometh a beggar and loseth his caste.
Touch not at all the feet of those

24: *He spends all his time in the mosque, so as to receive more alms.*

25: *The Yogi*

Who call themselves gurus and pirs, and go begging.
They who eat the fruit of their labor and bestow something
in the name of Lord,
O Nanak, recognize the right way."
(Sarang ki Var, Slok Mohalla 1, p-1245)

COMMON FREE KITCHEN- GURU KA LANGAR:

Every one worked for his living and gave a part of his earning for the free kitchen called Guru ka Langar. All people, the Brahman or the Sudra, the king or the commoner, the Muslim or the Hindu, had to sit in the same row and eat the same food.

COMPOSITION AND COLLECTION OF BANI:

These were the years when most of the Guru's disciples received religious instructions from him and who recorded what they received. Many devotees, it is said, copied the daily prayers and hymns. These collections were called 'Bani Pothis' (books of hymns). The Bani Pothi compiled during his life time was passed on to the second Guru, Guru Angad Dev.

FURTHER TRAVELS FROM KARTARPUR:

Although the Guru had settled down at Kartarpur, but he still took small tours within the radius of 100 to 200 miles around Kartarpur. The Guru went many places and preached his gospel of Nam. At many of these places, the people became Guru's followers and they set up Gurdwaras in honoring the Guru.

GURU AT ACHAL BATALA:

About 25 miles from Kartarpur, there was a place called Achal Batala where on the occasion of Shivratri festival, hundreds of Jogis used to come to take part in the festival. The Guru also went to Achal Batala to preach his doctrine. Thousands of people came from far and near to see and hear him. There were three camps- one of the Jogis, another of the Guru and the third one of a party of musicians. More and more people gathered around the Guru's camp than that of the Jogis. This made the Jogis very angry and jealous and they were determined to humble the Guru.

Whatever the money the musicians were getting from the audience, they put it in a bowl. Somehow the Jogis stole their bowl full of money and hid it someplace thinking that the musicians would go to the Guru for help and if the Guru was unable to locate the bowl, he would be humbled.

Knowing about the greatness of the Guru, the musicians went to the Guru for help to find their bowl of money. The wonderful Guru told them about the mischief of the Jogis and recovered their bowl from the hiding place. Thus the Jogis suffered a tremendous defeat.

Next attack from the Jogis came through a discussion. As mentioned before the Guru after his travels, laid aside the pilgrim's apparel and had put up ordinary dress of a family man. The Jogis said,"O Guru, you are a holy man but you are wearing the garb of a family person. Why does a holy man lead a family life?" Jogi Bhagarnath[26] further asked the Guru,"When the milk becomes sour, no butter is produced by churning it, why have you cast away your hermit's dress and donned ordinary clothes?"

The Guru replied,"O Bhangarnath, your mother was an unskilled woman. She knew not how to wash the churn, and so spoilt the butter in producing thee. Thou hast become an anchoret after abandoning thy family life, and yet thou goest to beg to the houses of family men."

Upon this reply the Jogis were enraged and through their miraculous powers, they started to harass the Guru. One Jogi became a cobra to frighten the Guru, the other became wolf and other started rain of fire. The powerful Guru sat calmly unperturbed and unharmed. When the Jogis were beaten badly, Bhangarnath asked the Guru that he exhibited miracles to the world, why he was slow to exhibit the miracles to them?

The Guru replied that he had no miracles except the True Name, and he uttered the following Sabad:

"Were I to put on a dress of fire, construct a house of snow and eat iron;

26: *Bhangarnath was a head Jogi*

Were I to turn all my troubles into water, drink it, and
drive the earth as a steed;
Were I able to put the firmament into one scale and weigh it
with a tank[27];
Were I to become so large that I could be nowhere contained;
and were I to lead every one by the nose;
Had I such power in myself that I could perform such things
or cause others to perform them, it would be all in vain.
As great as the Lord is, so great are His gifts; He bestoweth
according to His pleasure.
Nanak, he on whom God looketh with favor obtaineth the
glory of the True Name."
(Majh di Var, Slok Mohalla 1, p-147)

The Jogis then finally complimented the Guru on his success and said,"**Hail, O Nanak, great are thy deeds! Thou hast
arisen a great being, and lit a light in this age of falsehood
(kalyug) in the world.**"

BHAI BUDDHA:

The Guru initiated Kirtan at the early hours of the morning
at Kartarpur. A boy seven years of age started to come to listen
Kirtan and stood behind the Guru as a mark of respect. One day the
Guru asked the boy,"O boy, why do you come so early while your
age requires to eat, play and sleep." The boy replied,"Sir, one day
my mother asked me to lit the fire. When I put fire on the wood, I
observed that the little sticks burned first than the big ones. From
that time I am afraid of the early death. I am doubtful whether I will
live to be old and so I attend your holy communion." The Guru was
very much pleased to hear these words of wisdom from the lips of
the boy and said,"Although you are only a boy, yet you speak like
a 'buddha' (an old man)."

From that day the boy was called Bhai Buddha. He was
held in such high esteem that he was commissioned to impress the
saffron tilaks or patches of Gurudom on the foreheads of the first

---

27: *Tank is one weight measure in India. One tank is equal to the weight of 256 grains of Rice. It means
that if he is able to perform such a miracle.*

five successors of Guru Nanak.

Bhai Buddha's original name was Ram Das, and a village was named after him. The word Bhai means brother. Guru Nanak who disregarded caste and preached the doctrine of the brotherhood of mankind, desired that all his followers should be deemed brothers, and thus be addressed so. The title 'Bhai' is now bestowed on Sikh priests also.

DUNI CHAND:

The Guru once passed through Lahore. A millionaire, Duni Chand of that place, was performing Shradh[28] for his father. When Duni Chand heard the arrival of the Guru, he invited him too. The Guru reached his residence and inquired of the occasion. Duni Chand replied that it was his father's Shradh and he had fed one hundred Brahmans in his name. The Guru said,"It is now two days since your father had eaten anything and you claim that you have fed one hundred Brahmans in his name." Duni Chand asked,"Where is my father?" The Guru replied,"Your father when he was alive, had coveted meat which a Sikh was cooking, and had died in that desire. So after death his soul had entered a wolf. That wolf is in a clump of trees about six miles from here and he has not eaten for two days." Duni Chand realized that anything sent to our forefathers via priests, would never reach them. Such rites were mere customs under blind faith.

Duni Chand had amassed wealth and was always after adding more to it. The Guru gave him a needle saying,"Duni Chand, keep this needle with you and give it back to me in the next world."

Duni Chand asked,"How can we carry a needle with us beyond death?" The Guru replied,"If such a small needle cannot go to the next world, how can thy wealth reach there?"

Upon this Duni Chand fell on the Guru's feet and prayed for enlightenment. The Guru told him,"Give some of your wealth in God's name and feed the poor." Duni Chand became Guru's disciple and began to repeat the Name. The Guru uttered the following Sabad on the occasion:

28: *Shradhs are oblations of cakes and libations of water made to the spirits of deceased ancestors.*

"False are kings, false their subjects, false the whole world;
False are mansions, false palaces, false those who dwell
therein;
False is gold, false sliver, false he who weareth them;
False husbands, false wives, they pine away and become dust.
Man who is false, loveth what is false, and forgetteth the
Creator.
With whom contact friendship? The whole world passeth
away.
False is sweetness, false honey, in falsehood shiploads are
drowned-
Nanak humbly asserteth- Except Thee, O God, everything
is thoroughly false."
(Asa di Var- Slok Mohalla 1, p-468)

BHAI LEHNA:

Jodha was a disciple of the Guru who lived in a small town, Khadur, about 50 miles away from Kartarpur. Bhai Lehna was a son of a rich trader and was also living in Khadur. Bhai Lehna was a devotee of Durga- a Hindu goddess of energy, and he used to go every year to the temple of Durga in the Kangra Hills.

One morning, when Bhai Jodha was reciting Japji, Bhai Lehna heard him and was touched at heart by the ecstasy of Divine Word. He asked Jodha whose composition it was. Bhai Jodha explained in detail about his Guru and so Bhai Lehna was inspired to see the Guru.

On the annual occasion while his fellow devotees went on to the temple of Durga, Bhai Lehna stopped on his way to see Guru Nanak. On seeing the Guru, he was completely overtaken by love and compassion of truth. When Bhai Lehna told his name, the Guru said,"Thou Lehna is here, where else can it be found?" In Punjabi language Lehna means to pay dues or to receive. The Guru meant,"What thou desirest to receive- salvation, is here, and no-where else." After receiving some religious instructions from the Guru, he began to repeat God's Name.

It is said that Bhai Lehna in a vision saw a female in red

dress serving the Guru's house. Lehna asked who she was. She replied that she was Durga (goddess), and that she came once a week to do the service for the Guru. On this Bhai Lehna became convinced of the Divine Glory of Guru Nanak.

As the time went on, Bhai Lehna became more and more immersed in meditation and so became more and more close and obedient devotee of the Guru.

As the time of Guru's departure (from the world) was drawing near, it was becoming clear to Mataji (Guru's wife) that there would be succession to Guruship. As is the custom in the world, she always thought that her sons should be the heir of their father's property, the Guruship. One day she said,"My Lord, keep my sons in mind." This meant that the Guruship should be passed on to one of her sons. The Guru said,"Bring your sons." Both the sons were brought before the Guru. He then threw a bowl in a tank of muddy water, and asked his eldest son, Sri Chand, to go and recover the bowl from the tank. Sri Chand replied,"Why did you throw the bowl, if it had to be brought back?" So he refused to do the job. In the same way the younger son declined to act. Then the Guru turned to Bhai Lehna and said,"Lehnaji, go and bring the bowl." Bhai Lehna said,"Sat bachan (Yes Sir)." Bhai Lehna went and recovered the bowl without caring for his clothes getting soiled with mud.

One day the Guru asked Bhai Lehna to go home and settle his affairs. After some time when he returned from his home and arrived at the Guru's house, he was told that the Guru was in his fields and would be home by evening. Bhai Lehna went straight to the fields to see the Guru. The Guru had three bundles of grass for his cows and buffaloes and wanted to take them home. As the grass was wet and full of mud, his Sikhs shied away from the task. He then asked his sons to carry the bundles and they too evaded the duty. Bhai Lehna who had just arrived, made his obeisance and said,"Sir, give me this job." Bhai Lehna took all three bundles and walked in the company of the Guru to his house. When they arrived home, the Guru's wife complained,"It is not proper to impose such a menial labor on a guest, his clothes from head to foot are fouled with mud which has been dripping from the grass." The Guru replied,"This is not mud; it is the saffron of God's court, which marketh the elect." On looking again the Guru's wife observed that Bhai Lehna's clothes had really changed to saffron. The three bundles are considered by the Sikhs to symbolize spiritual affairs, temporal affairs, and the Guruship.

The Guru now began a systematic trial of the devotion of his Sikhs. One winter night, as heavy rain was falling, a part of the wall of Guru's house fell. The Guru desired that the wall must be repaired immediately. His sons refused to do the job right away saying it was cold and also mid-night but they would send for some masons in the morning who would do the job. The Guru stated that there was no need for masons as Guru's work should be done by his Sikhs. Bhai Lehna stood up and started to repair the wall. When he had finished the work somewhat, the Guru said,"That wall is crooked, pull it down and build it again." Bhai Lehna did it so but the Guru again professed not to be satisfied. Lehna again obeyed the Master's orders; but the Master again was not pleased. Upon this the Guru's sons told Lehna that he was a fool to obey unreasonable orders. Bhai Lehna humbly replied that a servant should make his hands useful by doing his Master's work. After that the Guru and his disciple grew close to each other and thus more pleased with each other. The Guru's sons grew jealous of the devoted disciple. They took no pains to conceal their dislike of him.

One day a Jogi came and congratulated the Guru on the large number of converts he had made. The Guru replied that he had only a few real Sikhs, as the Jogi would himself witness. The Guru and the Jogi started towards the forest to try the Sikhs who accompanied them. As the party proceeded they found the road covered with copper coins. Some Sikhs grabbed them and departed. A little further on, silver coins were found. Several Sikhs took them and returned home. As the party went ahead, they saw gold coins. Many of the remaining Sikhs took the gold coins and left the party. Only the Jogi, two Sikhs, the Guru and Bhai Lehna now remained.

On proceeding further they found a funeral pyre and four lighted lamps near the corpse. A sheet was covering the corpse which was emitting a foul smell. The Guru asked,"Is there any one who will eat this corpse?" The Sikhs recoiled at the frightening proposal, but Bhai Lehna remained firm in his faith in the Guru. Bhai Lehna with clasped hands asked the Guru,"Where should I begin to eat, the head or the feet of the corpse?" The Guru told him to begin at the waist. When Bhai Lehna lifted the sheet from the corpse, lo! Wonder of wonders, a dish of Parshad (sacred food) appeared instead of the corpse. Bhai Lehna offered the Parshad first to the Guru and said that he would partake of his leavings. The Guru stated,"Thou hast obtained my secret. Thou art in mine image. I shall give you the real spell which is the essence of religion. By this spell you shall have happiness here in this world and in the next hereafter." The following is the spell meant by the Guru, the preamble of Japji:

> There is but One God
> Eternal Truth,
> Almighty Creator,
> Unfearful, Without Hate and Enmity, Immortal Entity,
> Unborn, Self-Existent,
> By His Grace, shalt thou worship
> The One Who was True before the creation,
> The One Who was True in the beginning of the creation,
> The One Who is True now, and O Nanak,
> The One Who shall be True for ever.

Upon this the Jogi said,"O Nanak, he shall be the Guru, who is produced from thy 'ang', body." The Guru embraced Lehna and promised that he would be his successor.

The moral as the Guru enunciated here is that a Sikh must make a total unconditional surrender before the Guru. He must have total obedience for the Guru's order, then and only then the Sikh reaches his goal i.e becomes one with Him. The Guru's sons questioned him at every step, while Bhai Lehna submitted willfully without uttering even one word. The result being that Bhai Lehna was blessed with Guruship and became the embodiment of Divine Light. According to Guru's mandate and code of conduct, a Sikh must lead spiritual and moral life while conducting every day's business to earn Guru's blessing. The Guru's mandate is clear:

> "Hukam maniai howai parvan ta khasmai ka maihal paisi."
>   (Asa di Var+ pauri 15, p+471)
>   "By obeying His order, man is acceptable

And shall then reach the Lord's court."
(Translation of the above)

ASCENSION OF GURU NANAK:

The Guru, knowing that his time to depart was approaching, had to appoint his successor. His sons had not obeyed him and so they did not prove themselves to be worthy of Guruship. On September 2, 1539 (2 Asu, 1596 Asu vadi 5) Guru Nanak placed five Paise (Indian currency) before Bhai Lehna and bowed to him in token of his succession to the Guruship. He placed the umbrella of Spiritual Sovereignty over Bhai Lehna's head. **Thus, he created another Nanak and called him GURU ANGAD DEV.**

"Jot uha jugat sai seih kaya feir paltiai."
(Ramkali ki Var- Rai Balwand, p-966)

'Divine Light is the same
The Way and Mode are the same
The Master has merely changed the body.'
(Translation of the above)

When Guruship was passed on to Guru Angad, people realized that Guru Nanak was soon to depart bodily from the world (As a Divine Light and Spirit, the Guru is always present). The Sikhs, the Hindus and the Muslims came from all over to have holy glimpse of Guru Nanak.

After the proclamation of Guru Angad, the sons asked their father, what provision he had made for them. Guru Nanak replied,"O my sons, God is the Cherisher of His creatures; you shall obtain food and clothing in abundance, and if you repeat God's name you shall be saved at last."

Guru's Muslim devotees wanted to bury him after his death. His Hindu followers desired to cremate his body. When the Guru was asked for his decision, he replied," Let the Hindus place flowers on my right and the Muslims on my left. Those whose flowers are found fresh in the morning, may have the disposal rights of my body."

The Guru drew a sheet over him. When the sheet was removed next morning, body was not found underneath, but the flowers on both sides were afresh. The light blended with Light and the spirit went back and merged with the Master Spirit. It confirms that the Guru was not a body but it was the Divine Light.

The Hindus and the Muslims removed their respective flowers and cut the sheet into two. The former cremated the sheet and the latter buried it. It happened at Kartarpur on September 22, 1539 (23rd day of Asu, Vadi 10, Sambat 1596). He was about seventy and a half years of age.

The Sikhs built a Gurdwara and the Muslims a tomb in his honor on the bank of river Ravi. Both had since been washed away by the river, perhaps by a superact, so as to avoid idolatrous worship of the Guru's last resting place.

Rituals and superstitions earned the sanctions of old times. Religion had degenerated into ceremonial acts only. The life and teachings of Guru Nanak offer consistent evidence of fruitlessness of rituals. He exposed their hollowness and exhorted human beings to rise above such customs. With no sword or stick armed with Divine Word, he preached that only Impersonal Absolute is to be worshiped. Any religion which does not guard its values indicates a lower level of development and is deemed to disappear in the long run. Guru Nanak's religion excluded all senseless dogmas and meaningless rituals.

GURU ANGAD DEV
(1504-1552, Guruship- 1539-1552)

Guru Angad Dev was born on March 31, 1504 in a village called Harike in Ferozepur district of the Punjab. His father, Bhai Pheru was a trader. His parents called him Lehna. He was married at the age of fifteen. His wife, Khivi was a native of Mattei di Sarai in Ferozepur district. His father grew weary of Harike and with his family returned to his ancestral place, Mattei di Sarai and lived there. Bhai Lehna's wife gave birth to two daughters, Amro and Anokhi, and two sons called Dasu and Datu.

When Mattei di Sarai was sacked by the Mughals and Baloches, Bhai Lehna and his father moved to Khadur, now a famous town near Tarn Taran. Bhai Lehna grew very religious under the influence of his mother, Daya Kaur, and became a devotee of Durga, the goddess of Shakti. He used to organize yearly pilgrimage of devout Hindus to Jawalamukhi, a place of Durga temple in the lower Himalayas where fire issued from the mountains. He used to lead Durga dance around the fire in a harness of jingling bells.

Bhai Jodha, a Guru's Sikh, lived in Khadur and it was his daily routine to rise early every morning and recite Japji and Asa di Var. One day as Bhai Lehna attentively listened the Divine Sabad recited by Bhai Jodha, his mind obtained peace. After the day break he asked Jodha who had composed that stimulating hymn. Bhai Jodha then told him all about Guru Nanak, who was living at Kartarpur at that time. The touch of Divine Sabad made such an impact on Bhai Lehna's mind that he got impatient to meet the Guru. When he was on his annual pilgrimage to Jawalamukhi, he broke his journey at Kartarpur to offer his obeisance to the Guru. During his meeting, the Guru spoke to him of the True Creator, leaving such an impression on Bhai Lehna that he threw away the jingling bells, which he was carrying with him to dance before the goddess. He had obtained such a peace of mind that he decided to discontinue his pilgrimage and abide with the Guru. On seeing his increasing devotion, the Guru said to him one day that he should go home and settle his affairs and on his return he would initiate

him as his Sikh. Upon this Bhai Lehna returned to Khadur for some
time.

A detailed account has been given in the last chapter regarding the circumstances which led to his succession to Guruship.
One day as Sikhs assembled, Guru Nanak seated Bhai Lehna on his
throne, put five paise and a coco-nut in front of him and bowed
before him and then said to Bhai Buddha,"This is my successor-
Guru Angad; put a tilak on his forehead in token of his appointment to the Guruship." Bhai Buddha did so. The Guru then
ordered his followers to obey and serve Guru Angad; who was in
his own image. Bhai Gurdas describes the succession to Guru
Angad (Var 1, pauri-45):

> "Angad got the same tilak, the same umbrella over his
> head, and was seated on the same true throne as Guru
> Nanak. The seal of Guru Nanak's hand entered Guru Angad's,
> and proclaimed his sovereignty."

After his appointment to the Guruship, Guru Nanak directed
Guru Angad to return to Khadur. Upon this Guru Angad returned
to Khadur and lived there.

GURU ANGAD IN SECLUSION:

The Guru sat in a room locked from outside near Khadur,
and meditated on God without any distraction or interruption. He
did not eat or drink anything except a pot of milk daily. About six
months passed like this and the Sikhs did not know the whereabouts of the Guru. One day Bhai Lalo, Bhai Saido and Bhai Ajita
and other Sikhs came to Bhai Buddha and asked him the whereabouts of the Guru. They had searched Khadur and other places
but could not find him anywhere. It is said that Bhai Buddha
concentrated his thoughts on the Guru and was able to visualize
his place of meditation. Next morning they all went to the house
near Khadur where the Guru was sitting in seclusion. The owner
of the house gave them no information but went inside the house
and told the Guru about the visit of four Sikhs. The Guru told the
owner that they should be shown inside. The Guru embraced Bhai
Buddha and uttered the following Slok:

"Cut off the head which boweth not to the Lord, Nanak, take and burn the wretched body which feeleth not the pain of separation."

(Slok Mohalla 2, p-89)

Bhai Buddha requested him to take his seat as Guru and receive the Sikhs publicly. After this Guru Angad came forth from his seclusion. When the Guru came out, crowds went to see him and presented to him their offerings. Whatever he received, the Guru passed on to his kitchen. There were continuous preaching, singing of hymns and repetition of Name.

EMPEROR HUMAYUN COMES TO THE GURU:

Emperor Humayun succeeded his father Baber but he was badly defeated by Sher Shah. Humayun inquired for some saint who could help him regain his throne and kingdom. He was advised to seek assistance of Guru Angad. Upon this Humayun came to Khadur. At that time the Guru was in a trance and the minstrels were singing the hymns. The Emperor was kept standing unattended. Humayun felt offended and in moment of rage, he put his hand on the hilt of his sword with the intention of striking the Guru. The sword, however, did not come out of the sheath which gave Humayun time to repent his act. Upon this the Guru addressed to him,"Where was your sword when you were facing Sher Shah? Now when you have come amongst the priests, instead of saluting them respectfully, you want to draw your sword on them. In a cowardly manner you fled from the battle ground, now posing as a hero you wish to attack the priests engaged in their devotion." Humayun repented and begged for Guru's spiritual assistance. The Guru replied,"Hadst thou not put thy hand on the hilt of thy sword, thou shouldst at once obtained thy kingdom. Thou shalt now proceed for a time to thine own country, and when thou returnest thou shalt recover thy kingdom." Humayun went back to his country and having obtained a reinforcement of cavalry from the king of Persia, he returned to India. After fighting a pitched battle he recovered his empire and captured Delhi.

GURMUKHI SCRIPT:

Clipped or imperfect alphabet of Punjabi existed at the time of Guru Nanak, but Guru Angad modified and polished the existing script. Since the Guru had adopted the modified alphabet, it was called 'Gurmukhi'- spoken through the mouth of the Guru. The significance of the adoption of this script by Guru Angad lies in the fact that he rejected all other scripts, and adopted the script which was his own and suited to the language of the people. It also helped to enhance their culture. The Guru recorded everything onwards in Punjabi in Gurmukhi script.

BABA AMAR DAS COMES TO GURU ANGAD:

Baba Amar Das was living in a village called Basarka near Amritsar. He was a firm believer of Vaishnav faith and used to fast regularly. Every year he went to Hardwar for pilgrimage, bathed in the river Ganges and would give alms to the poor. It was the twenty-first year of his pilgrimage and he was sixty-two years old. He was coming back from Hardwar when he decided to lay down to sleep outside the village of Mihra. Here he met a Vaishnav Sadhu (a monk) with whom he became so intimate that they cooked for each other. As they continued their journey and as the monk found Baba Amar Das zealously discharging all the duties of a pious Hindu, he asked him (Baba) who his guru was who taught him such piety and wisdom. Baba Amar Das replied that he had no guru. On hearing this the monk said,"I have committed a sin by eating from the hands of a man who has no guru. My ablutions bathing in the Ganges are of no avail now. I can only be purified if I return to bathe in the Ganges again." After lamenting like this, the Sadhu departed.

This was a great shock to Baba Amar Das and he was jolted in his heart thinking he was a man of no guru (Nigura):

"Satgur bajho gur nahi koee, nigurei ka hai nau bura."
                    (Rag Asa Mohalla 3, p-435)

'Satgur is the competent guru and without that no other guru is worthy of acceptance but if a person has no guru at all, that person's name is sinful." (translated)

He started thinking seriously how he could find a guru and he prayed for that. One day early in the morning he heard a divine melody which thrilled his heart and he stood spell-bound listening to the hymn. This was voice of Bibi Amro, Guru Angad's daughter, who was recently married to his nephew. It was Bibi Amro's routine to rise early, bathe and recite Japji and other hymns of Guru Nanak. Bibi Amro had recited the following Sabad which was heard by Baba Amar Das:

> "Neither sisters, sisters-in-law, nor mothers-in-law remain
> with one;
> But the true relationship with the Beloved, when found
> through the Guru, shall never be sundered.
> I am a sacrifice to my Guru, I am ever a sacrifice unto him.
> I have grown weary of wandering so far without a Guru;
> Now the Guru hath united me with my Beloved.
> (Maru Mohalla 1, p-1015)

Baba Amar Das asked Bibi Amro whose composition it was. She replied that it was Guru Nanak's hymn and she had learnt it from her father who was the successor to Guru Nanak. Baba Amar Das then requested her to take him to the Guru. After some days he accompanied Bibi Amro to visit the Guru in Khadur. When Baba Amar Das arrived, the Guru on account of his relationship, wanted to embrace Babaji and receive him respectfully, but Babaji fell on the feet of the Guru and said,"Thou art as God and I am only a worm." Baba Amar Das was so much overwhelmed by Guru's darshan (holy sight) that it was unbearable for him to leave his presence. The love for the Master sprang so deep and intense in his heart that he wanted to serve him in every possible way.

One day meat was prepared for dinner and Baba Amar Das commented,"If the Guru is the knower of hearts, he should know that I am a strict Vaishnav and do not touch meat." Realizing this the Guru ordered the Sikh who was serving the dinner (langar) that only dal (bean-curry) not meat should be served to him (Baba Amar Das). Soon after that, Baba Amar Das realized that a disciple, whose practice differed from that of his Guru, must inevitably fail.

He told the cook that if the Guru were kind enough to give him his meat leaving, he would partake of it. In order to further remove his prejudices, the Guru instructed him,"These are the meats to abstain from- others' wealth, others' wives, slander, envy, covetousness and pride." The Guru then recited the Slok Mohalla 1 of page 1289 on the subject.

CITY OF GOINDWAL:

One day a man, Gobind, came to the Guru and said that if he became victorious in a lawsuit against his relations, he would found a city in honor of the Guru. Fortune favored him and he started to found the city on the bank of the river Beas. He started the work but what was done during the day, was in some mysterious manner undone at night. Gobind came to the Guru and prayed to him to grant him his desire to build the city.

Upon this the Guru sent Baba Amar Das to help him. Babaji prayed to God for His assistance. The city's work proceeded without any further delay and Baba Amar Das named it Gobindwal and later on it was called Goindwal. Gobind did not forget to build a palace in it for his benefactor Amar Das. When the work was successfully completed, Gobind went to the Guru to offer his thanks and to beg him to come and live in the newly founded city. The Guru did not wish to leave his town, so he ordered Baba Amar Das to go and live in Goindwal by night and come to him by day. Babaji obeyed the Guru and settled in Goindwal. In the process of time he took with him all his relations from Basarka and helped them in settling there.

Baba Amar Das was now living in Goindwal and his daily routine was- to rise very early in the morning, take a pitcher of water from the river Beas and proceed to Khadur which was about three miles away. The pitcher of water was for Guru Angad to bathe with. On the way he would recite Japji. There was a mid-way spot which was called Damdama or breathing place where he could rest for a while. A temple was erected on this spot later on. After attending the morning service, Asa di Var, he would fetch water for the Guru's kitchen, clean dishes and bring firewood from the forest. During the day he would learn Gurbani (Word) from the Guru. In the evening he would attend Sodar and evening Kirtan.

After putting the Guru to rest, he would return walking to Goindwal backwards in supreme reverence for his Master.

GURU ANGAD AND TAPA:

There lived a Sadhu (monk), Tapa in Khadur. He was worshipped as a Guru by the Khahira Jats only. Tapa had jealousy against the Guru and contended reverence shown to Guru by his followers. He maintained that he should be worshipped instead of the Guru since Guru was a family man and not an ascetic.

One year there were no monsoons and as a result there was a drought in the land. People were distressed and went to Tapa for his help to procure rain. Tapa told them that he was a monk, yet no one worshipped him and instead everybody worshipped the family man (Guru), and so he asked them to go to the Guru and ask him to procure rain for them. They went to the Guru who replied,"Be satisfied with God's Will." They came back to Tapa who told them,"If you expel the Guru from the town, I will bring rain within twenty-four hours." Ultimately the Guru left the town and went seven villages away from Khadur where Tapa had no influence.

When Baba Amar Das arrived in Khadur next morning, he found the Guru's house empty. On inquiry the people narrated the whole story to Babaji. In the meantime Tapa failed to bring any rain. Upon this Baba Amar Das asked the people if a lamp could be substituted for the sun. He asked them to punish Tapa if they wanted rain. It so happened that as Tapa was being punished, the rain came in torrents. After that the people went to the Guru to ask for forgiveness for their acts.

When Guru Angad heard of Tapa's punishment, he felt much grieved and addressed to Amar Das,"You have not obtained the fruits of my companionship, which are peace, forbearance and forgiveness." On hearing this Babaji fell at the feet of the Guru and humbly sought his pardon. He confessed that he got Tapa punished because he could not take Guru's insult and promised to obey the Guru's instructions in future.

One night in March 1552, it rained all night, cold winds blew and lightning flashed. Baba Amar Das brought a pitcher of water from river Beas for his Master. While he was coming to the Guru's house, he struck against a wooden peg which a weaver had driven into the ground, and he fell into the loompit. It was a weavers' colony and when they heard the thud of his fall, one of the weavers' wife said,"Who could it be at this early hour? It must be that homeless Amru who sleeps not, who knows no rest and who tires not. He is ever bringing water from the river and firewood from the forest; and what a Guru to serve!"

The Master felt the twitch and was deeply moved. He embraced Baba Amar Das who was seventy-three years old then and said,"My Amar Das, he will be the home of the homeless, the honor of the unhonored, the strength of the strengthless, the support of the supportless, the emancipator of the captive."

After that Guru Angad installed Baba Amar Das in his seat, put five paise and a coco-nut before him, and asked Bhai Buddha to put saffron tilak of Guruship on his forehead. He was then declared as Guru Amar Das:

"Jot uha jugat sai seh kaya pher paltiai."
(Ramkali ki Var- Rai Balwand, p-966)

'Divine Light is the same
Way and Mode are the same
The Master has only changed the body."
(Translation of the above)

Guru Angad directed him to live in Goindwal and left for his heavenly abode on March 29, 1552.

Submission to Guru's order and worship of God, was the guiding principle in selection of the Guruship. In spite of the opposition of his sons and relations, Guru Angad conferred the Guruship on Baba Amar Das who was proved to be the fittest and the most worthy for the Divine throne of Guru Nanak.

GURU AMAR DAS

(1479-1574, Guruship, 1552-1574)

Guru Amar Das was born on April 5, 1479 at Basarka village in Amritsar district. He was the eldest son of his parents, Bhai Tej Bhan and Mata Lakhmi. At the age of 24, he was married to Mansa Devi who gave birth to two sons, Mohan and Mohri, and two daughters, Bibi Dani and Bibi Bhani. The early history of Guru Amar Das has been given in the last chapter.

DATU'S ANIMOSITY:

Guru Angad's sons were upset because they claimed that after their father, they were the legitimate heirs to Guruship. Guru Angad's son Datu, therefore, proclaimed himself as Guru in Khadur; but the Sikhs did not accept him as such. Secondly under Guru Amar Das's strict dictum, it was mandatory that all persons, high or low, rich or poor, king or the commoner, Brahmans or Sudras, and Hindus or Muslims, must sit in the same row as equals to dine in the Guru's langar (kitchen). This had upset the Brahmans very much and they were on the search of an opportunity to rectify this situation. These Brahmans and other higher caste leaders saw some chance in Datu's revolt to capture the Guruship. Upon their support, Datu proceeded to Goindwal where the Guru was stationing.

Guru Amar Das was sitting on his religious throne and was delivering instructions to the congregation. Datu came along with a large number of his companions and kicked the Guru, who fell down the platform. Datu took possession of the platform and proclaimed himself as the Guru. Guru Amar Das got up and said in extreme humility,"Sir, pardon me, my hard bones might have hurt your tender feet." After this the Guru left Goindwal and went to his village Basarka. He confined himself in a house outside the town without letting anybody know about his whereabouts.

Datu sat on Guru's throne in Goindwal and was very proud of his position. The Sikhs, however, did not accept him as Guru, and all the pilgrims to Goindwal went away on hearing of the insult to their Guru. On seeing the Sikhs' contempt towards him, one day Datu loaded his newly acquired wealth on a camel and returned to Khadur. On his way he was encountered with some robbers who seized the camel with the load, and one of the robbers struck Datu on the same foot with which he had kicked the Guru. Datu's foot swelled up and caused him great pain.

The Sikhs were very much distressed at loosing their Guru. They searched all over but could not find him anywhere. Under the leadership of Bhai Buddha, they prayed and then let Guru's mare[1] loose and anxiously followed it for a short distance. The mare made her way to the Guru's house in Basarka, and stood before his door. It was written on the door,"Whoever openeth this door is no Sikh of mine, nor I am his Guru." They did not open the door, but made an opening in the wall and made supplication before the Guru. The Guru could not disregard the love and devotion of his Sikhs and returned to Goindwal. The Guru's return was celebrated with illuminations, rejoicing and feasting.

SOME NOTABLE SIKHS:

Bhai Paro belonged to a village, Dalla in Doaba, an area between the rivers Beas and Satluj. He received religious instructions and emancipation from the Guru. A rich Muslim horse-dealer of Delhi, Alayar, brought five hundred horses from Arabia and arrived at Beas. He could not continue his journey because the river Beas was flooded and the boatmen refused to take the risk in crossing the swollen river. Next morning Alayar saw Bhai Paro plunge his horse into the foaming river and reaching the opposite shore in safety. Alayar met Paro on his return and complimented his daring feat of crossing the river. Bhai Paro told him that it was through the blessings of the Guru that he could cross the swollen river. He further informed Alayar about Guru's glory. Alayar became anxious to meet the Guru. Next morning they both went to see him.

Alayar (Ala means God, and yar means friend) was delighted to see the Guru. Hearing his name the Guru said to him,"It is difficult to become friend (yar) of God (Ala), but I will make God thy Master and thee His servant." Alayar was blessed by the Guru

---

1: *Guru had a mare.*

and he became his disciple. Alayar was made incharge of the first Manji (diocese) of the 22 Manjis that were set up by Guru Amar Das later on to spread the fragrance of Name. There are numerous such stories of the Sikhs who were blessed by the Guru.

BAWLI AT GOINDWAL:

Guru Amar Das purchased some land in Goindwal and laid the foundation of a Bawli (a well with descending steps) in 1559. All Sikhs joined in the work of digging the Bawli. There was great activity throughout the construction of the Bawli.

Hari Das, a Khatri of Sodhi tribe, lived with his wife, Daya Kaur, in Chuna Mandi, a suburb of Lahore. Both husband and wife were very religious. After twelve years of their marriage, a son was born to them on September 24, 1534. They called him Ram Das, who was generally known as Jetha meaning first-born. He was very handsome having fair complexion with pleasing personality. As he grew up he liked the company of holy men. One day his mother boiled some pulse, put it into a basket and gave it to him to sell and make profit. Jetha went to the river Ravi. Soon he saw a company of holy men, and Jetha gave the boiled pulse to them and went home. The holy men were very much pleased and prayed for the boy.

One day Jetha saw a company of Sikhs singing the hymns and proceeding with great rejoicing. He asked whither they were going, one of them said,"We are going to Goindwal where Guru Amar Das holds his court. Every blessing in this world and the next is obtained by his favor. Come with us." On hearing this Jetha was delighted and he joined them in their pilgrimage.

On seeing the Guru, Jetha's heart was filled with love and devotion. When he made his obeisance to the Guru, he was attracted by his pleasing personality. The Guru remarked,"If you have come abandoning all worldly desires, you shall obtain a true sovereignty. Perform work and service." Jetha happily applied himself to the Guru's service. He worked in the kitchen, cleaned dishes, shampooed his Master and brought firewood from the forest. He worked in the excavation of the Bawli during his leisure time.

Guru's eldest daughter, Bibi Dani (also known as Sulakhni)

was married to Rama. The other daughter, Bibi Bhani was very
religious from the very childhood. When Bibi Bhani was of mar-
riageable age, her mother reminded the Guru that it was time to
search for a match for her. The Guru ordered the search. When his
agent was ready to depart, Bibi Bhani's mother saw a young person
standing outside and she said to the agent,"Search for a boy like
him." The Guru heard her remarks and exclaimed,"He is his own
parallel, for God had made none other like unto him." The young
man thus chosen was Jethaji (Ram Das).

At the time of marriage, the bridegroom was asked by the
Guru to choose a gift for himself, as it was customary to do so.
Jethaji replied,"Sir, bless me with the gift of Hari Nam." Bibi Bhani
not only considered the Guru as her father but her Guru also. In the
same way she served Jetha not only as her husband but as a saint
also. Prithi Chand was their first son and three years later Mahadev, the second son made his appearance. On April 15, 1563
Jetha and Bibi Bhani were blessed with their third son, Arjan, at
whose birth there were unusual rejoicing.

Meanwhile the Sikhs continued excavation of the Bawli.
After digging very deep they found large stones which hindered
the progress. The Guru asked the Sikhs if there was any one who
would be courageous to drive a peg into the base to remove the
obstruction. He had, however, warned that the operation had great
danger because if the person could not avert the gush of the water,
he might be drowned. All the Sikhs remained silent and no one
came forward to take such a risk. At last Manak Chand of Vairowal, who was married to a niece of the Guru, offered his services.
This was the same Manak Chand whose parents were blessed with
a son (Manak Chand) by Guru Nanak.

Manak Chand, invoking God's name and through the grace
of the Guru, was able to wedge through the stone and the stream
of water immediately overflowed the Bawli. Manak Chand was
overtaken by the gush of the water. He almost drowned but by the
grace of the Guru, he came to the top from where he was taken out
and was revived. Therefore, he was called 'Marjiwra' (revived after
death).

The Bawli when finished yielded sweet drinking water. The
Sikhs rejoiced at the successful completion of their labor. There
were eighty-four steps reaching down the Bawli. It is believed that

whosoever recites Japji attentively and reverently at each step, is saved from the cycle of transmigration.

GURU KA LANGAR (FREE KITCHEN):

Guru's free kitchen (Guru ka Langar) which was started by Guru Nanak and developed by Guru Angad, was further strengthened by Guru Amar Das. It was the injunction of Guru Amar Das that none would have his audience unless he had first eaten from the Langar. The Guru intended to remove the caste restrictions and prejudices of untouchability. It was, therefore, declared unequivocally that all persons of all castes, high or low, rich or poor, Brahmans or Sudras, Hindus or Muslims, must sit in the same line and eat the same food from Guru's kitchen. When Raja of Haripur or even Akbar, the Mughal Emperor of India, came to see the Guru, they had to sit with common people and dine with them before they could have audience with the Guru. In this way people were lifted above the hypocrisy of caste system and were able to look at one another as brothers and equals.

Mai Das was a renowned Pandit and a devout worshipper of Lord Krishna. He was a strict Vaishnav, he would eat only what he had cooked with his own hands within a purified square[2]. The Guru rejects these purified squares:

"All outlined purified squares are false; O Nanak,
Only God is pure."
(Maru ki Var, Slok Mohalla 3, p-1090)

When he came to see the Guru, he was informed that unless he had eaten from Guru's kitchen, he could not see him. Being a strict Vaishnav he could not do that, so he left for Dwarka where he thought to have a glimpse of Lord Krishna. On the eleventh day of lunar month Mai Das used to fast and would eat just fruits during that period. Due to winter season the fruits were not available in the forest. Mai Das wandered hungry in the forest looking for fruits but could not find them. Finally he started calling on his gods for

---

2: *A Brahman draws a small square and washes the spot with water and calls it a purified square. He then prepares his meals within the square. If anyone enters the square, it gets polluted and the food prepared inside the square then is deemed impure.*

help. At last he heard a voice,"You have not eaten food from the Guru's kitchen, and you have not had holy sight of him; therefore shalt thou not obtain perfection. If you desire to do so, then first behold Guru Amar Das."

Upon this Mai Das returned to Goindwal. He partook of food from the Guru's kitchen, and then was allowed to see the Guru. The Guru welcomed him,"Come, Mai Das, thou art a special saint of God." The Guru initiated him as his Sikh, blessed him with Nam and bestowed on him the spiritual power of conferring salvation on others. Mai Das held one of the 22 Manjis (dioceses) set up by Guru Amar Das.

EMPEROR AKBAR VISITS THE GURU:

Akbar, the Emperor of India, on his way to Lahore, paid a visit to the Guru at Goindwal. He was informed that he could not see the Guru until he had dined with others from the Guru's kitchen. Akbar partook of the food in the Langar, the more he had it, the more he relished it. After that the Emperor had an interview with the Master. It is said that the Guru rose to receive the Emperor in his arms, but Akbar spontaneously bowed to touch the feet of the Master. The monarch felt a thrill of joy and peace by the holy touch.

Having seen the large number of people fed from the Guru's kitchen, Akbar requested the Guru to accept his services and his offerings. But the Guru replied,"I have obtained lands and rent-free tenures from my Creator. Whatever comes daily is spent daily, and for the morrow my trust is in God." Akbar then replied,"I see you desire nothing. From thy treasury and thy kitchen count-less people receive bounties, and I also entertain similar wishes, I will grant these 84 villages to thy daughter, Bibi Bhani." This was the estate where Guru Ram Das built the city of Ramdaspur which is now called Amritsar.

A COMPLAINT AGAINST GURU TO AKBAR:

When the Brahmans and the Khatris failed in their mission to derail the Guru from Guruship by inciting Datu to declare himself as Guru, they made a special complaint to Emperor Akbar.

In their complaint they alleged,"Every man's religion is dear to him. Guru Amar Das of Goindwal has abandoned the religious and social customs of the Hindus, and abolished the distinction of the four castes. He makes his followers of all castes sit in a line and eat together from his kitchen irrespective of caste or religion. There is no offering of water to ancestors, no pilgrimages, no worship of idols of gods or goddesses. The Guru reverenceth not Jogis, Jatis or Brahmans. We, therefore, pray thee to restrain him now, else it will be difficult later on."

Akbar sent a high official to Goindwal to request Guru's attendance. The summons was not a brutal order of a modern court,"Herein fail not, but kindly grant me a sight of thee." The Guru sent Jetha saying,"Thou art in my image; Guru Nanak will be with thee and none shall prevail against thee. Fear no body and give suitable reply."

Jetha gave suitable replies to all the questions and satisfied the Emperor who then gave his decision,"I see no hostility to Hinduism in this man, nor do I find any fault with his compositions." The Brahmans left the court in utter defeat. Macauliffe qoutes 'Suraj Parkash', "Upon this the Emperor took Jetha aside, and told him to request Guru Amar Das, who before his conversion to Sikhism used to make yearly pilgrimages to the Ganges, to make one pilgrimage more in order to divert the wrath of the Hindus. The Emperor added that he would issue an order that no tax should be levied on the Guru's party...... The Guru in compliance with the Emperor's suggestion, and also in order to have an opportunity of preaching his religion, set out for Hardwar." 'The Guru's going to Hardwar for one more pilgrimage to avert the wrath of the Hindus', seems totally unfounded because it is against the tenets of the Guru who says:

"Tirath nawan jao, tirath nam hai
Tirath sabad bichar untar gian hai."
(Dhanasri Mohalla 1, p-687)

'What is pilgrimage? Pilgrimage is Nam,
Pilgrimage is contemplation on Word and realization of
inner knowledge.'
(Translation of the above)

"If mind is sinful, everything is sinful,
By washing the body, mind will not become pure."
                                    (Wadhans Mohalla 3, p-558)
It is not right to assert that Guru Amar Das went to Hardwar for
one more pilgrimage to please the Hindus. Guru Amar Das went
to Hardwar and Kurukshetra not to make a pilgrimage but to
preach his doctrine and gospel of Nam to the thousands of battered
souls.

ABOLITION OF SATI:

The status of women in Hindu society at that time was very
low. When the husband died, the wife either voluntarily burnt
herself on the pyre of her husband or was thrown into the fire
without her consent. In popular term the woman who did perform
this act was called Sati (truthful). Guru Amar Das carried out a
vigorous campaign against the practice of Sati. The Guru gave
special attention to the improvement of the status of women and
thus prohibited this practice. G.B. Scott acclaims the Guru as the
first reformer who condemned the prevailing Hindu practice of
Sati. The Guru advocated the following:

"Satis are not those who are burnt with husbands,
O Nanak, true Satis are whom pangs of separation can finish.
Those are considered Satis who live contented, embellish
                        themselves with good conduct;
And cherish the Lord ever and call on Him."
                            (Var Suhi ki- Slok Mohalla 3, p-787)

The Guru lifted the status of women as equal to men. He prohibited
the practice of Sati and preached in favor of widow marriage.

ESTABLISHMENT OF MANJI SYSTEM:

The Guru's following increased considerably. Steps were
taken to organize the scattered congregation into a unified whole
which was called Manji system. His whole spiritual domain took
the shape of 22 Manjis (dioceses). It was so named because the
incharge of a Manji sat on a cot (called Manji in Punjabi) to deliver

the message of the Guru. The incharge of each and every Manji was a devoted Sikh who was blessed by the Guru before he was appointed to that position. His function was to preach the mission of the Guru, to keep the Sangat (congregation) in touch with the Guru and he was also responsible for the offerings of the Sikhs which they made in token of their reverence to the Guru. The following were the twenty-two Manjis:

1. Alayar: Alayar also called Allah Shah was a Pathan trader whose story has been given earlier, became Guru's Sikh and was entrusted with the first Manji to spread Sikh faith.
2. Sachan Sach: He was a Brahman from Mandar village in Lahore district. He always used the word 'Sachan Sach' and so he was called Sachan Sach. One of the queens of Raja of Haripur became insane, and by the grace of the Guru, she recovered her sanity. The Guru married her to Sachan Sach. The couple preached Sikhism.
3. Sadharan: He was an inhabitant of Goindwal and was given a Manji for his devotion to the Guru.
4. Sawan Mal: He was a nephew of Guru Amar Das. The Guru sent him to Haripur in Kangra district to procure timber for the construction of houses in Goindwal. Sawan Mal propagated Sikh gospel in that area.
5. Sukhan: He was an inhabitant of Dhamian village in Rawalpindi district. He preached Sikhism in that area.
6. Handal: He was from Jandiala village in Amritsar district. He rendered great service in Guru's kitchen.
7. Kedari: Bhai Kedari was an inhabitant of Batala in Gurdaspur district. He was a very famous devotee of the Guru.
8. Kheda: He was from Khemkaran village in Lahore district. He was a devotee of Durga goddess before he became Guru's Sikh.
9. Gangushah: He was an inhabitant of Garh Shankar. The Guru sent him to preach Sikhism in Sarmaur state.
10. Darbari: Bhai Darbari was from Majitha village in Amritsar district.
11. Paro: Bhai Paro was a Sikh of Guru Angad. He was an inhabitant of Dalla. His devotion got him the eleventh Manji.
12. Phera: Bhai Phera was an inhabitant of Mirpur in

Jammu area. He was a disciple of the Jogis before he became Guru Amar Das's Sikh. He preached Sikhism in that hilly area.

13. Bua: Bhai Bua became Guru's Sikh and was blessed with Nam, the fragrance of which he spread around his area.

14. Beni: He was a learned Pandit of Chunian in Lahore district. He was proud of his knowledge of Hindu Shastras and he defeated many in the debate of that knowledge. When he came to Goindwal, he fell on the feet of the Guru and became his Sikh. The Guru entrusted him with the fourteenth Manji.

15. Mahesa: He was an inhabitant of Sultanpur and he performed missionary work in that area.

16. Mai Das: Mai Das's story has been given in the previous pages. He preached Sikhism in Majha area.

17. Manak Chand: His reference has been made in the previous pages. When he was drowned in the Bawli and then revived by the Guru, the Sikhs called him Marjiwra- the revived after death. His generation is called Marjiwre in Vairowal village in Amritsar district. Manak Chand was made a spiritual guide to Mai Das by the Guru.

18. Murari: He was an inhabitant of Khai village in Lahore district. His original name Prema and he was a leper. He heard about Guru Amar Das and came crawling all the way to Goindwal. By the grace of the Guru, he was fully healed. He was renamed as Murari. The Guru married him to Matho, daughter of Bhai Sihan. He was then sent out as one of the itinerant preachers of the Guru's gospel.

19. Raja Ram: He was a Brahman. He became Guru's Sikh. His generation now lives in Sandhma village of Jullundhur district.

20. Rang Shah: He was an inhabitant of Malupote village in Jullundhur district. He propagated Guru's faith in Doaba area.

21. Rang Das: He was from Gharooan village (near Kharar) now in Rupar district.

22. Lalo: He was an inhabitant of Dalla and was a famous Vaid (doctor). He became Guru's Sikh and preached Guru's gospel.

Guru Amar Das established another organization called Piri system. The incharges of the Piris were ladies whose objective was to lit the flame of Guru's word and spread the fragrance of Nam among women. Bibi Bhani, Bibi Dani and Bibi Pal were some of the most revered incharges of the different Piris. Guru Amar Das gave authority and power to 146 of his apostles to go to various parts of the country and unfold the glory of Nam. Out of these 146 persons, 94 were men and 52 were women. They were all glowing with Nam and filled with Divine Spirit.

COMPOSITION OF ANAND SAHIB:

One day a Sidh Jogi came to the Guru and complained that he performed every form of penance but did not obtain any peace of mind. He further showed his desire to abandon his body to be reborn in Guru's family so that he be happy worshipping God and singing His praises. His wish was granted. The Guru had two sons, Mohan and Mohri. Mohri's eldest son was Arth Mal and it is said that this Sidh Jogi was reborn as Mohri's second son. When the Guru heard of the Jogi's rebirth, he sent Bhai Ballu to bring the infant to him. On seeing the child, the Guru uttered the composition of Anand (Ramkali Mohalla 3, Anand) or the Song of Joy, and called the child, Anand. This composition (Anand Sahib) is now recited on the occasions of marriages and rejoicing.

SELECTION FOR GURUSHIP:

It should be remembered that Guru's eldest daughter, Bibi Dani was married to Rama who was a zealous Sikh. He used to work in Guru's kitchen and administer to the needs of the pilgrims. Jetha was his younger son-in-law. One day the Guru asked Rama and Jetha,"Each one of you make a platform by the side of Bawli. I will sit on one in the morning and on the other in the evening." When the platforms were completed, the Guru went to inspect them. Rama showed his work and thought that he had done well. The Guru told Rama,"Your platform is not straight, bring it down and rebuild it." Rama dissented but rebuilt another one. It still failed to please the Guru. Rama after long argument, pulled the platform down but refused to build it third time.

The Guru inspected Jetha's platform and said,"Jetha, I do not like it. Demolish it and build another one." Jetha built the second one which was also not of Guru's liking. He demolished it and rebuilt it. The Guru continued to find fault with it until it was demolished and rebuilt seven times. Jetha then fell at Guru's feet and begged, "I am a fool and lack understanding, while thou possesseth all knowledge. kindly bless me with the understanding so that I may be able to build the platform of your liking."

On hearing this the Guru smiled and embraced Jetha and commented,"Obeying my order, you have built the platform seven times, so seven generations of thine shall sit on the throne of Guru Nanak."

Bibi Bhani, Guru's youngest daughter, used to attend her father. She used to fan him, draw water and work in the kitchen. One day the Guru was sitting on his couch (chauki) in deep meditation, when Bibi Bhani noticed that one leg of his couch had broken. Fearing that his meditation would be disturbed, she put her arm in place of the broken leg to support the couch. When the Guru opened his eyes, he found blood coming out of Bibi Bhani's arm. On inquiry Bibi explained that broken leg might have caused disturbance in his meditation and so she thought herself fortunate to serve Guru by substituting her arm for the broken leg of the couch. The Guru commented,"Whosoever does good work, shall reap the reward thereof." He invited her to ask for any favor. She humbly requested that the Guruship should remain in her family. It is believed that the Guru told Bibi Bhani that the Guruship was not a bed of roses and he warned her of the trouble and torture that the later Gurus would have to go through. Bibi Bhani agreed to embrace all those troubles, and again requested to grant her the wish that the Guruship would remain in her family. So far the Guruship was earned by obedience and devotion to the Guru. Here again Bibi Bhani earned it, for her family, with her devotion and sacrifice. The Guru granted her the wish and the Guruship thereafter remained in Bibi Bhani's family.

Guru Nanak appointed his successor at Kartarpur but asked him to go and live at Khadur. Guru Angad asked his successor, Guru Amar Das to live in Goindwal. Guru Amar Das asked Jetha to search for a place other than Goindwal as a residence for the Sikhs. Jetha found an open land about 25 miles from Goindwal, and he established himself there. He built a house for himself and got a tank excavated which was called Santokhsar. It is also believed that the Guru asked Jetha to excavate another tank towards the east which would be called Amritsar- tank of nectar.

SUCCESSION OF GURU RAM DAS:

Guru Amar Das having tested Jethaji in every way, found him perfect and asked for special congregation. Then he asked Bhai Ballu to bring coco-nut and five paise. He asked Jethaji to bathe and clothe in new raiment. Then the Guru descended from his throne and made Jethaji seat on it and called him Guru Ram Das. Bhai Buddha, according to the custom, attached the tilak of Sovereignty to Guru Ram Das's forehead. Among great rejoicing, all Sikhs made offerings according to their means and saluted Guru Ram Das on his appointment. This ceremony was performed on August 30, 1574 at Goindwal.

GURU AMAR DAS'S DEPARTURE:

Guru Amar Das proclaimed,"God's summons hath come. Let there be no mourning when I have gone, sing God's praises, read God's Word (Gurbani), hear God's Word and obey God's Will." On the first of September, 1574, Guru Amar Das left for his heavenly abode and the spirit blended with the Master Spirit.

GURU RAM DAS
(1534-1581, Guruship, 1574-1581)

The early history of Guru Ram Das is referred to in the previous chapter.

Many writers have expressed their opinion that Akbar granted the land only to Guru Ram Das on which he founded the city of Ramdaspur (later known as Amritsar), and so they contend that the city of Amritsar was not founded during the time of Guru Amar Das. It is also a well-known fact of Sikh history that Emperor Akbar came to Goindwal and he dined with the common people in the Guru's langar before he could see the Guru. It seems that the Emperor granted the estate in the name of Bibi Bhani at that time, and Jethaji being her husband, was made incharge of the estate by Guru Amar Das. Guru Nanak awarded the Guruship to Bhai Lehna and not to his sons, and it is quite obvious that in order to avoid hostility of his sons towards his successor, he asked Guru Angad to move to Khadur instead of continuing to live in Kartarpur. The same circumstances prevailed during the reign of second and third Gurus. It is, therefore, quite likely that the planning of a new city was called for during the reign of Guru Amar Das as mentioned in the previous chapter.

Guru Ram Das left Goindwal for his new colony. Many Sikhs followed the Guru and settled there. At first this city was called Ramdaspur, which is now called Amritsar.

A revenue collector of Patti in district of Lahore had five daughters, the fifth daughter was very religious. One day the father asked who gave them to eat and drink. The first four daughters said that it were their parents who had provided them with food and other necessities of life, but the fifth daughter told her parents that God was the only Cherisher of His creation. On hearing this reply her father got very angry and remarked,"I shall see if God will protect you."

One day a crippled leper came to the town and the father married his fifth daughter to him to teach her a lesson. She willfully accepted him as her true husband. She put him in a basket and carried him on her head, and begged from door to door to maintain their livelihood. One day she left him under a tree near a pool of water and went to the nearby colony to beg for food. The leper saw some crows (black in color) dipping in the water and they turned white when came out of the water. The leper thought that the water had some miraculous healing property. So he left his basket and crawled into the water, and lo, the leprosy at once disappeared from the body except one finger which was left out of water. When the lady came back, she did not believe the story of the healed leper. Ultimately they went to Guru Ram Das, who confirmed saying that the pool possesseth such extraordinary efficacy which the man allegeth. Upon this the couple became Guru's followers and they worked in the excavation of the tank later on.

The tree under the shade of which she left her husband, is still standing there and is called 'Dukhbhanjni Beri'. The pool was known as Amritsar- tank of nectar, the place itself came to be known as the city of Amritsar. The work was not finished by Guru Ram Das but it was completed by his successor, Guru Arjan Dev.

GURU RAM DAS AND SRICHAND:

Baba Srichand, the eldest son of Guru Nanak, had founded a religious sect of his own known as Udasis. He visited Amritsar and came to see Guru Ram Das. On seeing Guru's long flowing beard, Baba Srichand asked him jocularly why he grew it that long. The Guru replied,"To wipe the dust from the holy feet of the saints like you." 'Your this sweet humility is the magic that makes you so great and makes me feel so small,' replied Srichand.

Baba Srichand promised the Guru his co-operation. After that the Udasis spared no pains to serve Sikh religion. It is said that after the death of Banda Bahadur, when the Mughal rulers decided to root out Sikh religion, it was the Udasis who kept the Divine spark of the Sikh faith alight.

FREE KITCHEN (GURU KA LANGAR):

Like his predecessors, Guru Ram Das carried on the work of Langar in a more elaborate and methodical way. As in the past strict adherence was made to the term 'Pangat' in Langar. Anybody irrespective of race, caste, creed, religion or sex, could partake of food without any hesitation. The caste system and pilgrimages were decried and superstitions were denounced.

NEW CUSTOMS:

Guru Ram Das composed a hymn known as 'Lawan' in Suhi Mohalla 4, page 773 of Guru Granth Sahib, and asked his Sikhs to recite them to solemnize marriages. The Sabad 'Lawan' embodies in itself a lesson for the couple to develop true love for each other. In reality this Sabad is for a human being to develop love for the divine bridegroom.

The Guru composed the following Sabad to instruct his Sikhs in the practice of their religion:

"He who calleth himself a Sikh of the true Guru, should rise early and meditate on God;
He should make an effort early in the morning, bathe in the inner tank of nectar;
Repeat God's Name under Guru's instruction, and all his sins and transgressions shall be erased;
At sunrise he should sing the Guru's hymns, and whether sitting or standing meditate on God's Name;
The disciple who at every breath meditateth on God, will be dear to the Guru;
The Guru imparteth instruction to that disciple to whom my Lord bestows His grace;
The servant Nanak prayeth for the dust of the feet of such a disciple of the Guru who himself repeateth God's Name and causeth others to do so."
(Gauri Ki Var- Mohalla 4, p-305-6)

SELECTION OF GURUSHIP:

Sahari Mal, Guru's cousin from Lahore, invited the Guru to grace his son's marriage. For some reason the Guru could not go, but he asked his eldest son, Prithi Chand to attend the marriage. Prithi Chand refused to go. His refusal is attributed to possibly two motives. It is said that he was incharge of the offerings that were made to the Guru and was able to furtively set aside much wealth for himself. If he had gone to Lahore, this illicit gain might have fallen in somebody else's hands. Secondly he thought that the time was fast approaching for the selection of a person to succeed his father as Guru and so he should remain in Amritsar. Mahadev, the Guru's second son, did not want to go because of his indifference to worldly affairs. The third son, Arjan Dev agreed to attend the marriage. He was instructed to stay on in Lahore after the marriage to look after the affairs of the Sikh Sangat of that place.

After some time he started feeling the pangs of separation for his father and the Guru, and wrote three letters, two of which were intercepted by his elder brother, Prithi Chand. A letter marked '3', reached the Guru and Arjan Dev was immediately recalled from Lahore. On his return he told his father that he had sent three letters. The truth came to light and Prithi Chand was forced to produce the other two letters. Thus Prithi Chand's actions were exposed.

Guru Ram Das embraced Arjan Dev, sent for five paise and a coco-nut, and placed them before him. He descending from his throne, seated him there before the whole assembly of the Sikhs. Bhai Buddha affixed the tilak of spiritual sovereignty to Arjan Dev's forehead, and thus he was proclaimed as Guru Arjan Dev. This happened in August, 1581.

Prithi Chand became so mad that he addressed his father in abusive language. He told Bhai Buddha that his father acted improperly in giving Guruship to his younger brother. He vowed that he would remove Guru Arjan and would seat himself on the Guru Gaddi (throne). The Guru counselled him not to quarrel about it, but Prithi Chand refused to submit and adopted an attitude of open defiance.

Having nominated Guru Arjan Dev, Guru Ram Das left for his old headquarters at Goindwal. After a few days Guru Ram Das left this world on the first of September, 1581.

GURU ARJAN DEV
(1563-1606, Guruship 1581-1606)

Guru Arjan was born in Goindwal, a small town in Amritsar district, on April 15, 1563. He was the youngest son of Guru Ram Das and Bibi Bhani. As a child, one day he found his way to the bed of Guru Amar Das who was then resting. His mother ran to fetch the child before he could disturb the Guru, but he had already awakened the Guru, who revealed,"Let him come to me; 'yeh mera dohita pani ka bohita howega'- this grandson of mine shall be a ship to take mankind across the ocean of the world."

Guru Arjan was married to Ganga, daughter of Krishen Chand, a resident of Meo village near Phillor in Jullundhur district. The marriage took place in 1589 when he was about 26 years old. Guru Ram Das began excavation of two tanks named Santokhsar and Amritsar and started the foundation of the city of Ramdaspur. After his father, Guru Arjan applied himself to the task of completing the tanks and extending the city. It was his practice to go every day and superintend the work.

MASAND SYSTEM:

Guru Nanak during his missionary tours had established Sangats at the various places throughout the country. The connection with the center was kept up by the constant visits of the Sikhs to the Guru. During Guru Amar Das's time the missionary work became more regular and methodical. He divided the Sikh spiritual kingdom into twenty-two Manjis. Guru Ram Das established the nucleus of a new order of missionaries called Masands. The word Masand seems to have come from 'Mas Nad' which is shorter form of 'Masnedi-Ali' or His Excellency, the title which the Mughal Governors often held. The purpose of this organization was to spread the Sikh faith at a rapid pace and also to collect money for the construction of tanks and the city of Ramdaspur. Guru Arjan organized Masand system afresh. He appointed new Masands of integrity and sincerity to look after the secular as well as spiritual affairs of the Sikhs. Masands were required to collect Daswandh (one-tenth of income) from the Sikhs which was then contributed towards the Guru's treasury (Golak) for the maintenance of the Sikh temples.

Some writers are of the opinion that Daswandh was raised under compulsion. Daswandh was never raised under any pressure nor it was considered 'a tax'. Whatever the Sikhs contributed or are contributing even today, is totally out of free will, love and devotion.

Masands were required to pay annual visits to Amritsar at the Baisakhi fair to receive instructions from the Guru and to hand over the amount of Daswandh collected. Regular accounts of these offerings were kept and receipts were issued.

Apart from financial duties, Masands were vigorous preachers. For the ceremony of initiation the ideal Charanamrit was the one administered by the Guru himself. Since it was not possible for the Guru to be present physically everywhere, the authority was delegated to the local missionaries to enrol new members of the Sikh Sangat by administering Charanamrit prepared by themselves in the prescribed manner. It attracted a large number of converts. During the time of Guru Arjan, there was hardly any place in India where the Sikhs were not found. Masands worked very hard to propagate Sikhism in every corner of the country.

COMPLETION OF CONSTRUCTION WORK:

Guru Arjan completed the unfinished work of excavation of tanks- Santokhsar and Amritsar. Bhai Buddha being the most trustworthy disciple, was appointed to supervise the work of construction. Santokhsar was completed in 1587-89. Having completed the tank of nectar, the Guru laid down the foundation of Hari Mandar which is now called Golden Temple, in the center of the tank. It is said that the Sikhs represented to the Guru that Hari Mandar should be the tallest building in the neighborhood. The Guru explained,"Hari Mandar should be the lowest because what is humble, shall be exalted. The more a tree is covered with fruit, the more its branches descend to the earth."

Mian Mir, a famous Muslim saint, was a friend and a devotee of the Guru. The Guru asked Mian Mir to lay the foundation stone of Hari Mandar. Thus, Mian Mir laid the brick in January, 1589. The head mason moved the brick to place it in order.

Whereupon the Guru prophesied that since the brick was moved by the mason, the foundation of the temple would be laid again in the coming times. His words were subsequently fulfilled as Ahmad Shah Abdali destroyed the temple and desecrated the tank in 1763. However two years later, the great army of the Khalsa recovered possession of the temple, relaid its foundation and reconstructed it.

Hindu temples were closed on three sides and their entrances were generally towards the east while Muslim mosques had entrances towards the west. Hari Mandar, the holy Sikh temple had entrance on all four sides. This denotes that God was in all the directions; and secondly four doors in the four directions (east, west, north and south) meant that all the four castes would have equal access to the temple. Whereas the Hindu temples were only open to the chosen classes, the Golden temple was open to all who would seek God. Muslim mosques were open only to Muslim men, the Golden temple was open equally to all men, women and children, irrespective of caste, creed, race, color, sex, religion or nationality. The Adi Granth, Sikh holy Scripture, was placed in the center of the temple.

When the construction of the tank and the temple was completed, Guru Arjan uttered the following Sabad in joy and gratitude:

> "The Creator stood in the midst of the work,
> And not a hair of any man's head was touched[1].
> The Guru maketh my ablution successful.
> And by repeating God's Name, sins shall depart.
> O saints, Ramdas[2] tank is beautiful,
> He who batheth in it shall save himself and the souls of his
>   family.
> The whole world shall congratulate him,
> And he shall obtain the reward his heart desireth.
> He who while meditating on his God
> Cometh to bathe here shall be made safe and whole.
> He who batheth in the saints' tank
> Shall obtain final salvation. Meditating on God's Name,

1: *Work was not interfered with from any direction.*

2: *Ramdas may also mean here God's servant*

Golden Temple, Amritsar

He shall not suffer transmigration.
He to whom God is merciful Knoweth divine knowledge.
His cares and anxieties shall depart
Who seeketh the protection of Baba Nanak and God."
(Sorath Mohalla 5, p-623)

NOTE: It should be pointed out here that bathing alone in the tank of Golden Temple cannot give the desired salvation. The above Sabad should not be taken for any pilgrimage of rituals. It does not mean a mere journey to holy place. Sikh faith rejects all ceremonial acts. In fact there are two tanks in Amritsar- outer tank and inner tank. First one is the outer tank full of water. It is customary for a Sikh to take bath every morning- to clean and purify his body before going in the 'presence of God', that is meditation. Thus outer tank in Amritsar serves that purpose. A Sikh's mission does not complete here. Guru Amar Das confirms this:

'If mind is sinful, everything is sinful,
By washing the body, mind will not become pure.'
(Wadhans Mohalla 3, p-558)

Then there is the inner tank called Hari Mandar. That tank is 'Gurbani'- Guru Granth Sahib which is full of 'Praise and Prayer'- NAM. After washing outerself in the outer tank, a Sikh goes to the inner tank to cleanse his sinful mind in the tank of Nam. **That is what Guru Nanak calls pilgrimage:**

"Pilgrimage is Nam.."
(Dhanasri Mohalla 1 Chhant, p-687)

Without Nam immersing in water countless times, will not deliver salvation. This process of cleansing sinful mind in the inner tank of Nam is the pre-requisite for spiritual growth. It leads to graduation to spiritual consciousness- a breakthrough to Eternal illumination. After cleaning his inner and outer-self, a Sikh realizes the glory of Nam and enters a stage of eternal bliss, and thereby merges with the Eternal Being. **A body is dead without life, and life itself is dead without Nam.**

What is then Amritsar?

When there was no sign of the city of Amritsar, Guru Nanak asked his disciples to bathe in 'Amritsar':

a) "Bikhia mal jai amritsar navo Gur santokh paya."
   (Maru Mohalla 1, p-1043)
   'All sins are washed away by bathing in Amritsar And by Guru's grace, contentment is obtained.'
   (Translation of the above)

b) "Gur sagar amritsar, jo echhai so phal pai."
   (Maru Mohalla 1, p-1011-12)
   'Divine Word (Gurbani) is Amritsar
   Whosoever batheth in it, will get his desire fulfilled.'
   (Translation of the above)

c) "Untar nirmal amritsar nai."
   (Asa Mohalla 3, p-363)
   'Impurities of mind are washed away by bathing in Amritsar.'
                                      (Translation of the above)

d) "Undro trisna agan bujhi Har amritsar nata."
   (Mohalla 3-pauri, p-510)
   'The inner fire of desires gone When bathed in Amritsar.'
   (Translation of the above)

e) "Meil gaee man nirmal hoa Amritsar tirath nai."
   (Mohalla 3, p-587)
   'Impurities gone and mind becometh pure
   When batheth in the pilgrimage of Amritsar.'
   (Translation of the above)

All the above verses of Guru Nanak and Guru Amar Das give reference of 'Amritsar' when there was no trace of the city or the tank of Amritsar. That means that Amritsar actually and literally means Tank of Nectar which is Gurbani, the Divine Word. Thus pilgrimage of Amritsar means the pilgrimage of one's mind in the Divine Word, the NAM. Without Nam,   bathing hundreds of times cannot purge mind of its impurities and therefore salvation cannot be achieved:

"Mal haumai dhoti kivai na uterai je sau tirath nai."
(Sri Rag Mohalla 3, p-39)

The Guru says that without Nam, all other acts to attain salvation, are futile:

"Nam bina phokat sabh karma jiun bajigar bharm bhulai."
(Parbhati Mohalla 1, p-1343)

'Without Nam, all acts are futile
As an actor's role in drama,maketh him not real.'
(Translation of the above)

When the tank and the temple were completed, there were great rejoicing. The enormous exertions and sacrifices were made by the Sikhs. The Guru honored all those Sikhs who had put in dedicated service to ensure the completion of the projects. Eminent among those people were: Bhai Buddha, Bhai Bhagtu, Bhai Bahla, Bhai Kalyana, Bhai Ajab, Bhai Ajaib, Bhai Umar Shah, Bhai Sangho, Bhai Salho and Bhai Jetha. Bhai Buddha was made incharge of the Hari Mandar. Bhai Bhagtu was instructed to preach Sikh doctrine in the Malwa region and Bhai Salho was made the superintendent of the city to look after its development. City of Ramdaspur was, in the course of time, called Amritsar. Because of Guru's residence and the central place of worship, Amritsar became the center of the Sikh activities.

ANIMOSITY OF PRITHI CHAND:

As referred to in the previous chapter, Prithi Chand was superseded and the Guruship was conferred on his youngest brother by his father, Guru Ram Das. Upon this Prithi Chand adopted an attitude of open defiance. He met Sulhi Khan, a revenue officer of Lahore province and told him that he was filing a complaint to the Emperor against his youngest brother for superseding him. Next he conspired with the headmen of the area who then told Guru Arjan that being the eldest son, Prithia had the right to the property of his father. The Guru gave the property to Prithia and some of it to Mahadev, the other brother, and reserved the voluntary offerings of the Sikhs for himself.

Prithi Chand in alliance with Sulhi Khan found ample opportunities to harass the Guru. However Wazir Khan, Akbar's assistant prime minister, interposed on behalf of the Guru and prevailed on Sulhi Khan to bring the two brothers to a compromise. By listening to Guru's Sukhmani (The song of Eternal peace compiled by Guru Arjan), Wazir Khan was restored to perfect health from dropsy ailment. This was the reason why Wazir Khan supported the Guru's cause. Although the compromise had been affected, yet Prithia continued to create every possible trouble for the Guru. Ultimately the Guru decided to leave Amritsar and make a tour of Majha, an area between the rivers Ravi and Beas.

PREACHING TOURS OF GURU:

The Guru first visited Khadur and then proceeded to Sarhauli where he sought to obtain land to build a dwelling for himself.

A Sikh from the village Bhaini invited the Guru to visit him. When he arrived there, it was late at night. The wife of the Sikh prepared a dish of broken bread with butter and sugar and laid it before the Guru. He enjoyed the dish prepared with love and devotion. He stayed there a few more days and in return he gave the village his own Chola and renamed the village as Chola Sahib.

The Guru then visited village Khanpur, situated between Goindwal and the present city of Tarn Taran. He was accompanied by five Sikhs including Bidhi Chand and Bhai Gurdas. It was a cold night and wintry winds were blowing hard. Bidhi Chand saw a lofty building and requested the Guru to go to that building, but the Guru objected saying that it would be better to stay where they were rather than to go to a place where evil people were dwelling. Bidhi Chand did not agree with the Guru and went to the lofty building and asked the owners for shelter, which they refused and called the Guru and his Sikhs hypocrites. Hema, a devout Sikh of that village, came and requested the Guru to visit his poor dwelling and bless it with his holy presence. Seeing his love and devotion, the Guru accepted his hospitality. Hema cooked and supplied his best food for the party. He took his sole blanket and put it under the Guru as bedding, who seeing Hema's devotion uttered the following Sabad:

"Very beautiful is the hut in which God's praises are sung,
While the mansion in which God is forgotten is of no avail.
There is a pleasure even in poverty when in the company of
saints God is remembered,
May that grandeur which is bound up with mammon, perish!
Blessed is turning a handmill or wearing a coarse blanket,
if the heart is happy and contented.
That empire is of no avail which conferreth not satisfaction,
Those who wander even naked in the love of one God obtain
honor.
Vain are silks and satins, attachment to which maketh man
covetous.
Everything is in Thy power, O God; Thou actest and causest
to act.
May Nanak obtain the gift of remembering Thee at every
breath."
(Rag Suhi Mohalla 5, p-745)

The Guru stayed there for some time. During his stay, Hema obtained his desire and went to his final rest. After Guru's departure, the Emperor's viceroy, who for some reason became dissatisfied with the inhabitants of Khanpur, sent his army and razed the village to the ground and massacred its chief residents.

From there he proceeded to the village of Khaira where he was attracted by the natural environments. He had a very warm welcome from the headmen. They afterwards assisted him in obtaining land from the villagers on which he laid down the foundation of what is now the famous city of Tarn Taran; and he proceeded to construct a tank there. This happened in 1590. The Guru, at a great expense, built brick-kiln for baking the bricks. The local officer named Nur-ud-din seized the bricks for the construction of a Sarai that was being built at Government expense. The Sikhs resented and requested the Guru to write to the Emperor against this high-handedness of Nur-ud-din, but the Guru refused to take notice of the outrage. He left quietly and waited for better times for the completion of the project. After sometimes the tank was completed.

The Guru then crossed the river Beas and proceeded to Jullundhur area where he purchased land to build city to be named as Kartarpur (city of Creator). The Guru with his own hands cut the first sod for the construction of the city and a well to supply water to the inhabitants. The well was called Gangsar.

Thence he went to Nakka at the invitation of his devotees. He visited Khemkaran, Chunian and other villages. Then he reached Jambar and remained there for some time. He made many converts in that area.

At the invitation of his Sikhs, the Guru went to Lahore. People of all classes flocked to see him. Jogi Shambhunath, Shah Husain, Shah Suleman and others came to see the Guru beseeching soul-saving religious instruction. The Guru uttered the following Sabad on that occasion:

> "O wise men, think of the Lord in your hearts,
> The true King, the Releaser from bondage, dwelleth in the
> hearts by the mind's affection.
> Nothing is equal in value to the sight of God.
> Thou art the pure Cherisher;
> Thou art the Lord great and Incomparable.
> Give me Thy hand, O Brave One, Thou art the only one to
> assist me.
> O Creator, by Thy power, didst
> Thou create the world; Thou art Nanak's prop."
> (Tilang Mohalla 5, p-724)

This Sabad, when heard by the Viceroy of Lahore, produced a profound impression on his mind. He asked the Guru if he could render any service to him. Upon his consent, the viceroy got a Bawli excavated.

From there he went to the shrine of Guru Nanak at Dera Baba Nanak. After that he proceeded to Barath to visit Sri Chand, Guru Nanak's son.

After that the Guru returned to Amritsar but Prithia still continued to create problems for him. Prithia's wife was very much sore and complained,"The eldest son has been superseded. The youngest one obtained the Guruship and the whole world, both

Emperor and the common man, worships him." Prithia replied,"Arjan has no son and so his prosperity is short-lived. Our son Meharban will be the next Guru." Guru's wife heard this conversation and reported it to the Guru, and prayed that he should grant her a son. He bade her to pay no heed to the remarks of Prithia or his wife but should continue to repeat true Name. One day again she requested the Guru,"O King, they who seek thy protection, obtain happiness in this life and salvation in the next. My married life would be most happy if you grant me a son."

The Guru always blessed his Sikhs and then most of the religious acts were performed through them. When his wife continued pressing for the gift of a son, he told her to go to his revered Sikh, Bhai Buddha and pray for the desired gift.

Next day the Guru's wife set out in great state to see Bhai Buddha. She took her attendants and the wives of the headmen of Amritsar and rode in carriages with great pomp and show. She carried plates of sweets as offering to the saint. When Bhai Buddha saw the procession he remarked,"What happened! Is there a stampede from Amritsar that the inhabitants have left the city and are coming here?" She placed plates of sweets before Bhai Buddha and prayed for his blessing. Bhai Buddha replied,"Respected lady, I am only a servant of your house. It is only the Guru who is an ocean of supernatural power, who fulfills every one's desires. I am also not worthy of these savoury dishes. Were I to eat them, how could I, afterwards, think of cutting the grass?"

So she came back very much disappointed and related the whole story to the Guru, who then remarked,"The saints and the true Guru are not pleased with display of pomp. If you desire anything from them, appear before them not in a state of superiority but in a humble manner. If you still desire the saint's blessing, then with devotion in thy heart, prepare bread with your hands, dress yourself like an ordinary person and go alone on foot."

As instructed by the Guru, she proceeded all alone next day. On seeing her Bhai Buddha said,"Hail O lady! Give me what you have brought." While eating he said,"The Guru is the owner of the storehouse, but I have received instructions to open it. As you have given me food of my heart's content, so shall you have a son of thy heart's content." On her return she told the Guru about the graciousness of Bhai Buddha.

When Prithias learnt the news of Guru's wife's pregnancy, they got very upset and instigated Sulhi Khan against the Guru. To avoid conflict, the Guru moved to village Wadali, about six to seven miles away from Amritsar.

On 19th of June, 1595 (21st of the month of Har, Sambat 1652), Guru's wife gave birth to a son[3] named Har Gobind at Wadali. On the birth of his son, the Guru uttered the following Sabad:

"The True Guru sent me a son;
A long-lived son hath been born by destiny.
When he took his dwelling in the womb,
His mother's heart was exceedingly glad.
The destiny recorded in the beginning hath become manifest
                                                                to all.
By God's order the boy hath been born in the tenth month.
                                        (Asa Mohalla 5, p-396)

On hearing the birth of Har Gobind, Prithias were very much saddened. They immediately began to hatch conspiracies to put an end to the life of the infant Har Gobind. Several attempts were made to this effect. Prithia hired a nurse to poison the baby. She applied poison to nipples of her breast and went to Wadali. In the meantime the child was said to have stopped breast suckling due to some indisposition. The nurse first congratulated the Guru's wife on the birth of the child. She then caressed and fondled the baby trying to breast feed him. The child refused suckling. At that time, for some mysterious reasons, nurse fainted and fell backwards. When she regained her consciousness, she repented and disclosed that Prithia had hired her to kill the infant. The story of Prithia's ill scheme spread from house to house.

Prithia then hired a snake-charmer and induced him to kill the child by exposing him to a cobra. He promised the snake-

---

3: John Clark Archer writes in his book, 'The Sikhs' that Har Gobind was not a real son of Guru Arjan but he was an adopted son. As we see in the above narrated Sabad, the Guru thanked God for His blessing over the birth of his son. Also the entire Sikh world believes that Guru Har Gobind was Guru Arjan's son. God knows what was Archer's source of such a misleading information. He should have shown some sense of responsibility while writing on such a sensitive subject. There are many such serious irregulatrities in his book and we take a very serious note of them.

charmer a great sum of money if he succeeded in the plot. The snake-charmer found a chance and let a black cobra loose in the court-yard. It is said that Har Gobind took the hissing cobra in his hand and killed it immediately.

Sikhs from distant places visited Amritsar during the absence of the Guru. Prithia made efforts to convince them that he was the real Guru but could not succeed in his mission. When Har Gobind was two years old, some prominent Sikhs came to Wadali and requested the Guru to return to Amritsar which he did.

Har Gobind became ill with small-pox of very virulent type. The people suggested to the Guru to make offerings to the goddess of small-pox but he rejected their advice to worship the goddess for the recovery of his son's illness. He, rather, stressed the worship of only one God who is the Creator and the sole Cherisher. The Guru uttered many Sabads in Rag Bilawal and Sorath on this subject. By the grace of God, Har Gobind recovered fully in a few days.

Prithia took another shot and induced Har Gobind's male nurse to poison the child. Next day the servant slipped poison in the baby's milk. The child, however, turned away from the poisoned milk and refused to drink it. The servant tried to fondle Har Gobind in feeding the contaminated milk but in vain. When the baby started crying, the Guru inquired of the cause of his weeping. The servant replied that he did not drink the milk and when he pressed him to drink, he began to cry. Then the Guru, himself tried to feed the baby who insisted on refusing to drink. Upon this the Guru took a sample of that milk and fed it to a dog which fell immediately sick and died. The servant realized his ill doings and confessed to the Guru and disclosed the murderous designs of Prithia.

Prithia became very furious and went to Delhi with Sulhi Khan to complain against the Guru to the Emperor. Before his departure to Delhi, Guru's other brother, Mahadev and Bhai Gurdas tried to restrain Prithia but he would not listen. Sulhi Khan presented the complaint to the Emperor who decided not to interfere in the affairs of religious men and secondly he concluded that the charges were not true. Prithia was crushed by his disappointment.

When Har Gobind became of a suitable age to receive instructions, he was entrusted to Bhai Buddha for his education. Bhai Buddha gave him adequate lessons and also taught him the use of offensive and defensive weapons, riding, chemistry, astronomy, medicine, agriculture, administration and other sciences. The Guru offered acknowledgement to Bhai Buddha for his successful and comprehensive instructions.

COMPILATION OF ADI GRANTH:

Prithia was composing his own religious hymns which he described as compositions of Guru Nanak and his successors. The ignorant people did not have sufficient intelligence to discriminate. Guru Arjan, therefore, felt the need to lay down rules to guide his followers in their daily religious duties. He made plans for the compilation of Adi Granth. For that purpose he chose a secluded spot outside the city which is now called Ramsar. He got a tank excavated there. Tents were erected for the accommodation. Guru Arjan took abode near the tank and dictated hymns to Bhai Gurdas who wrote them down. The verses were arranged according to Rags or musical measures. The hymns of the first Guru came first as Mohalla 1 (read as Mohalla pehla), then those of the second Guru- Mohalla II (read as Mohalla Duja) and so on. After the Bani of the Gurus, came the verses of the Bhagats or the Indian saints. The hymns of the Adi Granth were thus set according to thirty-one Indian Classical Ragas.

When the composition was completed, the Guru then wrote Mandawni as a conclusion and affixed his seal thereto:

"Three things have been put into the vessel[4]- truth, patience, and meditation.
The ambrosial Name of God, the support of all, hath also been put therein.
He who eateth and digesteth it, shall be saved.
This provision should never be abandoned; ever clasp it to your hearts.
By remembering God's feet, we cross the world of Maya;
Nanak, everything is extension of God."
(Mundawni Mohalla 5, p-1429)

4: *Means Guru Granth Sahib.*

After this the Guru uttered the following Slok:

"I can't appreciate what Thou didst for me, and yet Thou
madest me worthy. I am virtueless;
I possess no merit, and yet Thou Thyself
hast compassion on me.
Thou showest compassion and kindness unto me; I have
found true Guru, the friend.
Nanak, If I obtain the Name, I shall live, and my body and
soul shall be refreshed."
(Slok Mohalla 5, p-1429)

A Muslim might never like to read a hymn of a Hindu saint,
and by the same token a Hindu might not like to hear the religious
verse of a Muslim saint. The Hindus did not allow a saint, born in
low caste family, to enter the Hindu temple. This was the religious
fanaticism prevailing at that time. Guru Arjan, therefore, created
an ocean in which all rivers and rivulets could fall and assume the
appearance of the ocean itself. The composition of such an ocean
was completed on Bhadon Vadi 1, Sambat 1661 (1604 A.D.) and
was called Adi Granth. It was by no means a bible for the Sikhs
alone, but it is universal in character. It contained no life story of
the Gurus but only the Universal Truth, each and every word of
which was dedicated to the Glory of the Almighty God only.

The composition of Adi Granth consisted of the hymns of
the first five Gurus, Hindu saints (Brahmans as well as Sudras) and
Muslim Sufis. These saints were: Beni, Bhikhan, Dhanna, Farid, Jai
Dev, Kabir, Nam Dev, Parmanand, Pipa, Ramanand, Ravidas, Sain,
Sadhna, Sur Das and Trilochan. It also contained the hymns of
Minstrels (Bhats and Bards). These minstrels were all Brahmans
and then became Sikhs of the Guru, they were- Kal, Jalap, Bhika,
Sal, Bhal, Nal, Bal, Gyand, Mathura, Kirat and Harbans. It also
consisted of Var of Satta and Balwand, Ramkali Sad by Sundar and
five Sabads of Mardana, the minstrel of Guru Nanak.

On Bhadon Sudi first, Sambat 1661 (1604 A.D.), Adi Granth
was installed in the Hari Mandar and Bhai Buddha was appointed
as the first Granthi (priest).

PRITHI CHAND'S JEALOUSY CONTINUED:

Prithia addressed the Qazis and the Pandits who had enmity towards the Guru on account of his compilation of Adi Granth and he induced them to make a complaint to the Emperor that Guru Arjan had compiled a Granth in which Muslim and Hindu prophets were reviled. Upon this the Emperor sent for the Guru and the Granth. The Guru did not go himself but sent Bhai Buddha and Bhai Gurdas to read to the Emperor from the Granth. Various stanzas (Sabads) were read to him and Emperor Akbar was very much pleased and said,"Except love and devotion to God, I find neither praise nor blame of any one in the Granth. It is a volume worthy of reverence." Guru's slanderers and enemies were stunned. Akbar gave Siropas (dresses of honor) to Bhai Buddha and Bhai Gurdas, and promised to visit the Guru on his way back from Lahore.

As promised Akbar visited the Guru on his return journey to Delhi. He was charmed and fascinated with Guru's saintly bearing. The Emperor partook of the Guru's hospitality and prayed that he be allowed to make contributions to secure spiritual and temporal welfare and happiness. The Guru replied,"The welfare and happiness of monarchs depend on cherishing their subjects and doing justice." The Guru then stated that there was a severe famine in the land and cultivators required His Majesty's consideration. The Emperor remitted the revenue of the Punjab for that year. The Guru's fame and influence had largely increased owing to the respect the Emperor had shown to him. This became a cause of greater agony to Prithia.

MARTYRDOM OF GURU ARJAN:

During the rein of Guru Arjan, crowds were converted to Sikhism in Punjab and in various other parts of India and even in the neighboring countries. It is said that the hilly Rajas of Kulu, Suket, Haripur and Chamba visited the Guru and became his followers as did the Raja of Mandi. Guru's fame and influence became widely spread.

At that time Chandu Lal was Emperor Akbar's Diwan or financial advisor. He was a Khatri by caste and was originally an inhabitant of Rohela village in Gurdaspur district of Punjab. His official duties necessitated him to reside in Delhi. He had a young daughter of extreme beauty. Her mother, one day, said to her father,"Our daughter is growing to maturity. We should search for a husband for her." Chandu Lal, therefore, sent his family priest and barber[5] in search for a suitable match for his daughter. The priest and the barber searched every city in the Punjab but could not find a satisfactory match. One day again Chandu's wife insisted that they should continue their efforts. So the priest and the barber were again despatched for the purpose. They searched and searched and when they reached Lahore, they heard about the Guru's young son, Har Gobind. They went to Amritsar and found Har Gobind as the most descent match for the young girl. They came back and reported to Chandu accordingly. They gave their analysis on the excellence of Har Gobind and the enormous respect that his father was commanding in the city of Amritsar. Chandu was not pleased hearing praises of the Guru, so he asked the priest and the barber,"Do you think him equal to me? Guru's caste is inferior to me. You desire to put the ornamental tile of top storey into a gutter! Where am I, the imperial finance minister; and where is the Guru, though he may be an object of veneration to his followers?"

After the husband and wife had argued the whole night over the matter, it was decided that Sada Kaur (their daughter) should be given in marriage to Har Gobind. The marriage presents were, therefore, dispatched to Amritsar.

It came to the ears of the Sikhs of Delhi that Chandu had used derogatory expressions for the Guru. They sent a messenger with a letter explaining Chandu's utterances and prayed to the Guru to reject his alliance. The Sikhs of Delhi as well as of Amritsar prayed that the alliance of a haughty head like Chandu should not be accepted. The Guru was obliged to accept the advice of his Sikhs and so with utmost humility he told the matchmakers,"I am contented with my humble lot and desire not an alliance with the great. An ornamental tile should not be put in a gutter."

While the matchmakers were still remonstrating, a Sikh,

5: *It was customary in those days to send the family priest and the family barber to find suitable match.*

Narain Das, a grandson of Bhai Paro (a famous Sikh of Guru Amar Das) stood in the congregation and beseeched the Guru,"O king, I am the dust of thy lotus feet. I have a daughter whom my wife and I have vowed to offer to thy son. If you make her the slave of thy feet, I shall be fortunate. I am a poor unhonored Sikh and thou art the honor of the unhonored." The Guru replied,"If you have love in your heart, then your proposal is acceptable to me." Narain Das at once went and purchased the marriage presents and betrothal ceremony was performed. Upon this another Sikh, Hari Chand stood up and appealed,"O true king, I have vowed to give my daughter to thy son. If my petition please thee, I will give my daughter as a servant to Har Gobind." The Guru though unwilling at first to accept a second wife for his son, felt that he could not reject the offer of a faithful Sikh[6].

All this happened in the presence of Chandu's matchmakers who went back to Delhi and disappointed their master with sad news. Chandu was very much incensed and he wrote a letter to the Guru apologizing for his thoughtless expressions. He pleaded with the Guru that if he accepted his alliance, he would give large dowry to his daughter and he would have many favors conferred on him (Guru) by the Emperor. In the end he wrote that he was already on bad terms with his brother Prithi Chand and if he fell out with him too, it might ignite a blazing fire which would be difficult to extinguish.

He despatched the letter with the priest. The Guru having read it, stated,"It is the pride that ruins men. Man suffers for his acts. They whom the Creator joineth, are united and they whom men joineth, are not. It is the Guru's rule to comply with the wishes of his Sikhs. Their words are immutable[7]. As for his threats, I have no fear because God is the guardian of all." The priest returned with this message. This set the stage for Chandu's evil designs

6: *The Gurus were held in such high esteem that religious people frequently thought it their duty to vow to them their lives, their children, and their property. Several Sikhs used to register oaths on the birth of their daughters that they would only bestow them on the Guru or his relations. None would marry them except those to whom they were vowed. The Guru, therefore, felt bound to meet the wishes and vows of his Sikhs.*

7: *The Guru is always supreme but the Guru honors the Sangat (congregation of his followers). It is said that the Guru is twenty Biswei (a measure) and the Sangat is twenty-one Biswei Chandu's alliance was rejected by the Sangat and it was, therefore, obligatory for the Guru to accept the Sangat's decision.*

against the Guru.

The Emperor Akbar died soon after and was succeeded by his son Jahangir. Akbar had nominated his grandson Khusro in supersession of his son. Khusro claimed Punjab and Afghanistan which his father, Jahangir, was unwilling to concede to him. Jahangir ordered Khusro's arrest but the latter escaped and went towards Afghanistan. On his way he visited the Guru at Tarn Taran and told him that he was unfriended, needy, poor and had no travelling expenses. So he begged the Guru for pecuniary assistance.

Khusro had previously visited the Guru accompanying his grandfather Akbar and was, therefore, very well known to him. Secondly in Guru's house everybody- friend or foe, king or pauper, is treated equally. The Guru knew what was coming, but seeing the plight of the prince, he gave Khusro financial help[8]. Khusro was, however, seized while crossing Jehlum, by the imperial forces and was brought in chains to his father.

Prithia continued to retain the assistance and co-operation of Sulhi Khan against the Guru. On the pretext of collecting revenue in the Punjab, Sulhi Khan obtained leave from the Emperor. On his way he visited Prithia at his village Kotha where they concocted plans for the Guru's destruction. In the meantime, however, Prithia took Sulhi Khan to show his brick-kilns, where Sulhi Khan met with his accidental death by his sudden fall in the live brick-kiln.

Prithia was very much saddened at the death of his ally in evil. In those circumstances Chandu came to his rescue and filled the gap. Chandu wrote to Prithia to use his influence to bring his daughter's alliance with Har Gobind. Prithia was ready to assist Chandu in his nefarious designs against the Guru. He wrote back that the Guru who had deprived him of his right over Guruship, was already his enemy; and he would only be too happy to assist in meting him with adequate punishment. In his letter he begged Chandu to use his influence with the Emperor to bring the Guru to justice. So they both concocted a plan to induce the Emperor by

---

8: As we will see later on, Jahangir wrote that the Guru made a tilak (patch) of saffron on Khusro's forehead which implied that the Guru had blessed Khusro with Emperorship. This was not true. It seems that it was a concocted story of Guru's enemies to excite Jahangir against him.

some means to visit Punjab where they would have an opportunity to enter into some conspiracy against the Guru.

Chandu's scheme was successful and in a short period of time the Emperor came to Punjab. He told the Emperor that Guru Arjan was acting as his rival in Punjab by entertaining thieves and exercising independent authority. Upon this the Emperor sent an order to the Guru through Sulabi Khan, the nephew of late Sulhi Khan, to abstain from such practices. On his journey to Amritsar, Sulabi Khan confronted with some Pathans and was killed. When Chandu heard the death of Sulabi Khan, he convinced the Emperor that it had been done through the machinations of the Guru. He added that he had done many such misdeeds. For example the Guru had deprived his elder brother Prithi Chand of his rights over Guruship and had also endeavored to deprive Hindus and Muslims of their religions. The Emperor immediately sent for Prithia who was overjoyed with the invitation. He made preparations to go to the Emperor but after the dinner he got a cramp in his stomach and died the same night.

Meharban, son of Prithia, wasted no time after the death of his father in informing Chandu who in turn informed the Emperor that the Guru had blessed Khusro and had promised that he would become the Emperor. The Emperor was also notified that the Pundits and the Qazis were enraged at the compilation of Adi Granth which blasphemed the worship rules of the Hindus and the prayer and fasting of the Muslims. By such accusations, Chandu induced the Emperor to summon Guru Arjan.

Emperor Jahangir writes in his autobiography:

"In Goindwal, which is on the river Biyah (Beas), there was a Hindu named Arjan, in the garments of sainthood and sanctity so much so, that he had captured many of the simple-hearted of the Hindus and even the ignorant and foolish followers of Islam, by his ways and manners, and they had loudly sounded the drum of his holiness. They called him Guru and from all sides stupid people crowded to worship and manifest complete faith in him. For three or four generations (of spiritual successors) they kept this shop warm. Many times it occurred to me to put a stop to this vain affair or to bring him into the assembly of the people of Islam.

At last, when Khusro passed along this road, this insignifi cant fellow proposed to wait upon him. Khusro happened to halt at the place where he was, and he came out and did homage to him. He behaved to Khusro in certain special ways, and made on his forehead a finger-mark of saffron which the Indians call Qashqa and is considered propitious. When this came to my ears and I fully knew his heresies, I ordered that he should be brought into my presence and having handed over his houses, dwelling places, and children to Murtaza Khan (Sheikh Farid Bukhari) and having confiscated his property I ordered that he should be put to death with tortures."

The following events led to the Guru's summons by the Emperor resulting in martyrdom:

To begin with, it was his elder brother, Prithi Chand who devoted his whole life to harm the Guru in every possible way. Secondly Chandu's animosity over his daughter's non-alliance with the Guru's son, is considered the main fuel. These men with jealousies in their hearts, concocted the real story of Khusro to rouse the ire of Emperor Jahangir which added fuel to the blazing fire. Along with these circumstances Guru's increasing influence to convert crowds of Hindus and Muslims, created a stir in the minds of the Pundits (Brahmans) and the Qazis (Muslim priests). The compilation of Adi Granth was considered a serious blow to other religions. Through all these circumstances Guru Arjan fell a victim to the bigotry and inhumanity of the Mohammadan Emperor.

Before his departure to Lahore, the Guru appointed his son, Har Gobind as his successor and gave suitable instructions. He took five Sikhs, Bhai Bidhi Chand, Bhai Langaha, Bhai Piara, Bhai Jetha, and Bhai Pirana, with him. Some writers say that Emperor Jahangir had gone to Kashmir before the arrival of the Guru in Lahore.

The Emperor Jahangir addressed the Guru,"Thou art a saint, a great teacher, and a holy man; You look on all, rich and poor, alike. It was therefore, not proper for you to give money to my enemy Khusro." The Guru replied,"I regard all people, whether Hindu or Musalman, rich or poor, friend or foe, as equals; and it is on this account that I gave your son some money for his journey, and not because he was in opposition to you. If I had not assisted him in his forlorn condition, and so shown some regard for the kindness of thy father, Emperor Akbar to myself, all men would have despised me for my heartlessness and ingratitude, or they would have said that I was afraid of you. This would have been unworthy of a follower of Guru Nanak."

The Guru's reply did not sooth Jahangir's feelings and he ordered him to pay two lakhs of rupees (two hundred thousand rupees), and also to erase the hymns in his Granth which were opposed to the Hindu and Muslim religions. The Guru replied, "Whatever money I have is for the poor, the friendless and the stranger. If you ask for money, you may take whatever I have; but if you ask for it by way of fine I shall not give you even a penny, because a fine is imposed on the wicked worldly persons and not on priests and saints. As regarding the erasure of hymns in the Adi Granth, I cannot erase or alter an iota. I am a worshipper of the Immortal God. There is no monarch save Him; and what He revealed to the Gurus, from Guru Nanak to Guru Ram Das, and afterwards to myself, is written in the holy Granth. The hymns contained in the Adi Granth are not disrespectful to any Hindu incarnation or any Mohammadan prophet. It is certainly stated that prophets, priests, and incarnations are the handiwork of the Immortal God, Whose limit none can find. My main object is to spread the truth and the destruction of falsehood; and if, in pursuance to this objective, this perishable body is to depart, I shall account it great good fortune."

The Emperor left and the Guru was placed under the surveillance of Chandu. Some writers say that Guru Arjan's execution was nothing except usual punishment of revenue defaulter. It seems that these writers are totally ignorant of Sikh tradition. When the Sikhs of Lahore came to know about the fine of two lakhs of rupees, they decided to raise the money to discharge the Guru's obligation of fine. The Guru issued a stern warning to his Sikhs that whosoever contributed to pay the fine imposed on him, would not be his Sikh. It was a matter of principle as mentioned in the Guru's reply above, and not a matter of two lakhs of rupees which could have been collected in twinkling of an eye. Fines are for thieves, robbers, slanderers and the wicked. Men devoted to religion did not belong to that category. It is, therefore, baseless to say that Guru's execution was usual punishment of revenue defaulter. The Qazis and Brahmans offered alternatives to the Guru to exchange death for expunging the alleged objectionable passages in Adi Granth and inserting the praises of Mohammad and of the Hindu deities. The Guru did not budge from his position.

Guru Arjan was made to sit on the red hot iron pan and burning sand was poured over his bare body. He was seated in red-hot caldron, and was bathed in boiling water. Guru's body was burning and was full of blisters.

His friend and devotee, Mian Mir, a Muslim saint, rushed to see him. When Mian Mir saw the ghastly scene, he cried out and said,"O Master! I cannot bear to see these horrors inflicted on thee. If you permit me, I would demolish this tyrant rule (Mian Mir is said to have possessed supernatural powers at that time)."

The Guru smiled and asked Mian Mir to look towards the skies. It is said that Mian Mir saw Angels begging the Guru's permission to destroy the wicked and the proud.

The Guru addressed Mian Mir,"Mian Mir, you are per-turbed too soon. **This is the Will of my Master (God), and I cheerfully submit and surrender to His Sweet Will." The Guru repeated and exemplified in action the meaning of this verse:**

**"Tera kia meetha lagei
Har Nam padarath Nanak mangei."**
(Asa Mohalla 5, p-394)
**'Sweet be Thy Will, my Lord
Nanak beseecheth the gift of Nam.'**
(Translation of the above)

**The Guru bore all this torture with equanimity and never uttered a sigh or a groan.
The Guru was unruffled!
The Guru remained calm and unperturbed like a sea!
The Guru was in Absolute Bliss!
This was the wonder of the Lord-an unparrallel example**

in the history of mankind.

Mian Mir asked, why was he enduring the suffering at the hands of his vile sinners when he possesseth superpowers? The Guru replied,"**I bear all this torture to set an example to the Teachers of True Name, that they may not lose patience or rail at God in affliction. The true test of faith is the hour of misery. Without examples to guide them, ordinary persons' minds quail in the midst of suffering.**" Upon this Mian Mir departed commending the Guru's fortitude and singing his praises.

The Guru was again addressed to comply with the demands of his enemies. When he was threatened with further torture, he replied,"O fools! I shall never fear any torture. This is all according to God's Will, any torture wherefore affordeth my pleasure." He is said to have uttered this Sabad:

"The egg of superstition hath burst; the mind is illumined;
The Guru hath cut the fetters off the feet and freed the
captive.
My transmigration is at an end.
The heated caldron hath become cold; the Guru hath given the
cooling Name.
Since the holy man hath been with me, Death's myrmidons,
who lay in wait for me, have left me.
I have been released from him who restrained me; what shall
the judge do to me now?
The load of karma is removed; I am freed therefrom.
From the sea I have reached the shore; the Guru hath done me
this favor.
True is my place, true my seat, and truth I have made my
special object.
Truth is the capital; truth the stock-in-trade which Nanak
hath put into his house."
(Maru Mohalla 5, p-1002)

Chandu thought to suffocate him in a fresh cowhide, in which he was to be sewn up. Instead the Guru asked for a bath in Ravi river which flowed embracing the walls of Lahore city. Chandu revelled at the thought that the Guru's body full of blisters, would undergo greater pain when dipped in cold water. So he permitted him to bathe in the river. The soldiers were sent to escort the Guru. The Master's disciples saw him. He looked at them still forbidding any action. He said, "Such is the Will of my God, submit to the Divine Will, move not, stand calm against all woes."

Crowds watched the Master standing in water and having a dip. **Lo! The light blended with Light and the body was found nowhere. Hail to the Master! Thou art Wonderful- Martyr, the greatest. Thou art the Greatest!**

SALUTE TO THE MIGHTY KING!

This was the fourth day of the light half of the month of Jeth, Sambat 1663 (May 30, 1606 A.D.).

GURU HAR GOBIND
(1595-1644, Guruship 1606-1644)

Guru Har Gobind was born to Guru Arjan Dev on June 19, 1595 at Wadali, a village near Amritsar. The period of Guru's early life is alluded to in the previous chapter.

After the Martyrdom of his father (Guru Arjan), the Guru caused the Adi Granth to be read by Bhai Buddha and the musicians of the temple sang the Guru's hymns. This lasted for ten days. When the final rites were over, Bhai Buddha started the ceremony of Guruship. It should be remembered here that when Guru Arjan's wife went to Bhai Buddha for boon of a son, she had prepared the meals with her own hands, and she took bread with onions. Bhai Buddha while eating had said,"The Guru is the owner of the storehouse, but I have received an order to open it. As you have given me food to my heart's content, so shall you have a son to your heart's content. He shall be very handsome and brave, possess spiritual and temporal power, become a mighty hunter, ride on royal steeds, wear two swords, be puissant in battle, and trample on the Mughals. As I crush these onions you have brought to me, so shall your son crush the heads of his enemies, and be at once a great warrior and exalted Guru. His shall not be the humble seat of a village Guru, but a gorgeous imperial throne." As usual Bhai Buddha placed before the Guru a seli (a woolen cord worn as a necklace or twisted round the head by the former Gurus) and a turban, as appurtenances of his calling. The Guru ordered the seli to be placed in the treasury and reminding him about his prophecy said to Bhai Buddha,"My endeavors shall be to fulfil thy prophecy. My seli shall be a swordbelt, and I shall wear my turban with a royal aigrette. Give me a sword to wear instead of seli." The sword was brought but Bhai Buddha placed it on the wrong side of Guru Har Gobind. The Guru said,"Bring another one, I shall wear two swords." He wore two swords which were emblems of Spiritual and Temporal authority- Piri and Miri- the combination of 'Bhakti and Shakti'.

AKAL TAKHAT:

The martyrdom of Guru Arjan was an unparallel act in the history of mankind. The Guru had all the superpowers. He could have averted the situation in any way he liked, but he went through all that torture to show to the world how in all thick and thin one should cheerfully submit to the sweet Will of God. As a matter of fact, the contents of the Adi Granth were not meant for the Yogis, Sidhas and Sanyasis or the Muslim Suffis only, who sit in seclusion in the caves of the Himalayas and worship the Almighty by denouncing the world. Instead the teachings of the Adi Granth were meant for the family men. Leading the family life, the Gurus gave practical examples as how to live according to Guru's Word.

The cruel and torturous execution of Guru Arjan aroused a very strong wave of angry feelings among the masses. The enlightened, but not passive, sufferings of the Guru instilled a new spirit and life into the people and they resolved to exert and sacrifice themselves for the sake of righteousness. For centuries, countless Hindu men, women and children had fallen under the Muslim sword and this did not soften the stone hearts of their oppressors; but rather they had become more cruel and brutal. Sometimes it might be possible to reform the evil doer by opposing untruth and injustice through non-violent methods. The silent resistance and suffering for righteous cause might sometimes enable the tyrant to see his evil actions and he might be improved. History stands witness that no amount of non-violence can succeed against a tyrant who is hardened and steeped in criminal oppressive ways and who pays no heed to basic values of moral and civilized conduct. Against such men, non-violence is only another name of disgraceful cowardice in their dictionary. Such power drunk men must be faced bravely with a stick bigger than theirs. After the inauguration, some Masands represented to the Guru's mother that the preceding five Gurus never handled arms; if Emperor Jahangir heard about this, he would be angry and where would they (Sikhs) hide? She showed courage to the Masands, however, she remonstrated with the young Guru,"My son, we have no treasure, no state revenue, no landed property and no army. If you walk in the way of your father and grandfather, you will be

happy." The Guru recited the following verse:
"The Lord who is the Searcher of all hearts
Is my own Guardian."
(Bhairon Mohalla 5, p-1136)
and said,"Have no anxiety and everything shall be according to the
Will of God."

The Guru issued an order to the Masands that he would be
pleased with those who brought offerings of arms and horses
instead of money. He laid down the foundation of Akal Takhat
(Timeless Throne) in 1606 (the fifth day of light half of month of
Har, Sambat 1663) just in front of Hari Mandar, and it was completed in 1609. Akal Takhat was built of solid bricks on a raised
platform of about ten feet in height and looked like a throne. The
Guru took his seat on it. He built Akal Takhat a few yards in front
of Hari Mandar with a view that a Sikh at Akal Takhat should not
forget that spiritual elevation was as essential as his social obligations. As a matter of fact, the Guru wanted his followers to be
'saint-soldiers', extremely cultured, highly moral with spiritual
height and be ever-ready to measure swords with demonic forces.
Bhai Buddha on seeing the Guru in military harness, mildly remonstrated with him. Instead the Guru replied,"In the Guru's house
religion and worldly enjoyment shall be combined- the caldron to
supply the poor and the needy, and the scimitar to smite the
oppressors." (This should be noted by those Sikhs who say that
worldly and practical affairs should be kept separate from religion
in our Gurdwaras).

Several warriors and wrestlers came to the Guru for service.
He enrolled fifty-two heroes as his body-guard and this formed the
nucleus of his future army. About five hundred young persons
came from all over the Punjab to enlist in his service. He made Bhai
Bidhi Chand, Bhai Jetha, Bhai Piara, Bhai Langaha, and Bhai
Pirana, each captain of a troop of one hundred horse. People began
to wonder how the Guru could continue to maintain such an army.
The Guru quoted:

"God provideth every one with his daily food; why, O man,
art thou immersed planning;
He putteth their food even before the insects which He

created in rocks and stones."
(Gujri Mohalla 5, p-495)

Akal Takhat grew into an institution which symbolized in
itself the idea that the use of sword for the protection of righteousness and for self-defence was called for. Here the Guru sitting on
his throne, would watch wrestling bouts and military feats of his
disciples performed in the open arena opposite to the Akal Takhat.
As all intricate cases and disputes were finally decided here by the
Guru, the Akal Takhat served the purpose of a Supreme Court for
the Sikhs. Besides throne, the Guru adopted all other emblems of
royalty- the umbrella, the swords, the crest and the hawk, and thus
the Sikhs called him a true king or 'Sacha Padshah'- a king in all
appearance but in deeds and in purity as holy and great as
previous Gurus. People looked towards Akal Takhat for guidance
in their secular affairs. This custom became so significant that the
decision once taken at Akal Takhat was followed by the Sikhs
enthusiastically and this was the reason that they were always able
to overcome every peril. The development of this custom contributed a lot towards the consolidation of the Sikh Movement.

Some writers charge that lure of politics and glamour of
arms led the Guru away from the true path of a religious and
spiritual leader. Their judgement is altogether unfounded. There
was no political motive of Guru Har Gobind to begin with and the
time proved none whatsoever. Secondly his daily routine was to go
to Hari Mandar, listen Asa di Var and then give religious instructions to his followers. He took keen interest in propagation of his
religion and appointed preachers in the various regions of the
country. He himself undertook tours to various places in Punjab to
propagate his faith. However the policy of the Guru symbolized in
itself the response to the challenge of the time. Bhai Gurdas justifies
the Guru's change in the policy under peculiar circumstances:

"Just as one has to tie pail's neck while taking out water,
Just as to get 'Mani', snake is to be killed;
Just as to get Kasturi from deer's neck, deer is to be
killed;
Just as to get oil, oil seeds are to be crushed;
To get kernel, pomegranate is to be broken;

Similarly to correct senseless people, sword has to be taken
up."
(Bhai Gurdas, Var-34, pauri 13)

Guru Har Gobind appears to have been the first Guru Who
systematically turned his attention to the chase. His daily routine
at Amritsar was:- He rose before day-break, bathed, dressed in full
armor, and then went to Hari Mandar to worship. There he heard
Japji and Asa di Var being recited. He then preached to his Sikhs.
After the concluding prayer, breakfast was served indiscriminately
to the Guru's troops and followers as they sat in rows for the
purpose. After that he would rest for some time and then would go
to the chase, accompanied by an army of forest beaters, hounds,
tamed leopards and hawks of every variety. Late in the afternoon
he sat on his throne and give audience to his visitors and followers.
Minstrels sang the Guru's hymns and at twilight the 'Sodar' was
read. At the conclusion of the service musical instruments of many
sorts were played. After that all adjourned for their evening repast.
A sacred concert was afterwards held in which hymns were sung.
Next followed the minstrel Abdulla's martial songs to inspire the
Sikhs with love of heroic deeds and dispel feelings unworthy of
warriors. The Sohila was then read after which the Guru retired to
his private apartment.

BANDI CHHOR- THE GREAT DELIVERER:

Chandu was fearful that the Guru might avenge his father.
His daughter was still unmarried and he wrote to the Guru for her
alliance which was again refused. He, therefore, once again represented to Emperor Jahangir against the Guru. Upon this Jahangir
summoned the Guru to Delhi through Wazir Khan[1]. After careful
consideration the Guru agreed to go to Delhi and assigned the
secular duties of the Hari Mandar to Bhai Buddha and its spiritual
duties to Bhai Gurdas. He instructed,"The Har Mandar is specially
devoted to God's service, wherefore it should ever be respected. It
should never be defiled with any impurity of the human body. No

1: *Wazir Khan was the viceroy of Punjab at the time of Guru Arjan. He was suffering from dropsy and*
was completely restored to health by hearing the recitation of Sukhmani, upon which he became Guru's
follower.

gambling, wine-drinking, light behavior with women, or slander, should be allowed therein. No one should steel, utter a falsehood, smoke tobacco, or contrive litigation in its precincts. Sikhs, holy men, guests, strangers, the poor and the friendless should ever receive hospitality from Sikhs. My people should ever be humble, repeat God's Name, promote their faith, meditate on Guru's words, and keep all his commandments." The Guru then went to Delhi.

Through the good offices of Wazir Khan, the Emperor received the Guru with great apparent respect. Seeing him very young and already installed as Guru, the Emperor had a good deal of spiritual discussion in order to test his knowledge of divinity.

The Emperor having heard that the Guru loved the chase requested him to accompany him one day on a hunting excursion. In the forest a tiger rushed towards the Emperor. Elephants and horses took fright, bullets and arrows were discharged towards the tiger but in vain. The Emperor was completely paralysed with fear and called upon the Guru to save him who alighted from his horse, and taking his sword and shield ran between the tiger and the Emperor. As the tiger sprang, he dealt him a blow with his sword and the tiger fell lifeless on the ground. The Emperor thanked his God that he was saved by the Guru through his heroic endeavor.

It was time for the Emperor to visit Agra and he invited the Guru to accompany him. He, after repeated invitations, consented to go. When they both arrived in Agra, the Guru was received with great rejoicing by the people. Seeing increasing friendship between the Emperor and the Guru, Chandu said to himself,"The Guru will take revenge on me whenever he finds an opportunity. I shall only be safe if by some means I succeed in having broken this friendship or having him imprisoned, and thus I should apply all efforts to that end."

The Emperor fell ill and he sent for his astrologer to check upon his stars and find the remedy. Chandu took advantage of the situation and bribed the astrologer heavily to sever connection between the Guru and the Emperor. The astrologer accordingly suggested that a holy man of God should go to the Fort of Gwalior and pray for the Emperor's recovery there. Chandu on the other hand advised the Emperor that Guru Har Gobind was the holiest of men and thus played double role. Jahangir requested the Guru to go to Gwalior, the latter accepted it without hesitation as another mission awaited him there.

There was a joy in the Fort when it was known that the Guru was coming. There were fifty-two Indian princes (Rajas) imprisoned in the Gwalior Fort who were spending their days in lamentation and misery. They believed that they would be released by the Guru's intercession. Hari Das, the governor of the Fort, was happy too, since he had been longing to have 'darshan' (holy sight) of the Guru. He went forth to receive the Guru and prostrated before the Master. The Guru met the princes, comforted them and gave them peace, making them happy even in adversity.

Chandu wrote couple of letters to the governor of the Fort, urging him to poison the Guru and put an end to him. Hari Das, however, put all letters before the Guru as he received them; since he had become his devotee. The Guru recited the following Sabad at that time:

> "The slanderer shall crumble down
> Like a wall of Kallar; hear, ye brethren, thus shall be
> known.
> The slanderer is glad when he seeth a fault; on seeing
> anything good he is filled with grief.
> He meditateth evil all day long, but it befalleth not; the
> evil-minded man dieth meditating evil.
>
> The slanderer forgetteth God, and when death approacheth,
> quarrelleth with God's saint.
> The Lord Himself preserveth Nanak, what can wretched
> man do?"
> (Bilawal Mohalla 5, p-823)

Jahangir recovered from his illness. The Guru was still in the Gwalior Fort. When the Emperor heard Wazir Khan's pleading on behalf of the Guru (some say, also the pleading of Mian Mir), he ordered that the Guru should be presented to him. On hearing this the imprisoned Rajas were very much distressed. The Guru would not leave the Fort unless all the Rajas were also released. The Emperor conceded to his wish and released all the fifty-two princes. From this the Guru is still remembered in Gwalior as Bandi Chhor-the Great Deliverer, the holy man who freed the prisoners. There still stands a shrine 'Bandi Chhor' in the historic Fort of Gwalior[2]. Mian Mir brought home to the Emperor the innocence of Guru Arjan and how under his cruel orders, the great divine Master had been tortured to death. The Emperor, however, washed his hands clean of this sin and held Chandu entirely responsible for this crime, who was then arrested by the Emperor's order and taken to Lahore to be executed there. He was paraded through the streets of Lahore, people threw filth on him, and cursed him. A grain-parcher struck him on the head with an iron ladle and Chandu died. When the Emperor heard Chandu's death, he remarked that he richly deserved this fate. The Guru, however, prayed that as Chandu had suffered torment for his sins in this life, God would pardon him hereafter.

Sujan, a Masand from Kabul who had amassed great wealth from tithes and offerings, heard that Guru Har Gobind had great love for the horses. He looked far and near and ultimately found a horse of rare beauty and speed which he purchased for a lakh of rupees to make an offering to the Guru. When Sujan was crossing the river Indus, the eye of an officer fell on the horse which was of a rare strain and beauty and he ultimately took away the horse saying that the animal should go to the Emperor. Sujan told the Guru how he was robbed of the horse. The Guru recommended patience and predicted that nobody but himself (Guru) would ride that horse.

When the Emperor desired to mount, the horse shook its head which was considered a bad omen. After sometimes the horse fell ill and would neither eat nor drink. All known medicines were tried but in vain. When the horse was on the verge of death, the head Qazi (Rustam Khan) suggested that if the holy Quran was read for him, he might recover. Upon this the horse was presented to the Qazi.

When the Qazi was leading the horse home, the animal neighed as it passed through the Guru's tent (Guru was at Lahore at that time). Through negotiations with the Qazi, the horse was purchased for ten thousand rupees. The Guru patted on the neck

---

2: *Some writers charge that the Guru was imprisoned on account of money due. If this or any other case was the cause of his imprisonment, how could he get the release of fifty-two Rajas from the Fort? The Guru was on good terms with the Emperor. On his illness Jahangir requested the Guru to go to the Gwalior Fort and in return the Emperor conceded to the Guru's wish to release the princes.*

of the horse and it started recovering its strength.

KAULAN:

The Qazi had a beautiful daughter, Kaulan[3] who was a disciple of Mian Mir. From her childhood she had occupied her mind praising God's Name and remembering Him in the company of the saints. Through the holy company of Mian Mir, she had heard praises of Guru Har Gobind and she praised the Guru in the midst of her own family. This incensed her father very much who addressed her,"O Infidel, you praise an infidel (Guru) and obey not the law of Mohammad, according to which it is forbidden, under penalty of death, to praise an infidel." Kaulan replied,"Father dear, the law of Mohammad does not apply to holy men. Saints are God's servants." On hearing this from her daughter, the Qazi burnt with bigotry and indignation. After consulting his brother Qazis, he issued an order for the execution of his daughter, Kaulan for her sin of transgressing the Mohammad law.

Kaulan's mother informed her daughter and Mian Mir about the order of the Qazi. Mian Mir recommended to Kaulan,"There appears no means of saving you here. It is better if you go to Amritsar and seek protection of Guru Har Gobind. None else but he can save your life." Kaulan heeded Mian Mir's advice and went to Amritsar.

Kaulan began her life at Amritsar under the protection of the Guru. She was given a separate building to reside. Kaulan found consolation in repeating following Sabad:

"O mother, I awake by association with the saints;
On seeing the love of the Beloved, I repeat His Name which
                                                    is a treasure.
Thirsting for a sight of Him, I long and look for Him;
I have forgotten my desire for other things.
I have found Guru, the giver of composure and peace;
On beholding him, my mind is wrapped up in God.

3:*Kahan Singh, a Sikh historian, writes that she was a Hindu girl named Kamla. Qazi Rustam Khan purchased her and kept her as slave. She was taught Islam.*

On seeing God pleasure hath arisen in my heart; Nanak dear
to me is His ambrosial Word."
(Kedara Mohalla 5, p-1119)

Quite a bit of time passed in this manner until one day she
took all her jewels and placed them before the Guru and said,"O
friend of the poor, please apply the price of these jewels to some
religious object by which my name may be remembered in the
world for sometime." The Guru got a tank excavated in her name
with that money in 1621. The tank is still famous as Kaulsar in the
city of Amritsar. Guru Har Gobind also constructed another tank
called Babeksar commemorating the deliverance of his spiritual
address on that spot to his followers. There are now five sacred
tanks in Amritsar in the vicinity of Golden Temple: Santokhsar,
Amritsar, Ramsar, Kaulsar, and Babeksar.

MUGHAL FORCES AND THE GURU:

Emperor Jahangir had died in Kashmir and his son Shah
Jahan became the Emperor of India.

When Prithia's son, Meharban heard Chandu's death, he
was greatly distressed. Meharban said to himself,"Sulhi Khan died
when he set himself against the Guru. My father died as he was
against the Guru. Now Chandu has died. What magic the Guru
possesseth that no one may withstand him." Meharban exchanged
turban with Karam Chand, Chandu's son, in token of life-long
friendship, and then discussed ways with him how to bring about
the Guru's ruin. They started poisoning Shah Jahan's mind against
the Guru. Guru Har Gobind sent his revered Sikhs to Meharban to
dissuade him from his hostile and evil designs. He also went
himself to Meharban to strike a conciliatory note but in vain.

Shah Jahan pursued a different religious policy. He served
to orthodoxy, and religious fanaticism was at a considerable height
during his reign. He took keen interest in the welfare of new
converts to Islam. If any Muslim gave up his religion, he was
severely dealt with. Some temples under construction in Punjab
were demolished and mosques were raised in their places. His
mind was poisoned against the Guru by his enemies and soon the
ties of cordial relations as they had been since 1611, were snapped

and a period of open hostility started towards the Sikhs.

On his way to Pilibhit, the Guru visited Kartarpur where he met some Pathans of village, Wadamir, equipped with swords and shields who offered their services to him. With them was a tall and powerful youth, Painde Khan. His parents were dead and he was living with his uncle. The Guru enlisted Painde Khan on his personal staff and continually pampered him to increase his strength. He could, without the aid of a rope or bridle, arrest a horse running at full speed. No wrestler would engage with him.

The Guru practised all martial exercises and collected arms of every description. He hunted and witnessed exhibitions of strength by Painde Khan and others. He presented to Painde Khan the offering made by the Sikhs. This caused great heart-burning and worry to others. A deputation of Sikhs went to Bhai Gurdas who in turn sent them to Bhai Buddha. Bhai Buddha represented to the Guru," Thou art like the Ganges, like the sun and like the fire. The river Ganges swallows corpses and bones of the countless dead, and yet remains pure; the sun draws noxious vapors towards it, and yet remains pure; fire burns the dead, yet remains pure. Thou art like all three. The Sikhs seeing your love and enthusiasm for sport and military exercises, fear for you. Therefore, please abandon them." The Guru laughed and replied,"I have done nothing improper. I am only fulfilling your prophecy and elevating the conditions of my Sikhs."

Preparations were made for the marriage of the Guru's daughter, Bibi Viro, and sweets were prepared and stored in a room. A company of Sikhs came from the west to behold the Guru and present their offerings. They were weary and hungry and reached late at night when kitchen was closed. The Guru desired that the sweets stored for the marriage should be served to his visitors. The key of the room was with Guru's wife, Mata Damodri who refused to give the sweets to any one till the bridegroom's party had partaken of them. The Guru again asked but his wife adhered to her determination. Upon this the Guru predicted,"My Sikhs are dearer to me than life. Were they the first to taste the sweets, all obstacles to the marriage would be removed, but now the Mohammadans shall come and possess themselves of the sweets and marriage be interrupted." This prophecy became true. In the meantime a Sikh brought sweets which were served to the

Guru's visitors.

Emperor Shah Jahan went hunting from Lahore towards Amritsar. The Guru also went in the same direction[4]. A clash took place between the Sikhs and the royal soldiers over the issue of a royal hawk. One of the royal hawks who was flying after a victim, strayed away and fell in the hands of the Sikhs. The royal soldiers came to recover the hawk but because of their arrogance and abusive language, the Sikhs refused to hand over the hawk and this started the trouble. The royal soldiers were driven away with a slaughter. They hastened back and reported to the Emperor about the seizer of the hawk and the violence of the Sikhs. The enemies of the Guru found a good opportunity to revive the charges against him and to remind the Emperor of Guru's alleged misdeeds.

The Emperor sent Mukhlis Khan, one of his trusted generals with seven thousand soldiers to punish the Sikhs. The Sikhs of Lahore hearing of the military expedition against the Guru, sent immediately a messenger to Amritsar to apprise the Guru of the attack. There were great rejoicing going on at the palace of the Guru on account of his daughter's marriage. The Guru's family was immediately removed to a house near Ramsar. Early next day it was decided to send the family to Goindwal. It so happened that the coming day was fixed for Viro's marriage. Thus the Guru ordered that his family and all the non-combatants of the city should halt at Jhabal, a town about seven miles south-west of Amritsar and the marriage should be celebrated there before going to Goindwal. Two Sikhs were sent to stop the bridegroom's procession, lest it should fall in the hands of the enemy.

There was a small fortress, Lohgarh, outside the city. It was a kind of raised platform (serving as a tower) where the Guru used to hold his court in the afternoon and it was surrounded by high walls. Twenty-five Sikhs were posted there in an anticipation of the attack. The Guru went to the temple and prayed for the victory. He repeated the following verse on the occasion:

"Wicked men and enemies are all destroyed by Thee, O Lord, and
Thy glory is manifested.

4: *Some writers say that it was neither Shah Jahan nor the Guru, but there were only their respective men.*

Thou didst immediately destroy those who annoyed Thy saints."

(Dhanasri Mohalla 5, p-681)

The Sikh detachment at Lohgarh though courageous were too few to stop the Mughal army. After destroying hundreds of the enemy soldiers, they fell martyrs to the Guru's cause. The enemy soldiers proceeded to the Guru's palace in search of him but became furious finding the palace empty. They searched the house and took care of the sweets. With the day break, began the conflict, the clashing of swords and the hissing of the bullets. Brave men fell and died, blood flowed in profusion, corpses were piled over one another, heads, bodies, arms, and legs were separated and horses without riders careered around the city.

Bhai Bhanu was the commander-in-chief of the Guru's army and Shams Khan was one of the chiefs of the imperial army. Shams Khan's horse was killed. Bhai Bhanu then dismounted, and he and Shams Khan engaged in a single combat. Bhai Bhanu told Shams Khan,"I will not allow you to escape now." Shams Khan replied,"Defend yourself, I am going to strike." Bhai Bhanu received the sword on his shield, and putting forward all his force, beheaded Shams Khan with one blow. The Mohammadans seeing their commander slain, rushed to Bhai Bhanu and surrounded him from all sides. He cut down the enemy as if they were radishes. At last he was struck by two bullets which passed through his body and the brave commander of the Guru's army left for his heavenly abode.

Bhai Bidhi Chand, Painde Khan and Bhai Jati Mal had been committing great havoc among the Mohammadan army. They, lifting their lances, made their enemies' horses riderless. The Guru himself fought so bravely that no one when struck by him, asked for water again. Painde Khan was equally successful in the combat. He made Didar Ali, the last survivor of Mukhlis Khan's personal staff, bite the earth.

Mukhlis Khan, now left alone, thought nothing remained for him but to engage the Guru himself. He said,"Let you and me now decide the fight by single combat, and none else approach." In order to please him, the Guru warned his own men to stand aside. He then discharged an arrow which killed Mukhlis Khan's horse.

The Guru dismounted and said,"Show thy skill and strike the first blow." Mukhlis Khan aimed a blow which the Guru avoided by a swift movement. The next blow fell on the Guru's shield. The Guru then warned,"You have made two strokes which I have parried. Now it is my turn." The Guru then lifting his powerful arm dealt Mukhlis Khan such a blow that his head was cut off in two.

Painde Khan, Bhai Bidhi Chand and Bhai Jati Mal killed the enemy soldiers who held the ground but the majority of them fled without looking behind. After that the Guru's victory was complete and the drums of victory were joyously sounded. This battle was fought in 1628 (some date it as 1634). The battle was extended to a distance of about four miles to the south of Amritsar and a dharmsal called the Sangrana was erected to commemorate the Guru's victory. A fair is held every year on this spot.

After completing the last rites of his brave soldiers, the Guru went to Jhabal and performed the marriage ceremony of his daughter.

FOUNDATION OF SRI HAR GOBINDPUR CITY AND SECOND BATTLE:

On hearing the death of Mukhlis Khan and the defeat of his army, Shah Jahan called a council of his chiefs at which it was decided that the Guru should be captured or killed lest he should seize the reins of the empire. Wazir Khan, a follower of the Guru, defended him and said,"Sir, the Guru is not a rebel and has no designs on thine empire. Had he ever got such a design, he would have followed his victory, seized some fortress, taken some territory or plundered some of thy treasuries. Is it not a miracle that with only seven hundred men he destroyed the army of seven thousand?" These and many such arguments of Wazir Khan were supported by the friends of the Guru at the court. The Emperor was convinced and agreed to forget the past. After the conflict the Guru went to Kartarpur. Painde Khan soon became a concern to the Guru as he began to boast,"It is I who conquered the countless hosts opposed to the Guru at Amritsar. With my arrow I skewered them like trussed fowl. Had I not been there, no one would have had the courage to oppose them. The Guru's Sikhs would have all fled." The Guru heard this. Painde Khan who used to wait on the

Guru whole day and go to his quarters just to sleep, was ordered by the Guru to remain at his home and visit him only occasionally. This was Guru's reprimand for Painde Khan's boasting. It was a rainy season and the Guru after crossing the river Beas, went to the right side of the bank which was lofty. He observed that the land dwellings were only in one direction and the rest of the land was unoccupied. He considered it a good site to found a city. The people received the Guru with open arms but the landlord and Chaudhry, Bhagwan Das Gherar was not in favor of him. Gherar started the hostilities towards the Guru. At some point Gherar used abusive language against the Guru. Upon this a clash broke between the Sikhs and Gherar's men in which Gherar was killed.

Having secured the goodwill of the people, the Guru made preparations for the city. He cut the first sod himself and summoned masons and laborers from the neighboring villages. The city subsequently was called Sri Har Gobindpur in honor of the Guru.

Rattan Chand, son of the Gherar, vowed to avenge the death of his father. He went to Karam Chand, Chandu's son, and urged him to join him against the common oppressor (Guru). They both then went to Abdulla Khan, the Subedar of Jullundhur. Rattan Chand poured his grievances and represented how pleased the Emperor would be if the Guru were put into his hands and what high promotion the Subedar would receive.

The Subedar and his advisors were convinced by Rattan Chand's arguments and an immediate expedition was planned and organized against the Guru. When the Guru heard about the expedition, he simply said," What pleaseth God is best." The Subedar had an army of ten thousand men. He disposed his forces into eight divisions, five for his generals, two for his sons and one for himself. The Guru gave his command to Bhai Jattu, Bhai Bidhi Chand, Bhai Jati Mal, Bhai Mathura, Bhai Jaganath, Bhai Nano and others.

Under the favoring glance of the Guru, the Sikhs who had formerly been weak as hares now became strong as lions. No matter what their birth or previous calling, they all proved themselves as gallant heroes in the field. After all the generals of Abdulla fell in the battle field, he resolved to conquer or die. Karam Chand, Rattan Chand and Abdulla Khan all three came on the

Guru. The Guru asked Karam Chand and Rattan Chand," What think you on? Now avenge your fathers. Retreat not like cowards. Be brave and stand before me; otherwise go where your fathers have gone." The Guru struck Karam Chand with his shield and made him stagger and fall. Rattan Chand ran to his aid. The Guru drew a pistol and shot him. Abdulla struck few blows which the Guru received on his shield. Then gathering his strength he drew his falchion on the Subedar, and severed his head from his body. By this time Karam Chand recovered his consciousness and rushed towards the Guru. There ensued a sword-play between the two until the sword of the latter was broken. The Guru as a holy man desiring to take no mean advantage of his adversary, put his own sword into his scabbard, and engaged with him in a wrestling combat. At last the Guru, seizing Karam Chand by both arms, swung him around and dashed his head to the ground. The Subedar and all his generals were slain and his army had fled, the battle was ended and victory kissed the feet of the Guru.

THIRD BATTLE:

Two Masands, Bakhat Mal and Tara Chand had been deputed to Kabul to collect funds for the Guru. They returned with a company of Sikhs who brought the offering and two horses of supreme beauty and speed, were Dil Bagh and Gul Bagh. Both of the horses were seized by the Emperor's officials who presented them to the Emperor. The Sikhs were much dismayed to see that they were robbed of the horses which they had bought for the Guru.

Bhai Bidhi Chand before entering the services of Guru Arjan, had been a very famous highwayman and robber and several of his exploits in that capacity were recorded. Afterwards he became Guru's follower. The Sikhs thought that as there were no horses like Dil Bagh and Gul Bagh in the world, so there was no one like Bidhi Chand who could secure possession of the horses. Ultimately Bidhi Chand decided to do the job. He got ready, uttered a prayer and went to Lahore to recover the horses. There lived a Sikh carpenter, Jiwan in Lahore and he stayed with him.

Bidhi Chand started the work of a kasiara (grass-cutter). He cut beautiful soft grass, made a bundle and took it to the market.

The grass was beautiful and Bidhi Chand was demanding very high price for that. Ultimately he reached Sondha Khan, the royal stable- keeper who on seeing the grass remarked that he had never seen such grass before. It was fit for Dil Bagh and Gul Bagh, and he ordered his men to adjust the price and buy it for the horses. Sondha Khan took Bidhi Chand with grass on his head to where the horses were tethered. The horses ate to their heart's content as if they had been fasting for a whole day. He continued this practice for several days before he was appointed grass-cutter for the Emperor's famous steeds for one rupee a day. He worked so hard and showed so much civility and sweetness in his words that Sondha Khan entrusted him with bridling and unbridling of the horses. The Emperor once came to see the horses and was very much pleased to observe their excellent condition and he admired Bidhi Chand for that.

One day one of his fellow-servants told him that he was drawing more money than any one of them but he never celebrated. Bidhi Chand agreed to their demand. He went to the market and bought the most potent liquor. A dinner was arranged. He served so much and so strong a liquor to his friends that they were disposed of for the night and Bidhi Chand was free for his action. He mounted on Dil Bagh and applying the whip he faced him towards the fort-wall over which he wanted the horse to leap. The horse which was never touched before, on receiving a cut with whip roused at unusual summons, gathered his strength and cleared without hesitation the high battlement with a bound, and plunged with his rider into the river (river was flowing by the side of the stable). Bidhi Chand, well skilled in horsemanship, steadied the horse in the water and reached safely to shore. He reached Bhai Rupa, a village where the Guru was staying.

The Sikhs noticed that Dil Bagh did not eat his corn well and he was missing his mate Gul Bagh. So Bidhi Chand set out to recover Gul Bagh too. When he reached Lahore, he heard that a reward was posted for the finder of Dil Bagh. Bidhi Chand changed his appearance and dress, reaching at the gate of the fort he claimed,"I am an experienced tracker and astrologer, and can trace anything that has been lost." Bidhi Chand under the pseudo name of Ganak, when presented before the Emperor, convinced him that he had the skill to interpret omens, discover tracks and read the stars and planets. The Emperor promised him lakhs of rupees if he pointed out where the stolen horse was. Bidhi Chand replied to the Emperor,"I know where the horse is, but I want to have a look at the place whence he was stolen, and then I will give all the information."

Upon this the Emperor along with his attendants took him to the stable. Some tried to dissuade the Emperor from trusting the stranger but the advice was disregarded.

Upon Bidhi Chand's advice all the horses were saddled in the stable, perfect solitude and tranquility was ordered and an embargo was put on the ingress and egress of the inhabitants of the fort. All this was done to make possible for Bidhi Chand to sit in perfect tranquility and make calculation. Macauliffe records Bhai Bidhi Chand's address to the Emperor,"Hear everything, consider not the thief a person to be forgotten. Thy father, by the power of his army, formerly took possession of an excellent horse intended for the holy and worshipful Guru Har Gobind, whose fame is like that of the sun, and thou hast now imitation of thy unjust father seized these steeds specially intended by the pious Sikhs for their beloved Guru. I have made reprisal and taken the first horse by my ingenuity. My name is Bidhi Chand; I am the Guru's servant. It was I who took home Dil Bagh, the horse thou art in search of. On account of separation from his mate, he wept copiously on his arrival, and we could only induce him to eat and drink with difficulty. Wherefore, in the guise of a tracker and with a love for dumb animals, I have come to take his companion to join him. I am the thief, the true King is my Master. Thou hast now given me Gul Bagh ready saddled. I have thoroughly gauged the wisdom of thy court. I will tell where the horse is, and in doing so remove all blame from myself. The Guru hath pitched his tent in the new village of Bhai Rupa. Know that Dil Bagh is standing there. Gul Bagh shall now go to join him."[5]

Upon this Bidhi Chand undid the ropes that tethered the horse to the peg and galloped it to Bhai Rupa where the Guru had encamped. Dil Bagh's name was changed to Jan Bhai (as dear as life) and Gul Bagh was called Suhela (companion). At this the Emperor got inflamed and he asked,"Is there any brave man who

---

5: *Some writers say that Bidhi Chand never met the Emperor.*

will undertake an expedition against the Guru?" Up rose Lala Beg, a high officer of the imperial army and said that he would lead the expedition against the Guru, and produce the stolen horses before the Emperor in a few days. Lala Beg's brother Qamar Beg with his two sons, Qasim Beg and Shams Beg, and his nephew Kabuli Beg also volunteered. Lala Beg and his companions were put in command of an army of thirty-five thousand horse and foot. The imperial army marched to Bhai Rupa and not finding the Guru there proceeded to his new headquarters, Lehra which was a few miles away from Bhai Rupa. The Guru chose this site because it was not connected with any city to provide rations and other requirements of war to the enemy and it had one well of drinking water which was firmly guarded by the Guru's army.

The Guru's army was commanded by Bhai Bidhi Chand, Bhai Jetha, Bhai Jati Mal, and Bhai Rai Jodh and there were about four thousand soldiers.

Rai Jodh with a thousand men went to oppose Qamar Beg. Showers of bullets thinned the ranks of the imperial army. They used their swords and guns. The Guru's troops caused great havoc upon the enemy. Rai Jodh finding an opportunity pierced Qamar Beg with his lance who fell and soon after died. After seeing his chiefs slain and his army disheartened, Lala Beg himself hurried to oppose Bhai Jati Mal, and discharged an arrow which struck Jati Mal on the breast and made him fall fainting to the ground. The Guru seeing Jati Mal fall, entered the battle field and invited Lala Beg to measure his strength with his. He shot Lala Beg's horse which fell with its rider. The Guru, on seeing the chief on the ground, dismounted so as not to take an unfair advantage of his adversary. Lala Beg assumed the offensive and aimed several blows of his sword at the Guru, who avoided them all. The Guru then putting forward his strength, struck the chief a blow which completely severed his head from his body. Kabuli Beg, the chief's nephew was the only one of imperial commanders remained in the field. On seeing Lala Beg fall down, Kabuli Beg jumped on the Guru. He slashed again and again at the Guru but every blow was evaded. The Guru then warned him,"It is now my turn, be on thy guard." He then dealt him with such a blow that his head was cut off. This ended the battle. The surviving imperial army soldiers fled for their lives. Twelve hundred soldiers of the Guru's army were slain or wounded.

The battle which had begun at midnight, lasted for eighteen hours on the 16th of Maghar, Sambat 1688 or 1631 A.D. (some date this battle in 1634). The Guru admired the bravery shown by Bhai Bidhi Chand, Bhai Jati Mal and Bhai Rai Jodh. In order to commemorate the victory, a tank called Guru Sar was built on the spot.

FOURTH AND LAST BATTLE:

The Guru went for a repose at Kangar and soon returned to Kartarpur. After a while a war broke between the Sikhs and the Mughals. This time the cause was Painde Khan. He went to Subedar of Jullundhur, Qutab Khan, and then both of them went to the Emperor and induced him to despatch a strong force against the Guru. Kale Khan, the brother of Mukhlis Khan, was given a command of fifty thousand men. Qutab Khan, Painde Khan, Anwar Khan and Asman Khan were commissioned to fight under Kale Khan.

Bhai Bidhi Chand, Bhai Jati Mal, Bhai Lakhu, and Bhai Rai Jodh ranged their troops on the four sides of Kartarpur. The imperial army chiefs advanced against them. The Pathans were, however, powerless against the brave Sikhs who were fighting for their religion and their Guru. Bidhi Chand engaged with Kale Khan, and Baba Gurditta, Guru's eldest son, with Asman Khan. Even Tegh Bahadur (later on the ninth Guru) who was only fourteen years old, had shown feats of valor in the field. Painde Khan with drawn sword confronted the Guru and used profane words for the Master. In the words of Mohsan Fani, a Muslim historian of that time, the Guru addressed him,"Painde Khan, why use such words when the sword is in your hand. Brave as you are my boy, come I give you full leave to strike first. I have no grudge against you. But you are full of wrath. You can wreak your rage by striking the first blow."

Painde Khan aimed a heavy blow at the Guru but it was parried off. He was allowed again to strike but in vain. Infuriated with his double failure, he gave a third blow but the Guru was able to avoid it. The Master then urged him,"Come, my boy, I will teach you how to strike. Not your way but this..." Saying this he gave him such strong blow that Painde Khan fell on the ground mortally wounded. From this blow he seemed to have regained his old sense of discipleship. The Guru told him,"Thou art a Musalman. Now is the time to repeat your kalma (creed)." Painde Khan replied,"O Guru, your sword is my kalma and my source of salvation." The Guru on seeing him dying was filled with pity, and by putting his shield over his face so as to shade it from the sun, he said,"Painde Khan, I cherished you, I reared you, and I made you a hero. Though men spoke ill of you, I forgot all your failings, and evil never entered my mind against you; but the evil destiny misled you so much that you brought an army against me. It is your own acts of ingratitude and insolence that have led to your death at my hands. Though you have been ungrateful and untrue to your salt, I pray the Almighty to grant you a dwelling in heaven."

After all his chiefs were slain, Kale Khan confronted the Guru. He discharged an arrow which whizzed past him. A second arrow grazed the Guru's forehead, and drops of blood bespattered his face. The Guru remarked,"Kale Khan, I have seen your science. Now see mine." At this he discharged an arrow which killed Kale Khan's horse. The Guru thought it a point of honor also to dismount and offer his adversary a choice of arms. Sparks of fire issued from clash of sword to sword. The Guru parried all his strokes and commented,"Not thus, this is the way to fence." He then dealt Kale Khan a blow with his two-edged scimitar which severed his head from his body. On this the imperial soldiers fled for their lives. Bidhi Chand and Jati Mal shouted slogans of victory.

It is said that several thousand Mohammadans were killed while only seven hundred of the Guru's brave Sikhs lost their lives in this battle. It ended on the 24th day of Har, Sambat 1691 (1634 A.D.).

Guru Har Gobind fought and won four battles. Since the Guru's purpose had always been defensive, he did not acquire even an inch of territory as a result of these victories. However this effected a great change in the character of the Sikhs who, side by side of their rosaries, girded up their loins and buckled on their swords in defence of their faith. A new spirit of heroism was risen in the land to resist the mighty and unjust power of the Mughal government who had embarked upon the policy of religious discrimination against non-Muslim subject. The Guru was looked upon by the Sikhs not only a divine messenger but as an accomplished swordsman, a hero and thorough master of the war.

PREACHING TOURS:

Guru Har Gobind was the first, after Guru Nanak, who went outside the Punjab to spread Sikh religion. He travelled from place to place and went as far as Kashmir in the north and Nanakmata, Pilibhit in the east.

A Sikh, Almast (means enthusiast) who had been preaching Sikh religion at Nanak Mata near Pilibhit, had been expelled from his shrine by the Jogis who had also burnt the sacred pipal tree under which Guru Nanak had held debate with the followers of Gorakh Nath. Night and day Almast read the compositions of the Gurus. He used to pray,"O searcher of hearts, true Guru, render us assistance." Enduring all hardships, Almast waited until the Guru came to repair and take possession of Guru Nanak's temple.

Ramo, the eldest sister of Guru's wife- Damodri, was married to Sain Das who lived in Daroli in the present district of Ferozepur. Sain Das was ever praying that Guru Har Gobind would visit his village. He built a mansion to receive him and vowed not to allow any one to live in it until the Guru had hallowed it by his presence. Sain Das prepared a beautiful bed, and over the pillow he put up a canopy. Every morning he used to lay flowers in the room and pray that the Guru would come to bless the place. Ramo used to press him to send for the Guru but he would say,"The Guru is omniscient and will come of his own accord."

On account of the troubles of Almast and the devotion of Sain Das, the Guru decided to visit Nanakmata and Daroli and taking with him a troop of his armed retainers. He went to Kartarpur and stayed there for some days. After that when he arrived in Nanak- Mata, the Jogis, seeing his retinue, thought that some Raja had come. Almast came forth and uttered thanksgiving that his spiritual master had arrived. The Guru constructed a platform and sitting on it recited the Sodar. He sprinkled saffron on the pipal tree which came back to its full bloom.

The Jogis came in a body and represented," Thou art a family man; we are well-known holy ascetics. Bearing the name of Gorakhnath, this place has been ours. Therefore leave it, and go and abide wherever it pleases you." The Guru replied,"Whom do you call a holy ascetic? I apply this name only to him who has renounced pride and who has the love of God in his heart. It is he, and not a man who wears an ascetic's garb, who will obtain salvation."

The Jogis, in order to terrify the Guru, made a show of their supernatural powers, but could produce no effect on the Guru, and thus retreated. Since that date the place is called Nanakmata, and remained in the possession of Udasi Sikhs. The Guru remained there for some time and occupied himself with preaching to his Sikhs, and set up a Sikh service organization under the guidance of Almast.

On his return journey the Guru proceeded to Daroli where his mother and wives were waiting for him. Sain Das and his wife Ramo begged for his blessings. The Guru replied,"God at all times assist those whose hearts are pure. With a pure mind meditate on His Name, and accept His Will, then you shall be happy."

The moon was full in the month of Kartik, Sambat 1670 (1613 A.D.) Mata Damodri gave birth to a son who was afterwards named Gurditta, and who bore a remarkable likeness to Guru Nanak. After that the Guru returned to Amritsar.

Sewa Das, a Brahman who was residing at Srinagar in Kashmir, had been a converted Sikh. His mother, Bhagbhari made a beautiful robe to give to the Guru when he would visit her. She continued praying and waited for the Guru who answered her prayer by deciding to proceed to Kashmir to see her.

On his way to Kashmir he reached Chaparnala near Sialkot, where he met a Brahman and inquired him where could he find water to drink and bathe in? The Brahman carelessly replied that the soil was stony and therefore, the water was very scant. Upon this the Guru drove a spear into the ground and it is said that a spring of pure water issued forth. The Sikhs constructed a tank at the spring and it was called Gurusar. The Brahman felt ashamed and asked for pardon for not having recognized the Guru's greatness. The Guru replied,"The sins of those who repent shall be pardoned."

The Guru continued his journey into the mountains of Kashmir. There he met Kattu Shah, a faithful Sikh who had visited him at Amritsar. He spent a night in his house and then proceeded to Srinagar, where Sewa Das was meditating and waiting for him. His mother said that she worshipped the very ground on which the Guru would tread. They received the Guru with great respect and enthusiasm. The Guru asked Sewa Das's mother to bring the dress she had made for him. He put it on and blessed her. Overwhelmed with devotion for the Guru, she recited the following Sabad:

"Who but Thee, my Beloved, could do such a thing?
Cherisher of the poor, Lord of the world, Thou hast put over my head the umbrella of spiritual sovereignty."
(Rag Bani Maru Ravdas, p-1106)

After this she and her son both drank some of the water in which the Guru had washed his feet, and the remainder she sprinkled over her house.

The Guru was paid homage by crowds of Kashmiris both from Srinagar and the surrounding villages and many embraced Sikhism. A very interesting story- a company of Sikhs came to behold the Guru from a distant village with an offering of honey. On the way they met Kattu Shah who requested them to let him have some of the honey, but they refused saying that they could not offer to the Guru Kattu Shah's leavings. When the Sikhs reached the Guru, the honey was found rotten and full of worms. The Guru remarked,"This is the result of not having given to my Sikh in whom is the spirit of the Guru." He ordered them to return and satisfy Kattu Shah. It is said that the honey became fresh and sweet when they returned to Kattu Shah. 'Hungry mouth is Guru's treasure.'

The Guru returned to Punjab through Bara Mula. The next day he visited the place where Rikhi Kashyap had dwelt, and where Vishnu was said to have incarnation of a swarf. Then he proceeded to Gujrat in the Punjab where he met Shah Daula, a saint of that city. Shah Daula was astonished to see the Guru with swords hanging on his both sides, aigrette attached to his turban and a hawk perched on his wrist. Shah Daula asked the Guru,"How can you be a religious man when you have wife and children and possess worldly wealth and have arms?" The Guru retorted,"A wife is man's conscience, his children perpetuate his memory, wealth enables him to live, arms are needed to extirpate the tyrants."

After that he proceeded to Wazirabad and thence to Hafiza-bad, both in the district of Gujranwala (now in Pakistan). Then he went to a village called Mutto Bhai and he preached the principles of his religion. He spent some time there. The Guru then reached Mandiali, a place about five miles from Lahore. Here Dwarka, a devout Sikh of the Guru married his daughter, Bibi Marwahi to the Guru.

While still at Mandiali the Guru was informed by his Sikh Langha of the sustained efforts of some of imperial officers and the Qazis to poison the Emperor's mind to destroy the sacred buildings of the Sikhs. The Guru took only a casual notice and proceeded to Talwandi, the birth place of Guru Nanak. He imparted religious instructions to the people who had gathered there in connection with the Namani fair. From there he proceeded to Madai. Next stop was at Manga in Lahore district. From there he returned to Amritsar where as usual great rejoicing were held in his honor.

During Shah Jahan's reign all those persons and groups who had enmity towards the Guru, were constantly on the look-out for some opportunity to strike the Guru and impede the onward march of Sikh movement. Tara Chand, the ruler of Hadur or Kehlur (Nalagarh) had waited upon the Guru and requested him to pay a visit to his state. In view of these circumstances the Guru had an idea of alternative headquarters. He sent his son Baba Gurditta to Tara Chand and promised him to visit his state later on. The Raja offered a piece of land for the Guru's permanent abode. Some writers say that the land was purchased from him. Baba Gurditta founded the town of Kiratpur on that piece of land.

Malwa region was still a vast tract of waste land and its people were still uncommitted to any religion. The Guru, therefore, undertook great tour of this region. He visited Zira, Rode Lande, Gill, Kotra and Hari. After that he visited Marajh, Dabwalli, Bhadaur, Mahal, Ded Maluke, Demru and then reached Darauli. Before his departure, he blessed the people of Darauli and gave them a 'pothi' and a small katar (a small sword) as monuments. Thence he visited Bara Ghar, Mado, Lopo, Sidhwan and then reached Sidhar. Rai Jodh, a big landlord of Kangar inspired by his wife Bhagan who was a daughter of Bhag Mal Gill, a devotee of the Guru, waited upon the Guru. He was so much impressed that he desired to enter the Sikh fold. The Guru initiated him, his brother Umar Shah and many others of their families.

The people came in flocks and embraced Sikhism specially in Malwa region. For the first time in history of Indian religions, the people were coming across a religious leader who was committed to the ideal of resisting all types of exploitations, injustice and tyranny. In fact the Guru's close identification with the lower and down-trodden classes and his constant endeavors for their welfare and uplift made him the cynosure of the masses.

GURU'S FAMILY:

The Guru had five sons and one daughter. They were:

Baba Gurditta was born to Mata Damodri in 1613.
Bibi Viro was born to Mata Damodri in 1615.
Baba Surj Mal was born to Mata Marwahi in 1617.
Baba Ani Rai was born to Mata Nanaki in 1618.
Baba Atal Rai was born to Mata Nanaki in 1619.
Baba Tegh Bahadur was born to Mata Nanaki in 1621.

There lived a Sikh, Gurmukh in Amritsar who had the only son, Mohan. Baba Atal and Mohan used to play together. One day they played until nightfall. The victory remained with Baba Atal and it was agreed upon that the play would be resumed the next morning. When Mohan went out, he was bitten by a cobra and the boy succumbed to death. Next morning Baba Atal Rai went to Mohan's house and was told that Mohan was dead. Baba Atal did not believe that he was dead and he lifted the dead Mohan to life. Upon this the Guru angrily addressed to his son," You must be working miracles, while I teach men to obey God's Will." Baba Atal replied," Great King, may you live for ages, I depart for Sachkhand (heaven)." By saying this, he left and went to bathe in the tank of nectar. After his ablutions, he circumambulated the Golden Temple four times. As he finished his morning devotions, his light blended with the Light of God when he was nine years old.

Guru Har Gobind narrated all the circumstances to his eldest son Gurditta and sent him to Budhan Shah, whose devotion he commended. Baba Gurditta took his wife Natti and his son Dhir

Mal and met Budhan Shah on the bank of river Satluj. Baba Gurditta reminded,"O priest, thou hast the milk that was entrusted to thee. Bring that to me. The Guru is my father, and he has sent me to taste it."[6] Budhan Shah gave the milk and it is said that it was as fresh as it had been set. Baba Gurditta and his wife Natti continued to reside in Kiratpur. A son was born to them on January 16, 1630 and they called him Har Rai.

BHAI BUDDHA:

Bhai Buddha remained in his village of Ramdas intent on his devotions. When he saw his end near, he asked for the Guru to come and fulfil his promise once he made to him. The Guru told him,"Bhai Buddha, you have lived long, you have been ever with the Gurus. Give some instruction." Bhai Buddha replied,"Great King, thou art a sun, I am a fire-fly before thee. You have come to save me, and to hear my dying words........I have been a servant of the Guru's house for six generations. Succor me in the next world, and allow me not to suffer when I enter death's door, which I fondly hope is the portal of salvation. Here is my son, Bhana at your service; take his arm and keep him at your feet." The Guru replied,"Bhai Buddha, you shall assuredly obtain bliss. Your humility is an assurance." The Guru then put his hand on Bhai Buddha's head and blessed him. He left for his heavenly abode. The Guru and his Sikhs sang congratulations on the event of Bhai Buddha's death after his long, holy and eventful life, and lauded him for the assistance he had given in the propagation and consolidation of Sikh faith. The Guru himself ignited his funeral pyre.

BHAI GURDAS:

Bhai Gurdas was a contemporary of the fourth, fifth and sixth Gurus and was acquainted with them and their contemporar-

---

6: *Some writers claim that it was Guru Har Gobind himself who asked Budhan Shah for milk. When Guru Nanak met Budhan Shah, he offered milk to the Guru as a mark of respect. The Guru promised that he would drink milk later on. Now Guru Har Gobind reminded Budhan Shah of the milk he promised to drink. Budhan Shah said,"You do not look like the Guru I gave the milk." Upon this Guru Har Gobind appeared in the appearance of Guru Nanak before Budhan Shah and accepted the milk to fulfil the promise.*

ies, especially Bhai Buddha, an aged Sikh who had survived from the time of Guru Nanak. The tenets of Sikh religion are given in Bhai Gurdas's Vars. There are forty Vars in number and each is divided in varying number of pauries (stanzas) and each pauri contains from five to ten lines.

One morning the Guru went to Bhai Gurdas whose end was now approaching. Gurdas begged pardon for any sins he might have committed. The Guru replied," I thank thee, Bhai Gurdas, for having assisted in laying out the road of the Sikh faith. Among the Gurus' Sikhs thy name shall be immortal." Having heard this Bhai Gurdas meditated on God and drew a sheet over him and closed his eyes in eternal sleep on Friday the fifth day of the light half of Bhadon, Sambat 1686 (1629 A.D.). After performing Gurdas's last rites the Guru returned to Amritsar.

GURU AT KIRATPUR:

The Guru lived in Kiratpur from 1635 to 1644. He chose Kiratpur, a city in the foothill of the Himalayas, which was not so easily accessible during those days of undeveloped and scanty means of transportation and communication, to ward off any further hostility between the Sikhs and the Mughal government after the confrontation of four battles. There were hilly Rajas who were great admirers of the Guru because he was instrumental in getting them released from the fort of Gwalior and some of them had developed veneration for Sikhism. These are some of the circumstances in which the Guru seemed to have set up his headquarters at Kiratpur.

When the Guru was busy in the battle field, Baba Gurditta was incharge to look after the organizational work. In 1636 the Guru asked Baba Gurditta to appoint four head preachers: Almast, Phul, Gonda and Baba Hasna. Almast was made the chief organizer of the proselytizing activities in the east. Baba Hasna who was the younger brother of Almast, established himself among the people of Pothohar, Kashmir, Chhachh and Hazara. Similarly Phul and Gonda were assigned the area of Doab to carry on the proselytizing work. All these four Udasis were founded in their allotted areas, preaching centers which were named as Dhuans or Hearths, to symbolize the flame of Sikhism. Besides this the Guru sent Bidhi

Chand to Bengal. He had also sent Bhai Gurdas earlier to Kabul and then to Banaras to enlighten the people on Guru's gospel and also to encourage trade in horses.

One day Baba Gurditta went for a hunting trip. It so happened that one of his Sikhs shot a cow by mistake for a deer. The shepherds came and arrested the offending Sikh. Baba Gurditta went to his assistance and offered to give compensation. The shepherds would have from the Guru's son (Gurditta) nothing less than the restoration of the cow to life. If he restored the cow to life, the Guru would be angry as he was before in the case of Baba Atal and if he refused to satisfy the shepherds, they would detain his Sikh as a hostage. He was at last persuaded to reanimate the cow. When it was reported to the Guru, he remarked,"It is not pleasing to me that any one should set himself up as God's equal, and restore life to the dead. Everybody will be bringing the dead to my door, and whom shall I select for reanimation?" Baba Gurditta replied," Mayest thou live for ever! I depart." He went to Budhan Shah's shrine, drove his cane into the ground, lay down, and left for his heavenly abode at the early age of twenty-four in 1638.

After this the Guru sent for Baba Gurditta's eldest son, Dhir Mal, from Kartarpur, and also for the Adi Granth which was in his custody. The Guru intended that the holy volume should be read for the repose of Gurditta's soul, and also that Dhir Mal should be present to receive a turban after his father's death in token of succession to his property and position. Dhir Mal declined the invitation saying,"My father is not in Kiratpur. To whom shall I go? It is through fear of the Guru my father died. I do not desire to die yet. I will myself have the Adi Granth read for my father." Thus he kept holy scripture thinking that whosoever had its custody would be the Guru. Bhai Bidhi Chand had unfinished copy of the Adi Granth which was read at that time.   One day the Guru's wife Mata Nanaki asked him,"O my lord, you always show great kindness to Har Rai, who is your grandson, but you never show regard to your own son Tegh Bahadur. Fulfil my wishes to put him on your throne." The Guru replied," Tegh Bahadur is a Guru of Gurus. There is none who can endure the unendurable so well as he. He has obtained divine knowledge and renounced worldly love. If you have patience, the Guruship shall revert to him."

A day was appointed for a great assemblage. When all were

present, Guru Har Gobind rose, took Har Rai by the hand and seated him on the throne of Guru Nanak. Bhai Bhana, son of Bhai Buddha, affixed the tilak to Har Rai's forehead and decorated him with a necklace of flowers. The Guru putting five paise and a coconut in front of him, bowed before him declaring him the Guru, and addressed the Sikhs,"In Har Rai now recognize me. The spiritual power of Guru Nanak hath entered him." Upon this the Sikhs shouted congratulations and minstrels began to sing.

After this Guru Har Gobind left this world in March, 1644 at Kiratpur.

When the last rites were completed, Mata Nanaki and her son Tegh Bahadur set out, according to the Guru's order, for Bakala, where they both lived until Tegh Bahadur obtained the Guruship.

GURU HAR RAI
(1630-1661, Guruship 1644-1661)

Guru Har Gobind had five sons and one daughter. The eldest son was Baba Gurditta who had two sons, Dhir Mal and Har Rai. Dhir Mal turned out disloyal and disobedient. He had some influence in the court of Emperor Aurangzeb and was in communication with the Guru's enemies. When Guru Har Gobind moved to Kiratpur, Dhir Mal with his mother, remained at Kartarpur and took possession of the Guru's property and also of the priceless original copy of the Adi Granth. He thought that as long as he had its possession, the Sikhs would look upon him as their religious leader and thus as mentioned in the last chapter, Dhir Mal refused Guru's invitation to come to Kiratpur on his father's death. Guru Har Gobind nominated Har Rai, younger brother of Dhir Mal, as his successor before he departed for the heavenly abode on March 3, 1644.

One day as a child, while passing through a garden, his loose flowing robes damaged some flowers and scattered their petals on the ground. This sight effected his tender heart and brought tears in his eyes. After that he always walked with his skirts tucked up, and resolved never to harm anything in the world. When he grew up, he carried the same spirit with him. He used Baba Farid's quotation frequently:

"All men's hearts are jewels; to distress them is not at all good;
If thou desire the Beloved, distress no one's heart."

Guru Har Rai was most magnanimous. His food was very simple, he did not desire dainty dishes. Whatever valuable offerings were made to him, he used to spend on his guests. On the advice of his grandfather, Guru Har Gobind, he kept twenty-two hundred mounted soldiers. In the afternoon he used to go to chase. The Guru took some of the animals he had obtained from the chase, freed them and protected them in a zoological garden, which he had made for the recreation of his followers. In the evening the

Guru used to hold his court, listen to hymns sung by his choir, and then give divine instructions.

The Emperor Shah Jahan had four sons, Dara Shikoh, Shuja Mohammad, Aurangzeb, and Murad Bakhsh. Dara Shikoh who was the heir-apparent, was very dear to his father. Aurangzeb was very clever, cunning and ambitious, and aimed at succeeding to the throne. It is said that Aurangzeb administered tiger's whiskers in a dainty dish to Dara Shikoh who became dangerously ill as a consequence. The best physicians were consulted but in vain. The Emperor, filled with anxiety, sent for astrologers and diviners from every country but of no avail. The wise men arrived at a conclusion that until tiger's whiskers were removed from Dara's bowls, there was no hope of recovery. They were of the opinion that if a chebulic myrobalan weighing fourteen chitanks (14/16th of a pound) and a clove weighing one masha could be administered to the patient, he would be restored to health. The Emperor searched for these articles everywhere in his empire but in vain. At last some one told him that the required items were available in the Guru's storehouse. On the advice of his courtiers the Emperor found it necessary to humble himself before the Guru, and accordingly addressed him the following letter:

"Your predecessor, the holy Baba Nanak granted
sovereignty to Emperor Babar, the founder of my dynasty;
Guru Angad was exceedingly well disposed to his son,
Emperor Humayun; and Guru Amar Das removed many
difficulties from my grandfather Akbar's path. I regret that
the same friendly relations did not subsist between Guru Har
Gobind and myself, and that misunderstandings were caused
by the interference of strangers. For this I was not to blame.
My son Dara Shikoh is now very ill. His remedy is in your
hands. If you give the myrobalan and the clove which are
available in your store, and add to them your prayers, you
will confer an abiding   favor on me."

A noble carried the letter to the Guru at Kiratpur, who commented,"Behold, with one hand man breaks flowers, and with the other he offers them, but flowers perfume both hands alike. Although the axe cuts the sandal-tree, yet the sandal perfumes the axe. The Guru is, therefore, to return good for evil." He sent the necessary medicine which was administered to Dara Shikoh. The medicine effected a speedy and complete cure. The Emperor was naturally very pleased, forgot all enmity against the Guru, and vowed that he would never again cause any annoyance to him.

One day during a ride, the Guru halted and knocked at the door of a poor woman and said,"Good lady, I am very hungry, bring me the bread you have prepared." The woman, throbbing with joy, brought out some coarse bread which he partook on horseback, without washing his hands, and relished it very much. He then blessed the woman and cut off the shackles of her transmigration. Next day the Sikhs prepared dainty dishes with great attention to cleanliness and offered them to the Guru at the same hour. He laughed and said,"O Sikhs, I ate food from that woman's hands because she was holy. This food which you have prepared with attention to ancient ceremonial is not pleasing to me." The Sikhs asked,"O true king, yesterday you ate bread on horseback from the hands of an old woman whom you did not know. There was no consecrated space and the food was in every way impure. Today we have prepared the food for you; no impurity is attached to it, yet you reject it. Be kind enough to explain the reason." The Guru replied," The woman with great devotion and faith prepared food for me out of what she had earned from the sweat of her brow. On this account the food was very pure, and I partook of it. The Guru is hungry for love and not for dainty dishes. In the matter of love for God, no rule is recognized. It is not what man eats that pleases God, it is man's devotion that is acceptable to Him."

GURU'S PREACHING TOURS:

Guru Arjan had practically completed the organization of his followers on peaceful lines and under Guru Har Gobind, Sikhism had added into itself an army. Apart from laying emphasis on the free kitchen and religious congregation and faith in the Adi Granth, Guru Har Rai undertook extensive tours in Malwa and Doaba regions of the Punjab. These regions provided good opportunities for the Sikh faith to sprout. Guru Har Rai made some notable conversions among the landed families of the Punjab who were, at that time, considered the natural leaders of the people.

On one of the Guru's tours, he stayed at Mukandpur in the present district of Jullundhur. There he drove a bamboo shoot into the ground in memory of his visit; and it still survives as a stately tree. From there he went to Malwa and visited the tank near Nathana where Guru Har Gobind had fought. There Kala and Karm Chand, two brothers of Mahraj tribe, came to him to complain that the people of Kaura tribe did not allow them to live among them. The Guru tried to settle the matter amicably but when Kaura tribe refused to listen, he helped the Mahraj brothers to take forcible possession of a piece of land and settle there. He remained for some time at Nathana preaching to the people, and Kala and his friends frequently waited on him. The Guru made many disciples. His hearers abandoned the worship of cemeteries and cremation grounds, and embraced the simple worship of God. One day Kala with his two nephews, Sandali and Phul, whose father was killed in the battle during Guru Har Gobind's time, went to visit the Guru. When the children arrived in his presence, Phul who was five years old, struck with his hands his own naked belly like a drum. When the Guru asked for the reason, Kala explained that he was hungry and wanted something to eat. The Guru took compassion on him and said," He shall become great, famous and wealthy. The steeds of his descendants shall drink water as far as the Jamna river; they shall have sovereignty for many generations and be honored in proportion as they serve the Guru." When Kala reached home and his wife heard Guru's benediction, she put pressure on him to take his own sons to him, and teach them to strike their bellies in token of hunger. When Kala and his own sons appeared before the Guru, he told him that he acted in obedience to his wife. The Guru said," The parents of these children are alive, but at the same time they shall have their own cultivation, eat the fruit of their toil, pay no tribute, and dependent on no one." This prophecy has been fulfilled and their descendants owned twenty-two villages called the Bahia. Phul had six sons. From the eldest, Tilok Singh, the Rajas of Nabha and Jind were the descendants. From Phul's second son, Ram Singh, the Maharaja of Patiala was the descendant. These three were known as the Phul ke Raje, or Phulkian chiefs. After India became independent in 1947, these states along with other hundreds of states in the county, were annexed by the Government of India.

The Guru, having been convinced of the deterioration of Masand system, evolved Bakhshishs or missionary centers. Six centers were manned by Suthrashah, Sahiba, Sangata, Mihan Sahib, Bhagat Bhagwan, Bhagat Mal and Jeet Mal. Bhagat Bhagwan was appointed as the incharge of the preaching work in the east, where he along with his followers, established as many as 360 gaddies (centers) to carry on these efforts. Bhai families of Kaithal and Bagrian were made responsible for missionary work in the land between the Jamna and Satluj rivers. Bhai Pheru was responsible for the area between the Beas and Ravi rivers. Another center was established in the central districts of Punjab. Bhai Aru, Sewa Das, Naik Das, Durga Chand and Suthra Shah were the important priests of the Guru's times who did missionary work in Kashmir.

THE GURU, HIS SON RAM RAI AND MUGHAL EMPEROR:

The Emperor, Shah Jahan, kept his eldest son Dara Shikoh near him. He made his second son, Shujah Mohammad, the governor of Bengal. The third son, Aurangzeb was appointed governor of Dakhan and Murad Bakhsh received the province of Gujrat. Their ambition was not satisfied and each one of them was eagerly seeking to become Emperor, and for that purpose they amassed wealth and armies in their respective regions. When Shah Jahan became ill and showed no signs of recovery, a war of succession broke out. Dara Shikoh dispatched Raja Jai Singh against Shujah Mohammad and sent Raja Jaswant Singh of Jodhpur to Dakhan. Jai Singh defeated Shujah Mohammad but combined armies of Aurangzeb and Murad forced Jaswant Singh to retreat. Upon this Aurangzeb prepared to retaliate and tried to seize the reigns of empire. Dara proceeded with great pomp and show to oppose Aurangzeb, and pitched his camp at Samugarh near the margin of the river Chambal. Aurangzeb soon appeared at the head of his own and Murad's armies and ensued a determined battle. Aurangzeb succeeded in capturing Dara's several nobles. Dara himself fled from the battle field. Aurangzeb came to Agra and imprisoned his father and his brother Murad, and then proceeded to Delhi. Dara fled towards Lahore.

Famous Muslim saint Mian Mir was Dara's priest from

whom he had heard Guru's praises. Dara's life was saved with the medicine from the Guru. In view of these circumstances Dara had great regard for the Guru. Since Dara became governor of Punjab, there were healthy relations between the Emperor and the Guru. Shah Jahan had an order against the Hindu temples while Sikh temples were exempt from such an order.

While Dara Shikoh was on his way to Lahore, the Guru happened to be in Goindwal. He met the Guru. Many writers give their own fanciful accounts of the assistance that the Guru gave to Dara. What type of assistance Dara asked or the Guru gave to Dara, is a big question? He had all the royal wealth, he had his generals and he had his army of thousand and thousand of men. He enlisted twenty thousand men in his army within days at Lahore. He had everything but he lacked a brave heart to fight in the battle-field. He fled from the field and ultimately was captured through a Pathan who betrayed him. He was brought to Delhi and was executed.

Having made his position secure on the throne of Delhi, Aurangzeb embarked on his religious crusade against the Hindus. After Dara the enemies of the Guru got a chance to poison the mind of Aurangzeb that the Guru had rendered assistance to Dara against him. Upon this Aurangzeb summoned the Guru to his presence in Delhi. The Guru had vowed not to see the Emperor. Instead he sent his eldest son Ram Rai to Delhi instructing him to rely on the divine power of the Gurus, not in any way recede from the principles of his religion, and in all his words and actions to fix his thought on God, everything would prove successful.

When the Emperor was informed that the Guru had not come himself but sent his son, he thought that if his object in trying the Guru was not fulfilled by the Guru's son, he would send for the Guru himself. It is said that Ram Rai performed seventy miracles. The Emperor sent him poisoned robes which he wore but was not hurt. In one interview a sheet of cloth was spread over a deep well so that Ram Rai when asked to sit, would fall into the well. The sheet did not give way and Ram Rai was miraculously preserved. The Emperor was shown the sight of Mecca while sitting in Delhi. After seventy such miracles were shown, Aurangzeb was almost convinced of Ram Rai's powers and became friendly to him. Then came the last question. The Qazis' asked Ram Rai," Ram Rai, your

Guru Nanak has written against the Muslim religion. In one place
he hath said,
   'Mitti Musalman ki peirei paee kumiar;
   Ghar bhandei itan kia, jaldi karei pukar.'
                              (Asa Mohalla 1, p-466)
'The ashes of the Mohammadan fall into the potter's clod;
Vessels and bricks are fashioned from them; they cry out as
                                                  they burn.'
                    (Translation of the above)

What is the meaning of this?"

        Ram Rai had won Aurangzeb's respect so much that he
perhaps did not want to displease him and forgot his father's
parting injunctions not to recede from the principles of his religion.
So in order to please the Emperor, Ram Rai replied," Your Majesty,
Guru Nanak wrote[1], 'Mitti beiman ki', that is the ashes of the
faithless, not of the Musalmans, fall into the potter's clod. The text
has been corrupted by ignorant persons and Your Majesty's religion and mine defamed. The faces of the faithless and not of the
Musalmans, shall be blackened in both worlds." All the Mohammadan priests were pleased with this reply. The Emperor then
conferred a mark of favor on Ram Rai and dissolved the assembly.
        The Sikhs of Delhi immediately sent an envoy to Kiratpur
and informed the Guru of the pomp and honor with which Ram
Rai had been received in Delhi, and detailed miracles he had
exhibited. The envoy then explained how he had made an altera-
tion in a line of Guru Nanak in order to please the Emperor. The
Guru was much distressed at the insult to Guru Nanak and
**remarked that no mortal could change the words of Guru Nanak
and that 'the mouth which had dared to do so should never be
seen by me.'** The Guru decided that Ram Rai was not fit for
Guruship. He confirmed," The Guruship is like a tigress's milk
which can only be contained in a golden cup. Only he who is ready
to devote his life thereto is worthy of it."

1: *It is also said that Ram Rai told Aurangzeb that Guru Nanak did not mean the ashes of
Musalman but he actually meant that of the 'beiman', the faithless. Ram Rai thus did not alter the
original verse but only changed the meaning of it.*

After Ram Rai had resided in Delhi for some time, he decided to go to Kiratpur and try to convince his father to reverse his decision regarding him. He pitched his camp near Kiratpur and wrote to his father for permission to visit him. He confessed that he had suffered for his sins and desired forgiveness. The Guru replied,"Ram Rai, you have disobeyed my order and sinned. How can you aspire to become a holy man? Go whither your fancy leads you. I will never see you again on account of your infidelity?"

The Guru feeling his end approaching thought of his successor and called for a meeting of his Sikhs. He seated his younger son, Har Kishen who was only five years old, on Guru Nanak's throne. He then placed a coco-nut and five paise before him, circumambulated him three times and had a tilak or patch put on his forehead. The whole assembly then rose and did obeisance to the young Guru. Guru Har Rai enjoined all his Sikhs to consider Har Kishen as his image, to put faith in him, and they would obtain salvation.

Guru Har Rai closed his eyes and went to his heavenly abode on October 6, 1661.

GURU HAR KISHEN
(1656-1664, Guruship 1661-1664)

Guru Har Kishen who was the second and the youngest son of Guru Har Rai and Mata Krishen Kaur, was born on 7th of July, 1656 at Kiratpur. The reason why Ram Rai was superseded has already been given in the last chapter. Guru Har Kishen was appointed Guru when he was five years and three months old.

Ram Rai was at the Emperor's court in Delhi and when the news of Guru Har Kishen's succession to Guruship reached Ram Rai, he was inflamed with jealousy. The masand Gurdas[1] who attended on Ram Rai comforted him," There is no need to be sad. Thou hast many disciples in this part of the country. Even the Emperor himself holdeth thee in honor." Ram Rai was not satisfied," Knowest thou not, when the Sikhs of this country learn that the Guruship hath been given to my younger brother, they will turn away from me and go to him." However Ram Rai acted on Gurdas's suggestion and sent his masands in every direction to proclaim his succession and bring him the offerings of the faithful. His masands went in all directions to announce his succession as Guru but the Sikhs who knew Guru's succession, refused to accept Ram Rai as their Guru. At that time Ram Rai decided to lay his case before the Emperor. Thus he addressed Aurangzeb,"Sir, my father has appointed my younger brother as successor to him, and now he has taken possession of his throne, his property and offerings. This misfortune has befallen me on account of my obedience to your Majesty. My father was opposed to you on that account, and at his death he ordered my younger brother never to be reconciled to you, and never to look upon your face. Now I pray thee to summon him to Delhi and order him to exhibit miracles as I have done."

This situation provided the Emperor with a good opportunity to realize his own religious mission. Aurangzeb wanted to convert all Hindus to Islam but he apprehended failure in Punjab because the people greatly revered the Guru there. If the Emperor could get Ram Rai the Guruship, and through him he would perhaps be able to spread Islamic faith in Punjab, or even if he were

---
1:*This Gurdas is different from Bhai Gurdas.*

successful to set both brothers at variance, they would die by mutual slaughter, his purpose should be served.

Aurangzeb having contrived this wicked plan, called Raja Jai Singh of Amber (Jaipur) and ordered him to summon Guru Har Kishen and said," I wish to see him, be careful that he (Guru) be treated with all respect on his journey." Ram Rai was delighted to hear the Emperor's decision to summon his brother.

Many writers have shown their disbelief over the fact that Guru Har Kishen being a child, possessed high attainments and he taught with all the confidence to those who asked him about truth. **Intelligentsia cannot understand the sanctity of Guruship as they attribute every happening to age, intelligence and experience of a person. It should be noted here that Guru Har Kishen because of his divine prerogatives, had the spiritual powers at the age of five. His spiritual attainments came with his status of Guruship.** As has been explained before, in Sikh Holy Scripture Guru means Jot or Divine Light, once the Guruship is installed, then a person's age, intelligence or experience has no value. It is then the Divine Light that works in that person. The power of Divine Light is beyond the reach of human intelligence. The intelligentsia cannot perceive or apprehend the power of Divine Light through the media of their technical knowledge. Our so-called technical knowledge or the intelligence, in reality is 'I-am-ness' or the veil of ego. God is everywhere and within us too, but this veil of ego separates us from Him and it hides the truth from us. According to Gurmat, human being as bride and God as bridegroom, live together but the veil of ego separates them. When by the grace of the perfect Guru, this veil of ego is broken, the bride meets the Beloved, God:

"Bride and the Bridegroom live together, but the screen of
ego hangs in between;
When the perfect Guru breaks the veil of ego, O Nanak,
we meet our Beloved, God."
(Malar Mohalla 4, p-1263)

It is only the Guru's grace that opens up our inner eyes with which we can perceive the **Incomprehensible and enter the stage of Eternal Bliss.**

"Bisman bism bhaey bismad, Jin bujhaya tis aya swad."
(Gauri Sukhmani Mohalla 5, 16-8, p-285)

'Man wondereth at the wonders upon wonders of Creation
But it is only he who knoweth God, who obtaineth bliss.'
(Translation of the above)

To reach that stage, a person first must seek Guru's grace. In order to do that, one must abandon the sense of egoism and the pride of technical knowledge; and then submit and surrender unconditionally before the Guru and beg for his grace. The answer to the question as to how the Guru at the age of five could possess attainments of such a high magnitude lies not in the reasoning of egoistic mind but in the spiritual vision. The answer to the spiritual power of the young Guru lies in the understanding that the Guru though human in body, is Divine in Spirit. Egoistic minds of the so called scholars prohibit them from understanding the Divinity of the Guru. As long as human mind remains under the intoxication of egoism, the cycle of arguments of intelligence will continue and a person can never perceive the power of Divine Light, cannot comprehend God and can have no knowledge of Him. The egoistic mind will then continue to wonder how a five years old Guru could perform those supernatural acts.

Raja Jai Singh had previously heard the Guru's praises and was, therefore, pleased at the prospect of making his acquaintance and of listening to his instruction. He sent his emissary to Kiratpur to request the Guru to come to Delhi. The Guru refused the invitation, for he had been forbidden by his father not to see the Emperor. Raja Jai Singh sent back this communication,"Raja Jai Singh humbly requests the Guru to come to Delhi so that he and the Guru's Sikhs may behold him. The Guru may act as he pleases regarding an interview with the Emperor." It was made clear by the emissary of Jai Singh that he (Guru) would not be compelled to go to the Emperor.

The Guru set out from Kiratpur. On his way he waited for some Sikhs who had come to Kiratpur after his departure. Among them were the maimed and the leprous, all of whom he cured by the imposition of his hands. At Panjokhra, a village near Ambala, came a proud learned Brahman, who without even saluting the Guru, sat down in his presence. He then said," Thou who callest thyself Sri Har Kishen, must be greater than Lord Krishna. Translate the Gita for me." At that time, there stood nearby a dumb and illiterate man, Chhaju who hailed from the same village as the Brahman. Chhaju was serving water in the kitchen of the Guru where he had encamped. The Guru asked the Brahman whether he should translate Gita himself or he should get it done from Chhaju. The Brahman thought, Chhaju who could not even talk, how could he translate it? So he replied after a little pause, that Chhaju should do it. The Guru was always carrying a stick with him. He called Chhaju, put his stick on his head and asked him to answer the Brahman's questions. To the utter amazement of the Brahman, Chhaju explained in detail each and every verse that the Brahman asked. Upon this the Brahman fell on the lotus feet of the Guru and apologized for his indiscreet behavior.

When the Guru reached Delhi, he was received by Raja Jai Singh who came bare footed to meet the Guru. He requested the Guru to stay at his palace. That palace is now known as Gurdwara Bangla Sahib in New Delhi. Thousands of people of Delhi came to have 'darshan' (holy sight) of the Guru. The sick were healed and those in distress were comforted at the very sight of the holy Master.

The Emperor sent presents at the arrival of the Guru and expressed a wish to see him but the invitation was refused. The Guru said," My elder brother, Ram Rai, is with the Emperor and he will transact all political affairs with His Majesty, and I better not meddle with him. My mission is to preach the true Name. Ram Rai bears enmity with me on account of Guruship, and if the Emperor shows any favor towards me , Ram Rai will become more hostile and grave dissensions in the family may better be avoided. For this and other reasons my father forbade me to meet the Emperor."

The next day the Emperor's son, prince Muazzam paid a visit and conveyed his father's desire to see the Guru. The Guru emphasized that he had already given the reason not to see the Emperor. If the Emperor desired any religious instructions, he would give it to the prince. If the Emperor understood the religious instructions and acted upon them, the blessing of Guru Nanak would light on him and he would be happy. The prince asked for the instructions and the Guru dictated the following Sabad of Guru Nanak:

"If the True God dwell not in the heart,
What is eating, what is clothing,
What fruit, what clarified butter and sweet molasses, what
                                        fine flour and what meat?
What dresses, What a pleasant couch for billing and cooing,
What an army, what mace-bearers and servants, and what
                                        palaces to dwell in?
Nanak, except the true Name all things are perishable."
                                    (Var Majh ki Mohalla 1, p-142)

On the instruction of Emperor Aurangzeb, Raja Jai Singh agreed to test the Guru whether he possessed any superhuman power. His head queen dressed like a maid servant and sat among other maid servants and queens. The Guru was requested to identify the head queen (Rani) which he immediately did. Upon this Raja Jai Singh and his queens acknowledged the Guru's spiritual power.

Cholera and small-pox were raging fiercely in Delhi at that time. The Guru ordered to spare all the offerings to reduce the suffering of the poor. The food, medicine and clothes were distributed among the poor and the sick. He won many followers in this way.

Shortly after the above occurrence, the Guru was seized with high fever which was followed by small-pox[2]. His mother sat by him and pleaded," My son, why art thou intent on thy death? Thou hast only lately been seated on the Guru's throne, thou art still a child, and it is too soon for thee to depart." The Guru replied," Be not anxious. My safety is in His Will. He is the Reaper of His crop; it is His pleasure, and sometimes He reaps it while it is still green, half-green and sometimes when it is ripe. The Creator will do what is best."

2:It is said that small-pox was so rampant in Delhi that the Guru out of human compassion took the small-pox to himself and absolved the inhabitants of Delhi of it. Raja Jai Singh got a tank excavated. The Guru dipped his feet in the water of the tank and after that whosoever took bath with that water, was cured from small-pox.

The Guru was ill for several days. He knew his end had arrived and called for five paise and a coco-nut. He waved his hand three times in the air in token of circumambulating his successor and said," Baba Bakale," which meant that his successor would be found at village of Bakala. He then breathed his last on 30th of March, 1664. His body was cremated on the bank of river Jamna where now stands the Gurdwara Bala Sahib.

GURU TEGH BAHADUR
(1621-1675, Guruship 1664-1675)

'Baba Bakale', was the only clue given by Guru Har Kishen for his successor. As this word reached the village Bakala, twenty-two Sodhis[1] including Baba Dhir Mal, the grandson of Guru Har Gobind, set up their shops and claimed themselves as the ninth Guru. The Sikhs were in great confusion as they could not know who the real Guru was. Makhan Shah Labana of Jehlem district was a trade merchant. When his vessel full of merchandise was sinking, he had invoked Guru Nanak and had vowed to offer five hundred gold mohars (coins) if the vessel reached the shore safely (some say that he vowed 101 gold mohars). Makhan Shah came to the village of Bakala to pay his offering to the Guru. He was surprised to find that twenty-two Sodhis had installed themselves as Gurus. In that state of confusion and uncertainty, he resolved to try the pretenders. He thought to put two mohars before each impostor and the real Guru being the searcher of hearts, would ask for the balance of his promised offering. He visited all the 22 impostors and made each of them offering of two gold mohars, but none of them asked for the balance.

He then inquired if there was any one else in Bakala. Some-one informed him about Guru Tegh Bahadur. Makhan Shah went and as usual made his offering of two gold mohars. Upon this Guru Tegh Bahadur asked," How now, O Sikh, thou art trying to wheedle the Guru by presenting him with only two gold mohars? Where are the balance of five hundred gold mohars you had promised when your ship was sinking?" Mukhan Shah was delighted and pros-trated himself before the Guru. He then went to the roof of the house and screamed," Guru Ladho! Guru Ladho!" 'I have found the Guru! I have found the Guru!'

Guru Tegh Bahadur was the fifth and the youngest son of Guru Har Gobind and was born on first of April, 1621 to Mata Nanaki at Amritsar, Guru ke Mahal. He was married to Mata Gujri, daughter of Lal Chand of Kartarpur in Jullundhur district. After

---

1:*Guru belonged to Sodhi clan.*

Guru Har Gobind, he with his mother, Mata Nanaki and his wife went to live in Bakala.

Makhan Shah's discovery of the genuine Guru put an end to the pretensions of the false Gurus. Dhir Mal could not reconcile with the situation and was determined to snatch the Guruship by force. One day he communicated his feelings to his masand, Sihan who promised to put an end to his enemy (Guru). Accordingly the masand, along with a score of people, set forth to kill the Guru. He fired and the bullet struck Guru's shoulder without serious wound who remained calm and full of composure. The other men plundered the property of the Guru and went away. When Makhan Shah heard of this incident, he proceeded with a body of Sikhs to Dhir Mal's residence. Dhir Mal closed his doors but they burst it open and seized him and his accomplices, tied his masand's hands at his back and brought them before the Guru. They brought back all the property of the Guru and they also took Dhir Mal's property. They brought back the original copy of the Adi Granth which was in the possession of Dhir Mal and placed it before the Guru. The masand Sihan fell at the feet of the Guru and asked for forgiveness for his sins. The Guru pardoned the masand and ordered Makhan Shah to return all the property of Dhir Mal including the Adi Granth. He preached Makhan Shah and his other Sikhs that the holy Guru Nanak gave them the wealth of Nam which was sufficient for all their wants.

GURU VISITS AMRITSAR:

When Guru Har Gobind shifted his headquarters to Kiratpur, most of his disciples had also moved to that place with him and the Golden Temple at Amritsar fell ultimately into the hands of the impostors like Harji Minas. In November 1664, Guru Tegh Bahadur went to Amritsar. He bathed in the sacred tank but the Pujaris (or the ministrants) closed the doors of the Har Mandar against him. He saluted it and remarked that it was they who were rotten within, who through greed of offerings, had entered the temple. When the news spread, the people of Amritsar went in a body and poured their souls at his feet. The women of the city took the lead, welcome him with the Guru's hymns and went with him singing all the way to the village Wadala (or Walla) where he stayed in the humble abode of a devout disciple. The Master blessed the women of Amritsar and Amritsar itself. On seeing their devotion he blessed them with these words,"God's love and devotion shall ever abide among you."

FOUNDATION OF CITY OF ANANDPUR:

Leaving Amritsar the Guru passed through the Majha and Malwa regions before reaching Kiratpur sometimes in May, 1665. He attended the last rites of Raja Dip Singh of Bilaspur and expressed his desire to build a new settlement near Kiratpur and also showed his inclination to buy a suitable land for that purpose. The Rani of Bilaspur offered to donate the site of Makhowal. The offer was accepted, a token price of about five hundred rupees was paid. The foundation stone of new settlement, Chak Nanaki was laid in June, 1665, after the revered name of Guru's mother. In the course of time, a beautiful town called Anandpur grew up around it.

GURU ON MISSIONARY TOUR:

After founding the new settlement, the Guru did not stay there long. However he entrusted the construction work to his trustworthy followers. It is said that the Guru undertook his missionary tour of the east in response to the invitation of his Sikhs from that area, Bhai Bulaki Das and Bhai Hulas Chand from Dacca and Bhai Darbara and Bhai Chain Sukh from Patna. These Sikhs had met the Guru at Kiratpur and begged him to visit their land in the east with his family. The Guru left Anandpur in August, 1665.

After leaving Anandpur he passed through Ghanauli, Rupar, Dadoomajra and Lung village and then reached Mulowal in Patiala state. The people of Mulowal complained to him that they did not have drinking water nearby and for that purpose they had to travel a long distance. There was a well nearby but its water was brackish and unwholesome. The Guru told them to first repeat God's Name, then draw water, and they would find it pure and sweet. From that day the well yielded sweet water and it is known Guru's well.

The Guru then proceeded to Pharwali, Handiaya, Bhandehar, Khiwa and Bhikki. He gave religious instructions wherever he stopped and instructed the people not to worship idols and tombs, but worship only One God, the Formless. He passed through the villages of Dhaleo, Alisheir, Khiala and reached Maur where he was awaited by a great concourse of people to whom he preached true Name. He induced the people to sink a well over there. He then went to Maisarkhana and thence to Sabo ki Talwandi, now known as Damdama Sahib and then travelled to Kot Dharmwala, Bachhoana, Gobindpura, Sangheri, Gurna and reached Dhamdhan in the Bangar tract. The Guru presented the Chaudhri of the village with funds to construct a well and a dharmsala for the reception of the travellers.

The Guru was accompanied by a Sikh, Ramdev, who was totally devoted to his service. He drew water, brought firewood from the forest for the kitchen, and performed all the services for the Guru. He always kept a cushion on his head to lift the burdens and it was continually wet from water and as a consequence his head festered. One day as he put his pitcher of water down, his cushion and turban fell off when maggots were seen from a sore in his head. It was brought to the notice of the Guru who sent for him. Being pleased with his devotion to service, the Guru gave him a robe of honor, named him Bhai Mihan and promised him that he would be a Mahant or a superior of religious order. On the Guru's instruction he preached Sikh religion. His generation is called today Mihan Shahi or Mihan Dasiay.

The Guru then proceeded to Tekpur and he stayed for a few days in the house of a carpenter who conducted him as far as Kaithal. Thence he reached Barna. He preached here against the use of tobacco.

GURU AT KURUKSHETRA:

The Guru reached Kurukshetra on the occasion of solar eclipse. He was received with great honor and distinction by all the holy men present there. During his stay he preached the true Name. From there he went to Bani Badarpur where he contributed money for the excavation of a well. Then he crossed the Jamna river and hunted on the way. He shot an animal and hung it to his saddle and reached Kara Manak where a saint called Maluk Das was living. Having heard that the Guru hunted and killed the animals, he refused to see him. It is said that when Maluk Das laid down food before his idol of worship next day, he found it turned into meat. He felt that it was a miracle wrought by the Guru. Then he wanted to see the Guru and bow before him, but he thought that the Guru being the searcher of hearts, should sent for him. The Guru knew what was going on in Maluk Das's mind, sent his Sikhs and a palki (litter) to fetch him. He went to the Guru, received religious instruction and initiation, and became one of the Guru's most devoted followers.

GURU IN UTTER PRADESH:

From Kara Manak the Guru proceeded to Mathura and thence reached Agra. There is a Gurdwara to symbolize Guru's visit. Through Itawa he reached Kanpur where there is a Gurdwara at the bank of the Ganges. Then he reached Priyag (Allahabad). The Guru's mother told him that her late husband Guru Har Gobind, had promised that a great being would be born in the house of Guru Tegh Bahadur and so she was awaiting for that event. He replied that her desire would soon be fulfilled but she had to meditate continually on Guru Nanak. The Guru stayed about six months at Priyag and to the great joy of his mother, his wife got pregnant. From Priyag he proceeded to Mirzapur where there is a Gurdwara on the bank of the Ganges. Thence he reached Banaras (Kashi) and stayed in Resham Katra where a Gurdwara marks the memory of the Guru. Hundreds of people came to behold him.

GURU IN BIHAR PROVINCE:

Then he reached the village of Sasram where lived a very devout disciple called Chacha Phagoo who had built a mansion and within it placed a superb couch for the Guru. Every morning he used to perfume it and then would close the doors declaring that he would not live in it until the Guru had come, entered and hallowed it with his footsteps. Chacha Phagoo's desire was fulfilled and he had the happiness to entertain the Guru in that mansion.

Thence he proceeded to Gaya. There the Brahmans met him in a body and explained the virtues of pilgrimage of Gaya. They said if barley rolls were offered to Brahmans at Gaya for the souls of ancestors, they would go to heaven even if they were already in hell. So they pressed the Guru to give money to perform such a ceremony for him. He refused to accept their argument rather exhorted them to meditate on God and instructed them on divine knowledge.

The Guru then reached Patna and encamped at first in a garden outside the city. That place is called Guru ka Bag. Bhai Jaita, a devout disciple, took the Guru to his residence. The Guru gave religious instructions to the people. One day he told his mother, Mata Nanaki that many Sikhs were waiting for him in a distant land, so he must go to them. He wanted the family to remain at Patna. On their remonstrance the Guru told his wife," The prophecy of my father is now about to be accomplished. A son shall be born to thee, who shall be great and powerful, extend the faith, establish Sikh supremacy, root out the wicked, and destroy the enemies of truth and true religion. You would suffer great hardship in travelling, so be happy here."

The Guru offered words of consolation to his mother and wife, thus, entrusting them to his brother-in-law Kirpal Chand, bade farewell and proceeded to Munger, Bhagalpur and Rajmahal.

GURU TO BENGAL:

The Guru then reached Maldah where he stayed with a Sikh who was a confectioner. Thence he went to Murshidabad and next halt was at Dacca. There lived a devout masand, Bulaki Das whose mother had prepared a beautiful couch for the Guru. Knowing about her devotion, the Guru went to her residence. She was overjoyed and fell on his feet. He blessed her for her devotion. The Sikh inhabitants came in crowds to behold the Guru and to receive his instructions and benedictions. He asked them to build a dharamsal (Gurdwara) in their city where God's praises should be sung.

Raja Ram Singh went to the Guru and said," The inhabitants of Kamrup and Assam became rebels against the rule of Delhi. The Emperor had recently sent Mir Jumla to subdue them but after some success, he died before reaching Dacca on his return journey. The Emperor has now ordered me to go and subdue the Kamrup country. If I conquer that country, it will be an addition to the Emperor's sovereignty; but if I am killed, the Emperor may annex my whole state of Rajputana. O true King, I have come to seek protection of thy holy feet."

The Guru replied," God's Name is the medicine for all diseases, so meditate continually on Name. Guru Nanak will assist you and you will conquer Kamrup."

Raja Ram Singh and the Guru left Dacca and reached Dhubri. The Guru encamped at Dhubri and Raja Ram Singh set out for the city of Rangmati on the right bank of the Brahamputra. Soon after the battle between Raja Ram Singh's army and the army of the king of Kamrup ensued. The decisive victory for the Raja's forces was not easy because of difficult mountainous terrain, climate and rainy season.

In addition to the attack, the king of Kamrup also began to make incantations and spells, and sent for all the women of his land who had magical skills, but none succeeded. After that he went to worship at the temple of goddess Kamakhsha. His mother-in-law saw in a vision, the goddess, who said," Guru Nanak has taken birth in this age. On his throne is now seated Guru Tegh Bahadur. Raja Ram Singh has become his disciple. The Guru is sovereign and nobody has the strength to oppose him. Go and make obeisance to him and ask for pardon otherwise your rule will perish."

The king proceeded to the camp of the Guru and after prostration he said that he had come by the order of the goddess to pray for pardon and protection. He begged the Guru not to allow him to fall under the power of the Muslims. The Guru replied that Raja Ram Singh was a very religious person and he should meet with him. He, however, told the king not to fear, his empire would be permanent.

The Guru sent for Raja Ram Singh and both of them were received by the king in a friendly manner. The Guru sat down placing the royal disputants on either side and effected a reconciliation. He putting his dagger in the ground declared," Let the territory on this side belong to the Emperor and the land on the other side belong to the king of Kamrup. Let both monarchs forget the enmity." Both sides agreed to the settlement and by the grace of the Guru serious bloodshed on both sides was avoided.

The Guru informed Raja Ram Singh that Guru Nanak had visited Dhubri and rendered it holy by his footsteps. He further asked that each soldier should bring five shieldfuls of earth to raise a tall mound in the memory of the founder of Sikh religion. A pavilion was erected at the top of the mound. The Guru spent a few more days there. Hearing his fame, the crowds came from far and near to behold him and also to receive religious instructions. Raja Ram of Assam, having heard Guru's praise, came to pay his homage. The Raja had no offspring and was desirous of a son. He brought his Ranis (queens) with him and after prostration beseeched the Guru," O true king, bring this sinking vessel to the shore." The Guru took off his signet ring and stamped its impression on the Raja's thigh and then said," The impression of my seal shall be on thy son's forehead. By this know it is Guru Nanak who hath mercifully granted thee offspring."

While in Assam the Guru also visited Cooch Behar, chander Bhanga, Kishen Ganj and Purnea.

BIRTH OF A SON:

While the Guru was at Dacca, a messenger arrived from Patna to inform him of the birth of his son. He was born on the seventh day of the light half of the month of Poh, Sambat 1723 (December 26, 1666) at Patna. Before his departure the Guru had directed his wife to name the child as Gobind Rai, who would be born in his absence. He wrote a letter of thanks to the Sikh Sangat of Patna for looking after his family.

There lived in the city of Kuhram a Muslim saint, Bhikan Shah. On the morning of Gobind Rai's birth, Bhikan Shah looked and bowed towards the east (towards Patna). His disciples asked why he bowed towards the east which was contrary to Muslim custom. He replied that there had just been born a spiritual and temporal king in the east who should establish true religion and destroy evil. Bhikan Shah set out for Patna along with his disciples to behold the young prince. When he reached Patna, the Muslim saint asked to have darshan (sight) of the newly-born child. When the infant was brought, Bhikan Shah bowed at the young prince's feet. He placed before him two earthen vessels covered with muslin, one containing milk and the other with water. The child touched both the vessels. Upon this Bhikan Shah thanked them for the opportunity given to him to behold the child and then prepared to leave. He was asked what he meant by the two vessels. Bhikan Shah explained that one vessel was marked for the Hindus and the other for the Muslims. He wanted to know whether he would favor the Hindus or the Muslims. As the child touched both the vessels, it meant that he should abide by both the Hindus and the Muslims and he should include both of them in his religion.

The Guru then left Assam early in 1670 and reached Patna via Bangaigaon, Siliguri and Kathiar. From there after giving instructions to his brother-in-law, Kirpal Chand left for Punjab. He travelled through Jaunpur, Ayudhya, Lucknow, Shah Jahanpur, Muradabad and reached Chack Nanaki (Anandpur). The Guru soon sent for his family who joined him later on at Anandpur.

AURANGZEB'S CAMPAIGN OF RELIGIOUS PERSECUTION:

As Aurangzeb ascended the throne of India by imprisoning his father and murdering his brothers, he decided to enlist the sympathies of the fanatical section of his co-religionists. His idea was to exterminate the idolatrous Hindus and to convert the whole of India to Islam. In order to achieve this objective he tried to go through four fundamental means to deal with the Hindus. Firstly he made peaceful overtures; secondly he offered money; thirdly he threatened punishment and lastly he tried to cause dissention among them. When all these measures failed, he resorted to forcible conversion. Orders were issued to the governors of all the provinces that they should destroy the schools and temples of the infidels and thereby put an end to educational activities as well as the practices of the religion of the Kafirs (non-Muslims meant Hindus). Many temples at Mathura and Banaras were destroyed. Even a Sikh temple in Buriya in Khizrabad pargna of Sirhind had been demolished and a mosque was built on the site. Some Sikhs, however, attacked the mosque and killed the priest. This type of incidents had become common occurrences. In order to force conversion to Islam, all possible means were adopted. In the field of taxation, the policy of discrimination was launched with great vigor. Jaziya and pilgrimage taxes were re-levied. Five percent custom duty was levied on the Hindus while the Muslims were charged only half of that.

The proselytizing zeal of the officials, with their campaign of religious persecution and their conversion at the point of the sword, had sent the wave of terror throughout the country. Sher Afghan Khan, the Emperor's viceroy in Kashmir, set about converting the Kashmiri Hindus by force and massacred those who opposed to embrace Islam. Even the Mohammadans who in any way assisted the Hindus, were mercilessly put to death. In extreme agony of too much slaughter, the Brahman priests of Kashmir prayed to their gods. It is said that the Kashmiri Brahmans heard a supernatural voice who told them," Guru Nanak is the spiritual king in this age. Guru Tegh Bahadur is now seated on his throne. Go to him, he will protect your honor and your religion."

KASHMIRI BRAHMANS COME TO GURU:

A deputation of Kashmiri Pandits (Brahmans) came to Anandpur and among tears of agony, they narrated their tales of woe and suffering to the Master. The Guru's eight years old son appeared on the scene and asked his father why those people had tears in their eyes. The Guru replied," The Emperor of India is converting the Hindus to Islam at the point of the sword and thus there is no end to the misery of these people."

"What is the remedy, father?" asked the son.

The Guru replied," This requires sacrifice- sacrifice of a holy and supreme soul." His son responded," O dear father, who is more holy than you in this age? Go and offer yourself and save these people and their religion." On hearing this the Guru asked the Kashmiri Brahmans to go to the Emperor and make the following representation to him," Guru Tegh Bahadur, the ninth Sikh Guru is now seated on the throne of the great Guru Nanak, who is the protector of faith and religion. First make the Guru a Musalman and then all the people, including ourselves, will of our own accord adopt the faith of Islam."

GURU SUMMONED TO DELHI:

The Pandits obeyed the Guru and conveyed the proposal to the Emperor. On hearing this proposal, the Emperor was very much pleased because he thought that it was much easier to convert one person than the whole lot. He retorted," If the Guru does not become Musalman, he will then at least show us a miracle." He was hopeful that once the Guru was converted, there would be a large accession of Hindu and Sikh converts. The Emperor, therefore, sent his emissary to the Guru to invite him to Delhi. The Guru received Emperor's message and wrote in reply that he would come to Delhi after the rainy season.

MARTYRDOM OF GURU TEGH BAHADUR:

The Guru took leave of his family and his devoted Sikhs and began his journey to Delhi sometimes in June-July. From Anandpur he passed through Kiratpur, Rupar and various villages before reaching Saifabad in Patiala state to see his Muslim friend Saif-ul-din. He stayed for sometimes with him. Saif-ul-din became Guru's disciple. Thence he went to Samana where he met another disciple called Mohammad Bakhsh. The Guru continued his journey through Kaithal, Lakhan Majra, Rohtak and other places, conferring temporal and spiritual favors on his disciples, and finally he reached Agra where he encamped in a garden outside the city.

After the rainy season, the Emperor again sent his messenger to hasten the Guru's presence to Delhi. When the messengers were unable to find the Guru, they reported that the Guru had fled[2]. Orders were issued all over the empire to find and arrest him. There are different views about the place of Guru's arrest. Some writers say that he was arrested at Dhamdhan; some say that he was arrested at Malikpur near Rupar and others say that the arrest was effected at Delhi while others still account for his arrest at Agra. According to Sikh accounts there lived a poor old man, Hasan Ali, at Agra. He knew that there were orders about Guru's arrest and the person who could effect his arrest, would receive one thousand rupees as a reward. Hasan Ali prayed," O true Guru, if

---

2: *It is said that Aurangzeb was at Hasan Abdal at that time but he was being continually reported about the Guru's activities.*

ever you want to get arrested, please do it through me. This will fetch me some money to bring my family out of the clutches of miserable poverty." The Guru being the searcher of hearts, came to Agra to get arrested through Hasan Ali.

The Guru saw a shepherd boy in the garden whom he gave his gold ring studded with diamonds and asked him to pledge it and bring him two rupees worth of sweets. When the boy told him that he had no cloth to wrap the sweets, the Guru gave him his valuable shawl for that purpose. The boy took his grandfather, Hasan Ali along with him and stopped at the confectioner's shop, gave him the ring and asked for sweets to be wrapped in the shawl. On seeing the ring and the valuable shawl, the confectioner was astonished and asked the boy from whom he had received those articles. The boy told him the truth but the confectioner became suspicious and took them to the police. The police went to the garden with the boy and asked the Guru who he was. When the Guru disclosed his identity, the police officer was delighted that he would get a large reward from the Emperor for his capture. The Guru was thus imprisoned. The Governor of the fort reported the arrest to the Emperor. Ultimately he was brought to Delhi. There were three Sikhs, Bhai Mati Das, Bhai Dayala and Bhai Sati Das with the Guru (Some writers account for five Sikhs- Mati Das, Gurditta, Uda, Chima and Dayala) who were arrested with him and were brought to Delhi.[3]

The Emperor explained that God appeared to him in a vision and told him to convert the whole world to Islam. Those who were to embrace Islam, would be rewarded with wealth, appointments, land revenue grants and lands. The Emperor tried to lure him," In this way you will have many disciples, and you will become a great priest of Islam. Therefore accept my religion- Islam, and you will receive from me whatever your heart desire." The Guru asked for one and one-quarter of maan (about 100 pounds) of black pepper. When it was brought, it was put into a heap and was ignited. The heap of pepper was let burning for twenty-four hours and was apparently reduced to ashes. The heap was then pounded

---

3:Some writers say that Emperor Aurangzeb was not at Delhi at that time as he had gone on an expedition to Hasan Abdal, but Guru's execution was carried on as per orders of him. Others say that all conversation took place directly between the Guru and Aurangzeb because this opportunity was unique and of utmost importance to achieve his goal of ultimate mass conversion to Islam.

and sifted. Three pepper pods came out as whole. The Guru addressed," O Emperor, you desire that there should be only one religion (Islam) out of two religions (Hinduism and Islam), but as these three pepper pods have been saved from the fire, God wishes to make three religions out of two. So there shall be three religions-Hinduism, Islam, and Sikhism in the future."

Upon this it was ordered that the Guru be imprisoned with sufficient guards around him. Again the Guru was sent for and was told that if he embraced Islam, every service would be performed for him otherwise he would be severely tortured. He replied that he would never embrace Islam and thus, remained in Delhi jail for eight days. He was given three choices: firstly to embrace Islam; secondly to perform a miracle; and thirdly to prepare himself to court death. The Guru responded that to show a miracle was against the Will of God and thus he would not consent to the Emperor's proposals and the Emperor might act as he pleased. The Guru was then put to extreme tortures.

It is said that there was conversation between the Guru and his disciple Bhai Mati Das. He told Mati Das that Guru Nanak had blessed Emperor Babar with the continuation of his empire for a long time. Since the Mughal Emperors started committing great enormities, their line would be exterminated if he (Guru) laid down his life. In consequence of this conversation which was overheard by a priest, Bhai Mati Das was bound between two pillars and his body was sawn asunder. When the executioners put saw on his head, he began to recite Japji (the first Bani in Guru Granth Sahib). It is said that when his body was cut into two, he continued reciting Japji and he was silent only when the recitation of Japji was complete. **This was a wonder of Guru's Grace.** Bhai Dayala was boiled to death in a cauldron of hot water. It is said that the third companion Bhai Sati Das was roasted alive with cotton wrapped round his body. The authorities thought that these tortures of his Sikhs might shake the Guru. Nothing could and nothing can shake the Divine Light (the Guru).

It is generally believed in Sikh circles that there was some communication between the Guru and his son when the Guru was being detained in Delhi jail before his execution. The story runs that Guru Tegh Bahadur foreseeing his execution, wanted to test the capability of his nine years old son and so he wrote the following couplet (Slok) and sent it through a messenger to Anandpur:

"All power shattered, humanity in fetters and availeth no
resource;
Saith Nanak, God is now only refuge; He should succor as He
did the elephant."
(Slok Mohalla 9 (53), p-1429)

It is being assumed that the Guru's nine years old son wrote back:

"With power, fetters break, availeth all in grace Divine;
Nanak, everything is in Thy power, it is only Thou Who canst
assist."
(Slok Mohalla 9 (54), p-1429)

It is the common opinion that upon receiving this reply, the Guru was convinced that his son was capable to take reigns of the Guruship.

Let us examine the merits of the above story which is prevalent in Sikh circles:

Firstly there are 57 Sloks (couplets) at pages 1426-29 of Guru Granth Sahib which begin under the heading 'Slok Mohalla 9'. This heading means that all the Sloks under this heading were uttered by the Ninth Guru.

Secondly how far it is valid to say that the Guru wanted to test the capability of his son? Being a Divine Guru and sitting on the throne of Guru Nanak, did he not know himself whether the son was capable? Did he have to ask him?

Thirdly if it is argued that the Guru was worried about the young age of his son to take command of Guruship, what about the eighth Guru? The eighth Guru was only five years old when he was installed on the throne of Guru Nanak. How much this argument of being too young holds good?

Fourthly as explained earlier also, in the case of Guruship, the age, experience and intelligence of a person did not matter. Once the person was invested with the Guruship, then the Divine Power worked itself, and the age, experience and intell igence of a person in question was of no consequence.

In the light of the above circumstances, it seems evident that all the 57 Sloks belong to the Ninth Guru and none to the Tenth Guru.

The final message was given to the Guru," You are to accept the religion of Islam or show a miracle. If you work a miracle, you may remain a Guru. If you accept Islam, then you will be advanced to an exalted position. If you fail to accept these offers, you shall be put to death. This is the final decision."

The Guru emphasized," I will never abandon my faith. I want no honor in this life; I want honor hereafter. The threat of death possesses no terrors for me. For death I am prepared and I cheerfully accept it."

Hearing this reply it was ordered that the Guru should be executed. Saiyid Adam Shah accompanied by courtiers and Muslim priests came with a warrant for the Guru's execution. Many people turned out to witness the execution. He was then taken out of his cage and allowed to perform his ablutions. He sat under the banyan-tree where he recited Japji. The executioner, Jalal-ud-din of Samana (some say it was Adam Shah) took his sword and in a split of second, severed Guru's head from the body. This happened on the afternoon of Thursday, the fifth day of the light half of the month of Maghar in Sambat 1732 (November 11, 1675) at Chandni Chowk, Delhi where now stands Gurdwara Sis Ganj in his memory. This Gurdwara was constructed by Sardar Baghel Singh Karor-Singheiye in 1790.

History has recorded that a furious storm raged immediately after this brutal deed which filled every one's eyes with dust. Bhai Jaita dashed out of the crowd and instantaneously took away the holy head of the Guru to Anandpur[4]. He reached Kiratpur on the 15th of November, 1675. From there the Guru's head was taken to Anandpur with full honor and on the 16th of November, 1675, it was cremated with full ceremonies. There is a Gurdwara called Sis Ganj at Anandpur where the hallowed head of the Guru was cremated. The tenth Guru received Bhai Jaita who belonged to backward classes, embraced him and said," Rangrettei Guru ke bettei" (Rangrettei were the sons of the Guru, Rangrettei was Bhai Jaita's caste). Bhai Jaita told the young Guru and his family how Guru Tegh Bahadur had sent for five paise and a coco-nut and bowed to his son Gobind Rai, made him the successor and infused his Light unto him.

Lakhi Shah Labana was a famous contractor in Delhi and he was also a follower of the Guru. He emptied his carts laden with lime near the Red Fort, taking advantage of the darkness and the carelessness of the Mughal sentries, and with the help of his sons, Nagahiya, Hema, Harhi and his friend Dhuma, whisked away the sacred body of the Guru, in one of their carts. Apprehensive of the government reprisal, Lakhi Shah and his sons then built up a pyre inside their own house and set fire to it. When the body was duly reduced to ashes, they cried out that their house had caught fire and called upon their neighbors to assist them in extinguishing it. Next day they collected the Guru's remains and buried them in a copper vessel called 'gaggar' in the earth under his funeral pyre. On this spot there stands a Gurdwara, Rakab Ganj, near Parliament House in New Delhi.

"Having broken his potsherd on the head of the king of Delhi,
he departed for Paradise;
No one else coming into the world acted like Tegh Bahadur.
The world was in mourning for the departure of Tegh
Bahadur;
There was weeping for him in the whole world, but rejoicing
in paradise."
(Guru Gobind Singh- Bachitar Natak)

4: It is said that the Guru had told Bhai Jaita that his head would fall into his lap, and he should fear nobody, take it to Anandpur and cremate it there. It is also said that Bhai Jaita shared this secret with his neighbor Bhai Nanu and he also took Bhai Uda, a resident of Ladwa, into confidence and three of them took Guru's head to Anandpur.

GURU GOBIND SINGH
(1666-1708, Guruship 1675-1708)

It may not be out of the way to say here that throughout the annals of human history, there was no other individual who could be of more inspiring personality than Guru Gobind Singh. At its climax the tenth Nanak infused the spirit of both the saintlihood and the undauntedness in the minds and hearts of his followers to fight oppression in order to restore justice, righteousness (Dharma) and to uplift the down-trodden people in this world. It is said that after the martyrdom of Guru Tegh Bahadur, the tenth Master declared that he would create such a Panth (nation) which would not be cowed down by tyrant rulers but it would rather challenge the oppressor in every walk of life to restore justice, equality and peace for mankind. He further resolved that he would feel worthy to be called Gobind Singh only when any single member of his Khalsa Panth would successfully and undauntedly challenge the army of one hundred and twenty-five thousand opponents in the field. This point was rightfully proven at Chamkaur Sahib when Sahibzada Ajit Singh (Guru's about 18 years old eldest son) challenged the Mughal forces and their allies, the hilly Rajas.

> "The Divine Guru hath sent me for religion's sake
> On this account, I have come into the world;
> Extend the faith everywhere
> Seize and destroy the evil and sinful.
> Understand this, ye holymen, in your minds
> I assumed birth for the purpose of spreading the faith,
>   saving the saints and extirpating all tyrants."
>   (Guru Gobind Singh- Chaupai, Bachitar Natak)

Guru Tegh Bahadur's martyrdom symbolized in itself the resistance to the tyranny of Muslim rule in favor of a new society. When evil is holding its head high, should a holy man knuckle under it or take up arms to combat and destroy it? The young Guru, Gobind Rai, decided in favor of the latter course i.e. to combat evil and uphold righteousness. He thus enjoined upon his followers to make use of the sword if all other means failed to liquidate the wicked and his wickedness. In order to achieve this mission, he issued 'Hukamnamas' (circular letters of authority) to his followers to present to him arms of different designs. The Guru's orders were obeyed with great zeal and devotion. He himself wore uniform and bore arms and induced others to practise archery and musket-shooting. He encouraged various muscle-developing and strenuous sports as part of the program of physical culture. Many followers with martial instincts whose forefathers had served the Guru's father and his grandfather, flocked to him. His principal companions at that time were his aunt Bibi Viro's (Guru Har Gobind's daughter) five sons, Sango Shah, Jit Mal, Gopal Chand, Ganga Ram, Mohri Chand; his uncle Suraj Mal's two sons- Gulab Rai and Sham Das; his maternal uncle Kirpal Chand; Bhai Daya Ram, the friend from his youth; and Bhai Nand Chand, a favorite masand.

The Guru instructed his followers to lead a well-meaning and disciplined life. He according to the customs of his predecessors, used to rise early in the morning and perform his devotions. He was particularly delighted to listen to Asa di Var. After daybreak, he gave divine instructions to his Sikhs and then practised martial exercises. In the afternoon, he received his followers, went shooting or raced horses; and ended the evening by performing the divine service of 'Rehras'.

The Guru's handsome exterior was much admired both by men and women. A person called Bhikhia from Lahore came to visit the Guru. Seeing the handsome young Guru, Bhai Bhikhia offered the alliance of his daughter Jito to him. The proposal was accepted and there were great rejoicing at Anandpur on the occasion of the betrothal ceremony. The twenty-third of Har, Sambat 1734 (1677 A.D.) was fixed for the marriage. The Guru sent orders in all directions for this occasion and the Sikhs thronged from various places including Lahore. A place was set up near Anandpur, which was called Guru ki Lahore where the marriage ceremony took place[1].

1: *One day a Sikh came and proposed to the Guru to wed his daughter, Sundri. The Guru did not desire the alliance but it was pressed on him by his mother. However it is believed that Sundri which means the beautiful, was an epithet of Jito and not a second wife of the Guru. It is also believed that Jito was the name given by her parents while Sundri was the name given to Mata Jitoji by the Guru's side. This frequently happens in the society*

VISIT OF DUNI CHAND AND RAJA RATTAN RAI:

Surging crowds of people with their hearts filled with love and devotion to the Master, thronged to see him. Some came from Kabul, Qandhar, Gazni, Balkh and Bukhara. They brought several priceless gifts- rugs, carpets, shawls and other valuables when they came to pay homage to their Lord. Duni Chand, one of the devotees, visited Anandpur in 1681 and presented to the Guru a woolen tent, 'Shamiana' or a royal canopy which surpassed in excellence. It was embroidered in gold and silver studded with pearls. It is said that its splendor surpassed that of the Emperor's canopy.

Through the grace of Guru Tegh Bahadur, Raja Ram of Assam was blessed with a son, Rattan Rai. Raja wanted to take his son to the Guru but he died soon and could not visit Anandpur. His last injunction to his Rani (wife) was that the prince should be brought up as a devout Sikh. The Rani faithfully carried out the behests of her husband and imparted the knowledge of the lives and teachings of the Gurus to the growing prince. When Rattan Rai, the prince, attained the age of twelve, he felt an inclination to see the Guru. Accordingly he with his mother and several of his ministers proceeded to Anandpur. He brought with him an offering of five horses with golden trappings, a very small elephant, and a weapon out of which five sorts of arms could be made, a pistol, a sword, a lance, a dagger, and a club.

The Raja was accorded a great reception. He offered his presents and prayed to the Guru to grant him the Sikh faith. He was granted all his desires. The Raja exhibited the traits of his presents. He caused the elephant to wipe Guru's shoes and placed them in order for him. At the word of command the animal took a chauri and waved it over the Guru. The Raja requested the Guru never to let the elephant out of his possession.

The prince and his party remained at Anandpur for five months and during this time, he enjoyed kirtan and felt uplifted by the Guru's sermons. At the time of departure, the Guru accompanied them to some distance and then bade them good-bye. They were sent off with presents. Besides these tangible gifts, the Guru gave Rattan Rai a RATTAN - a jewel of Nam, which was the

ultimate gift of life:
> "Nam is the priceless Jewel that the perfect Guru hath;
> If one dedicates oneself in love to the True Guru,
> He lights in one's heart the Light of Wisdom, and Nam is then
> revealed.
> Blessed is the fortunate one who goeth to meet the Guru."
> (Sri Rag Mohalla 4, p-40)

RANJIT NAGARA:

The Guru's army was swelling day by day and he was now set for the construction of a big beating drum which was deemed necessary to enthuse his army and without which he considered his equipment was incomplete. The work of the drum was entrusted to his Dewan, Nand Chand. In those days, only an independent chieftain was to use such a drum within the limits of his territory. The beating of the drum within the bounds of another chief's domain was an hostile act and meant an open invitation of war. The completion of the big drum which was called **Ranjit Nagara**, or victorious drum on the battle-field, was celebrated with prayers and the distribution of Parshad (sacred food). When it was beaten, the men and women of the city came to behold it and there were great rejoicing.

The Guru and his men went for hunting the same day and when they reached near Bilaspur, the capital of Kahlur, the drum was beaten and it sounded like a thunder to the hillmen who became apprehensive of some danger. Raja Bhim Chand of Kahlur consulted his prime minister who advised him that it was the Guru's drum who was worthy of worship, secondly, he maintained a large army and was greatly feared; and thirdly the Guru was brave, and such men were sometimes useful as allies. On hearing this Raja Bhim Chand desired to meet the Guru and despatched his prime minister to arrange for an interview which was granted. The Raja accordingly went with his courtiers to Anandpur.

RAJA BHIM CHAND AND THE GURU:

Raja Bhim Chand was received in Guru's darbar (court)

with great honor. He prayed to the Guru to let him see the gifts from the Raja of Assam. He was shown all the presents. Bhim Chand was astonished at the magnificence of the Kabuli tent. He was told that it was the offering of a pious Sikh from Kabul. During this conversation when the beautifully decorated elephant was let forward, Bhim Chand stood spellbound and expressed his unbounded admiration of all that he had seen. On his homeward journey his mind burned with jealousy of the Guru's state and wealth and he made up his mind to take possession of at least the elephant.

On his return to the capital, Bhim Chand disclosed his designs to his courtiers. It was decided that a message should be sent to the Guru that Raja Fateh Chand of Garhwal's party was coming with the object of betrothing his daughter to Bhim Chand's son, and Bhim Chand desired to borrow the elephant so as to make a display of his wealth to his guests. When the message was delivered to the Guru, he knew that it was only a trick to obtain permanent possession of the animal. He sent the reply to Bhim Chand," The Raja who presented the elephant, requested me not to let the animal go out of my possession. It is the principle of Guru's house to comply with such requests." It is said that the Raja sent his emissaries thrice, the last one being Kesari Chand, the Raja of Jaswal, but the Guru did not yield and therefore, Bhim Chand's demand was not met. So he got angry and wanted to take revenge.

Majority of the masands felt agitated at the Guru's warlike preparations and they represented to Guru's mother to dissuade him from such activities lest it should bring some trouble to him. When the Guru's mother talked to him about it. He replied," Dear mother, I have been sent by the Immortal God. He who worshippeth Him shall be happy; but he who acteth dishonestly and worshippeth stones shall receive well-merited retribution. This is my commission from God. If today I give Raja Bhim Chand the elephant, I shall have to pay him tribute tomorrow." Nand Chand then joined the conversation and said," Mother, hath a lion ever feared jackals? Hath any one ever seen the light of the firefly in bright sunshine? What availeth a drop of water in comparison with the ocean? The Guru is a tiger brave and splendid as the sun. Shall he fear Bhim Chand?" The Guru ended the discussion by saying,"Dear mother, heed not the evil advice of the masands.

They have become cowards by eating the offerings of the Sikhs."
    The Guru and his troops continued to practice archery and
devoted themselves to the chase. The Sikhs kept visiting continually and make offering of arms. Those who came for military
service, were readily received and were taught the profession of
arms. In this way the Guru collected a considerable army.

GURU LEAVES FOR PAUNTA SAHIB:

        In the meantime the Raja Medani Parkash of Nahan, invited
the Guru to visit him. The invitation was accepted and he left for
Nahan. Gulab Rai and Sham Das were made in charge for the
defense of Anandpur. The Raja came to greet and welcome the
Guru and then took him to his palace. One day he took the Guru
on hunting excursion and complained that Raja Fateh Shah of
Garhwal had often quarrelled with him over the ground on which
they were then standing. He suggested that he would be very
pleased if a fort were to be constructed on the spot for protection
against the enemy. The Guru erected a tent on that spot and held a
darbar. He laid down foundation stone of the fort. With the help of
the Raja's army and with the zeal and energy of the workmen, the
fort was completed within a short time. The Guru named it Paunta,
and started to live there and continued to increase his army.
        Raja Fateh Shah of Garhwal arrived at the conclusion that
since the Guru started living near his territory, it would, therefore,
be politic to be on good terms with him and accordingly he decided
to pay a visit to the Guru. He was received with great honor in the
Guru's darbar (court). During his visit the Guru sent his uncle
Kirpal to him to suggest that it would be well if he and the Raja of
Nahan were on good terms. Raja Fateh Shah gave his consent
immediately. The Guru then sent for the Raja of Nahan. He
brought the two Rajas together in the open court, caused them to
embrace and form a friendship.
        In the meantime a hillman came with tidings of a fierce tiger
which was destroying cattle in the neighborhood. He requested the
Guru to free the country from the wild animal. He took the two
Rajas and others to the place where the tiger was said to be
residing. On hearing the huntsmen's footsteps, the tiger sat on his

haunches looking at his pursuers. The Guru called on any one who could engage the tiger with sword and shield. No one came forward. He then took his sword and shield and challenged the tiger. The tiger rose with a roar and sprang at the Guru, who received him on his shield and striking him on the flank with his sword, cut him in two. The Rajas and the hunting party were astonished and delighted at the Guru's strength and bravery.

RAM RAI'S RECLAMATION:

Ram Rai, the eldest son of Guru Har Rai, when sent to Delhi on behalf of the Guru, distorted the holy words of Guru Nanak in the court of Aurangzeb in order to please the Emperor. Upon this the Guru disowned him and excommunicated him from the Sikh faith. The Emperor gave him an estate where he founded the town of Dehra Dun and continued to live there. Ram Rai claimed himself as the real Guru. Being a willing tool in the hands of the Mughal Emperor, he continually tried to harm the cause of the Sikhs. Now since Guru Gobind Singh had come to Paunta, which was only thirty miles from Dehra Dun, Ram Rai became afraid of him and could not muster courage to face him. A discussion started in Ram Rai's assembly about all this. Hearing on Ram Rai's anxiety, the Guru sent Nand Chand and Daya Ram to reassure him that no harm would be done to him. Ram Rai on receiving the Guru's message, was very much delighted. He gave robes of honor to Nand Chand and Daya Ram and decided to be on friendly terms with the Guru.

It is said that a meeting between the Guru and Ram Rai took place in a ferry in the middle of the stream. Ram Rai touched the Guru's feet in obeisance and said," I am fortunate to have obtained a sight of thee. When I am gone, protect my family........my father Guru Har Rai used to say that someone would be born from our family who would restore and refit the vessel for the safe conveyance of the souls." He asked for forgiveness. Ram Rai while he was in trance, was cremated by his masands in defiance of the entreaties and prayers of his wife, Punjab Kaur. The Guru then responded to the request of Punjab Kaur and meted out strict punishment to the guilty masands and rewarded those who had remained faithful to her.

PIR BUDHU SHAH:

Pir Budhu Shah was a Muslim saint who lived at Sadhaura, about ten or fifteen miles from Paunta Sahib. He was well known for his piety and had a large number of followers. He had heard of Guru Nanak and his mission. He had also learned that Guru Nanak's throne was then occupied by Guru Gobind Singh who was staying in the neighborhood. Ultimately he decided to visit the Guru. The Guru seated the Pir near him who beseeched," Pray! tell us how one meets God Almighty." During the discussion the Pir humbly submitted to the Master. There was a glow in the eyes of the Guru which radiated Divine Light and the Pir exclaimed with sudden joy," Allah-hu-Akbar!" - Great is God Almighty. After a while the Pir confessed," Master, I was spiritually blind and you have shown me the Light." Blessed are the souls on whom the Guru bestows the divine grace.

THE BATTLE OF BHANGANI:

One day the Guru received an invitation from Fateh Shah of Garhwal to his daughter's marriage with the son of Raja Bhim Chand of Kahlur who nursed enmity with the Guru. He decided not to attend the ceremony himself but sent his Dewan, Nand Chand and Daya Ram with costly gifts for the princess.

The shortest route for the marriage party was through Paunta Sahib; the Guru refused to give them the passage because he had no faith in Bhim Chand who was accompanied by a large number of soldiers. After a lot of negotiations, the Guru permitted the bridegroom and a small number of his companions to cross the ferry near Paunta Sahib. The rest of the party including Bhim Chand had to follow a circuitous route to Srinagar, the capital of Garhwal state. This happening made Bhim Chand very mad and he began to look forward to the opportunity to give vent to his anger. He became still more enraged when he learnt that Guru's envoy was present at the bride's place to attend the marriage. Thus he refused to accept Fateh Shah's daughter for his son, if he continued his friendship with the Guru. Bhim Chand, therefore, asked Fateh Shah to choose between himself and the Guru. Fateh

Shah was obliged to yield. Nand Chand and Daya Ram had to bring their presents back as a result. On their way back Nand Chand and party were attacked by Bhim Chand's troops but they were able to return safe and sound. After the marriage was over, Bhim Chand held a conference with Fateh Shah and other hilly Rajas- Kirpal of Katoch, Gopal of Guler, Hari Chand of Hadur and the Raja of Jaswal who were present there. They all decided to attack the Guru on their way back.

The hilly Rajas ordered their troops to march upon Paunta Sahib. The news of the impending attack came fast before the army could move and so the Guru was not taken by surprise attack.

On the recommendation of Pir Budhu Shah, 500 Pathans were enlisted in the Guru's army under the command of five chieftains-Kale Khan, Bhikan Khan, Nijabat Khan, Hyat Khan, and Umar Khan. The Pathans became apprehensive of the scanty resources at the disposal of the Guru and they all except Kale Khan with one hundred men, deserted the Guru at the eleventh hour, and joined the hill Rajas. The Udasi Sadhus except their chief Mahant Kirpal, also took to their heels. The Guru informed Budhu Shah of the misconduct of the Pathan soldiers. Pir Budhu Shah looked upon their behavior as a personal disgrace. In order to compensate this loss, Budhu Shah accordingly placed himself, his brother, his four sons and seven hundred disciples at the Guru's disposal.

The Guru stationed his troops at an eminent place near Bhangani village about six miles from Paunta Sahib. The five sons of Bibi Viro- Sango Shah, Jit Mal, Gopal Chand, Ganga Ram and Mohri Chand organized the attack for the Guru's forces. They were ably backed by Bhai Daya Ram, Dewan Nand Chand, Guru's uncle Kirpal and Mahant Kirpal. While repeating his orders the Guru buckled on his sword, slung his quiver over his shoulders, took his bow in his hand, mounted his steed, and shouting 'Sat Sri Akal' in his loudest voice, proceeded to confront his enemies. It is recorded that the hoofs of the Guru's horse in their quick movement raised clouds of dust which obscured the sun, and that the cheers of his men resembled thunder in the stormy and rainy season. As mentioned Guru's forces were also joined by Pir Budhu Shah's troops and one hundred Pathans under the command of Kale Khan.

The enemy forces were led by Raja Fateh Shah who was

joined by Raja Hari Chand of Hadur, Raja Gopal of Guler, Raja of Chandel, Rajas of Dadhwal and Jaswal, and four hundred Pathans who had deserted the Guru's side. A severe and bloody battle was raged. Many brave soldiers were killed on both sides. Although the opposite army far outnumbered the Guru's men, but they did not have the same spirit of sacrifice, nor did they have the same devotion to their leaders, as the Sikhs had.

Mahant Kirpal hit Hayat Khan, Pathan chief, and killed the deserter. Jit Mal and Raja Hari Chand engaged in a single combat. The arrows lodged in their horses' foreheads and both horses fell. After a short breath when their swords clashed, Hari Chand fell fainting to the ground and Jit Mal dropped down dead. Sango Shah, another cousin of the Guru, and Pathan chief Nijabat Khan were engaged and both fell dead. Upon this the Guru mounted his charger and rode into the thick of the combat. He discharged an arrow at Pathan leader Bhikan Khan. It missed him but killed his horse, and Bhikan Khan fled away. Upon this Nand Chand and Daya Ram launched a fierce attack on the demoralized Pathans which resulted in great slaughter of the treacherous Pathans. When the hillmen saw the defeat of the Pathans, they began fleeing from the battle field. By this time Hari Chand regained his conscious and reappeared on the scene and shot many brave men with his arrows. On seeing this the Guru confronted Hari Chand and he describes the combat in Bachitar Natak:

"Hari Chand, one of the hill chiefs, in his rage drew forth the arrows. He struck my steed with one and then discharged another at me, but God preserved me and it only grazed my ears in its flight. His third arrow penetrated the buckle of my waist and touched my body, but wounded me not. It is only God Who protected me, His servant. When I felt the touch of the arrow, my spirit was kindled. I took up my bow and taking aim killed the young chief Hari Chand with my very first shot. I discharged arrows in abundance. Upon this my adversaries began to flee. The chief of Korari was also seized by death. Upon this the hill men fled in consternation and I, through the favor of God Almighty, gained the victory........" (Translated)

The Guru went to the site where lay the dead bodies of Sangho Shah, Jit Mal and other brave Sikhs. Two sons of Budhu Shah were also killed. The Guru ordered the slain on both sides be disposed of with great honor. The bodies of the Sikhs were cremated, of the Hindus thrown into the river and of the Muslims buried with all solemnity. Pir Budhu Shah presented himself and his two surviving sons to the Guru. At that time the Guru was combing his hair. Budhu Shah begged of him to give him the comb with his loose hair as a sacred souvenir. The Guru gave him the turban, the comb with hair and a small sword. The greatest gift of all, the Guru blessed him with Nam.

Significance of the battle of Bhangani:

The victory in the battle of Bhangani was of far reaching importance. It uplifted the spirit and strengthened the moral of the Sikhs. Since the Guru did not acquire even an inch of the territory or gained any material advantage, the cause he championed, received added strength. His fame spread far and wide with the result that the supply of arms and horses to the Guru increased abundantly and hundreds and hundreds of persons offered themselves to be enlisted in his army. The Guru's victory also did not go without causing concern to the Mughal rule at Delhi. The hilly Rajas also viewed the whole issue afresh. Although the Rajas and the Guru were poles apart in ideology, yet the Rajas being goaded by their self-interest of thwarting the Mughals over lordship and thus to be relieved of the burdens of payment of annual tributes to the Mughal Emperor, wanted cordial relations with the Guru. Therefore, their leader Raja Bhim Chand entered into agreement with the Guru.

RETURN TO ANANDPUR:

The Guru remained about three years at Paunta Sahib and his fame attracted poets, singers and learned people to his court. **During this period the Guru composed Jap Sahib, Swayas and Akal Ustat.**

The Guru ordered his army to return to Anandpur and he came back via Sadhaura and then encamped at Laharpur for a few days. Raja of Nahan sent his envoy to convey his desire to meet the Guru but he never did. Leaving Nahan the Guru entered Ramgarh state and stayed at Tabra for more than a week. He then went to Raipur[2] in response to the invitation of the Rani of that place. She showed him the greatest hospitality and presented him a beautiful horse with costly trappings, and a purse of Rupees as an offering. He gave her son a sword and shield. After this the Guru continued his journey to Anandpur. After passing through Toda, Nada, Dhakoli, Kotla, Ghanaula, Bunga, he reached Kiratpur. From there he reached Anandpur in October, 1687. The eldest son, Ajit Singh was born on the fourth day of bright half of Magh, Sambat 1743 (1687 A.D.).

EXPEDITION OF ALIF KHAN:

The south India was up in the arms. Emperor Aurangzeb, therefore, remained busy many years in suppressing the revolt in southern India. All the expenditure of such a long war was met by levying heavy tribute on the northern and eastern provinces of the country. At that time Mian Khan was a viceroy of Jammu. He sent his commander-in-chief, Alif Khan to levy tribute on the hill Rajas. First he addressed Raja Kirpal of Kangra," Either pay me the tribute or contend with me in arms." Raja Kirpal gave him certain presents and then told him that Raja Bhim Chand of Kahlur was the greatest of all the Rajas. If he pays the tribute first, all the rest will follow him. If Bhim Chand refused to pay, he (Kirpal) would support him. Raja Dayal of Bijarwal was persuaded by Kirpal to meet Alif Khan's demands.

Alif Khan adopted Raja Kirpal's suggestion and proceeded towards the capital of Bhim Chand's state. He halted at Nadaun and sent his envoy to Bhim Chand with his demands. Bhim Chand replied that he would defend himself rather pay the tribute. However his prime minister advised Bhim Chand that if he desired victory, it would be assured only if he had obtained Guru's assistance. Upon this Bhim Chand sent his prime minister to the Guru to seek his active support. The Guru agreed to support the move-

---

2: *Raipur is near Ambala. In the fort of Raipur is a Gurdwara on the spot where the Guru dined as the Rani's guest. There is also a Gurdwara outside the fort on the place where his tent was pitched.*

ment of non-payment of tributes which symbolized the spirit of defiance against the Mughal imperialism. The Guru came in person as the head of a strong contingent. The Rajas of Jaswal, Dadhwal and Jasrot also came to participate in the impending war. Bhim Chand opened the attack with sharp arrows but the shots could not make any impact on the enemy because of their position and they struck only the wooden rafters of the fortress. The troops of Bhim Chand began to grow indifferent. At this critical juncture the Guru played his part most effectively. He took his gun and aimed at Raja Dayal. Fighting bravely the Raja fell to the ground. The Guru shot arrows one after the other on the enemy. Arrows and bullets flew in abundance and the battle turned in their favor. Alif Khan and his men fled and Bhim Chand won the victory. He remained at Nadaun for sometimes where he reached an understanding with Alif Khan through Kirpal who acted as intermediary.

The Guru after staying about a week there, returned to Anandpur. His son, Jujhar Singh was born on the seventh day of month of Chet, Sambat 1747 (1691 A.D.).

DILAWAR KHAN'S ATTEMPT TO WEAKEN GURU'S POWER:

Dilawar Khan who attained power in Punjab while Aurangzeb was in the Daccan (south), became jealous about Guru's fame and success. He sent his son Khanzada with a force of one thousand men to curb the power of the Guru at Anandpur. Khanzada crossed the river Satluj under the cover of the darkness at about midnight when Guru's scout, Alam Khan hastened to give information to the Guru about the approach of a hostile force. The drum (Ranjit Nigara) was immediately beaten and Guru's men at once marched to the river. The quick formation of the Sikhs bewildered the enemy and the guns which began discharging volleys of shots, terrified Khanzada's men so much that they were constrained to reel back. However they plundered the village of Barwa on their way back. Khanzada through shame, could not answer to his father when he censored him for his cowardice. This happened at the end of 1694.

HUSSAIN KHAN'S EXPEDITION:

Dilawar Khan had a slave called Hussain who boasted that if he were given a command, he would sack the Guru's city of Anandpur and exact tribute from Bhim Chand and other hilly Rajas. The failure of Khanzada provoked Dilawar Khan to plan for a bigger attack on the Guru. So he sent Hussain Khan with a force of two thousand men. Hussain brought the Raja of Dadhwal to his knees and plundered Dun. Raja Kirpal of Kangra joined him. Bhim Chand too cast his lot with Hussain. He then with the help of Kirpal and Bhim Chand, planned to proceed to Anandpur. The Guru kept his troops ready for any eminent attack.

When Hussain was preparing to march towards Anandpur, Raja Gopal of Guler sent his envoy to make peace with him. Hussain replied that he would be glad to meet with Raja Gopal if he gave him a subsidy as other Rajas had done. Gopal went with some money but Hussain was not pleased with his contribution. Hussain's terms were payment of ten thousand rupees or he would put Gopal and his troops to death. Gopal pleaded his inability to pay that large sum of money and thus came back. At this point Gopal sent his envoy to the Guru to pray to him for a negotiated settlement with Hussain. The Guru sent his agent, Sangtia with an escort of seven troopers to negotiate a peace settlement between Gopal and Hussain. Two parties could not reach any settlement with the result that a battle ensued between Hussain, Kirpal and Bhim Chand on one side and Raja Gopal and Raja Ram Singh on the other. Having fought very bravely Hussain perished in the battle field. Raja Kirpal of Kangra was also slain. Himmat and Kimmat, two officers of Hussain Khan were also killed. On the other side the Guru's envoy Sangtia and his seven troopers were all killed. On seeing this Bhim Chand fled with his army. After his victory Raja Gopal went to the Guru with large offerings and thanked him for his grace which made him successful in the battle field.

A third son, Zorawar Singh was born to the Guru on Sunday, the first day of the second half of the month of Magh, Sambat 1753 (1697 A.D.).

The defeat irked Dilawar Khan and he then sent Jujhar Singh and Chandel Rai to Jaswan but they could not achieve the purpose. They, however, captured Bhalan, a strategic place in that state. Before they could proceed further, Gaj Singh of Jaswal fell upon them. Jujhar Singh and Chandel Rai both fought like lions but Jujhar Singh was killed and Chandel Rai fled from the field.

The defeat of the imperial forces caused anxiety to Aurangzeb and he sent his son Prince Muazzam, later known as Bahadur Shah, for restoration of order in the hills. The Prince took charge in August, 1696 and deputed Mirza Beg to teach lesson to hill Rajas. He inflicted defeat after defeat, set up villages on fire, plundered the territory. After Mirza Beg, the Prince sent four more officers who, side by side, chastised the hill Rajas, plundered the homes of the apostates who had escaped destruction at the hands of Mirza Beg.

In due time a fourth son, Fateh Singh was born to the Guru on wednesday, the eleventh day of Phagan, Sambat 1755 (1699 A.D.).   In the state of seclusion and tranquility of the mountains, the Guru translated Sanskrit works in Sambat 1755 (1698 A.D.). It was on the 14th of June of that year that the Guru according to his own version, completed his translation of the Ram Avtar from Sanskrit into Hindi. Most of the compositions that are said to be of the tenth Guru, are not his. Macauliffe writes:

> "What is called the Granth of the tenth Guru (Dasam Granth) is only partially his composition. The greater portion of it was written by bards in his employ. The two works entitled Chandi Charitar and the Bhagauti ki Var found in it are abridged translations by different hands (any one even moderately acquainted with Hindi can tell from inner evidence of style that these translations have been done by different persons) of the Durga Sapt Shatti, or seven hundred sloks on the subject of Durga, an episode in the 'Markandeya Puran' on the contests of the goddess Durga with demons who had made war on the gods."

There were fifty-two[3] bards in the court of Guru Gobind Singh to translate the Mahabharat, the Ramayan, and the gallant

---

3: *Fifty-two bards were permanent in his employ but this number went as high as 94 at some point of time.*

achievements of Rama, Krishna, Chandi, and others. It does not follow from this that the Guru worshipped those whose acts were thus celebrated; this was only done for the purpose of inciting bravery and dispelling cowardice, and filling the hearts of his troops with valor to defend their faith. This the Guru himself declares in his translation of the tenth canto of the Bhagwat," I have rendered in the vulgar dialect the tenth chapter of the Bhagwat with no other object than to inspire ardour for religious warfare."

The Guru **never put faith or worshipped anyone other than the One Immortal God.** In Akal Ustat he writes:

"Without Thee (God) I worship none Whatever boon I want,
get from Thee."

The Guru makes the above point clear in his thirty-three Swayas:

"Some fasten an idol firmly to their breasts; some say that
Shiv is God;
Some say that God is in the temple of the Hindus; others
believe that He is in the mosque of the Musalmans;
Some say that Rama is God; some say Krishna; some in their
hearts accept the incarnations as God;
But I have forgotten all vain religion and know in my heart
that the Creator is the only God."
(Swaya- XII)
"Why call Shiv God, and why speak of Brahma as God?
God is not Ram Chander, Krishan, or Vishnu whom ye
suppose to be the lords of the world.
Sukhdev, Prasar, and Vyas erred in abandoning the One God
and worshipping many gods.
All have set up false religions; I in every way believe that
there is but One God."
(Swaya- XV, Guru Gobind Singh)

CREATION OF THE KHALSA:

The Guru sent Hukamnamas to his followers all over the country to visit Anandpur at the Baisakhi festival to be held in

Sambat 1756 (1699 A.D.). It seemed as if the whole of Punjab was on the move; and they came from all parts of the country.

A small tent was pitched on a small hill now called Kesgarh Sahib at Anandpur and an open air dewan (assembly) was held. **The Guru drew his sword and in a thundering voice said," I want one head, is there any one who can offer me?"** This most unusual call caused some terror in the gathering and the people were stunned. There was dead silence. The Guru made a second call. Nobody came forward. There was still more silence. On the third call there rose **Daya Ram, a khatri of Lahore who said," O true king, my head is at thy service."** The Guru took Daya Ram by the arm and led him inside the tent. A blow and thud were heard. Then the Guru, with his sword dripping with blood, came out and said," I want another head, is there anyone who can offer?"

> **NOTE:** Most of the writers including many Sikh writers, state that the Guru had concealed five goats inside the tent on the previous night without letting anybody know.
> Therefore, when he took Daya Ram inside the tent, he cut off goat's head instead of Daya Ram's. It is difficult for these writers to perceive Guru's supernatural acts. They cannot comprehend that the Guru could behead Daya Ram, and then bring him back alive from the tent. They need to under stand that the Guru was a Divine Jot, sitting on the Divine throne of Guru Nanak. They are showing complete disrespect to the Guru by implying that he was incapable of performing supernatural acts. With these types of thoughts, these writers are committing sacrilege upon the Guruship. The Guru had the power to raise the dead. The Divine Word confirms:
>
> "Satgur mera mar jiwalei."
>   (Bhairon Mohalla 5, p-1142)
>
> 'My lord can raise the dead to life.'
>   (Translation of the above)
>
> This was not an ordinary feat, this was the most unparallel and supernatural act which was performed through the

direct Will of God. The Guru himself authenticates this act:

"Khalsa is the army of God
  Khalsa is created with the Will of God."
                    (Guru Gobind Singh- Sarbloh Granth)

Again on third call Dharam Das, a Jat from Delhi came forward and said," O true king! My head is at thy disposal." The Guru took Dharam Das inside the tent, again a blow and thud were heard, and he came out with his sword dripping with blood and re-peated," I want another head, is there any beloved Sikh who can offer it?"

Upon this some people in the assembly remarked that the Guru had lost all reason and went to his mother to complain. Mohkam Chand[4], a washerman of Dwarka (west coast of India) offered himself as a sacrifice. The Guru took him inside the tent and went through the same process. When he came out, he made a call for the fourth head. The Sikhs began to think that he was going to kill all of them. Some of them ran away and the others hung their heads down. Himmat Chand, a cook of Jagan Nath Puri, offered himself as a fourth sacrifice. Then the Guru made a fifth and the last call for a fifth head. Sahib Chand, a barber of Bidar (in central India), came forward and the Guru took him inside the tent. A blow and thud were heard.

The last time he stayed longer in the tent. People began to breath with relief. The Guru clad them in splendid garments. They offered their heads to the Guru, and the Guru had now given them himself and his glory. When they were brought outside, they were in the most radiant form. There were exclamations of wonder and the sighs of regret on all sides. Now people were sorry for not offering their heads.

Since the time of Guru Nanak, Charanpauhal had been customary form of initiation. People were to drink the holy water which had been touched or washed by the Guru's toe or feet. The Guru proceeded to initiate them to his new order by asking five faithful Sikhs to stand up. He put pure water into an iron vessel or

---

4: *Some say that Himmat Chand was the third Sikh to come forward and Mohkam Chand was the fourth.*

Bowl (Batta of Sarbloh) and stirred it with a Khanda (two edged small sword). While stirring the water with Khanda, he recited Gurbani or Divine Word (Five Banis- Japji, Jap Sahib, Anand Sahib, Swayas, and Chaupai). Sugar crystals called 'Patasas' which incidently the Guru's wife, Mata Sahib Kaur, had brought at that moment, were mixed in the water.

The Guru then stood up with the sacred Amrit (nectar) prepared in the steel bowl. Each of the five faithfuls, by turn, each kneeling upon his left knee, looked up to the Master to receive his Eternal Light. He gave five palmfuls of Amrit to each of them to drink and sprinkled it five times in the eyes, asking them to repeat aloud with each sprinkle, "Waheguru ji ka Khalsa, Waheguru ji ki Fateh." (This meant: Khalsa belongs to God and all triumph be to His Name) Then he anointed with five sprinkles in the hair. In this way Amrit was administered to the five faithfuls from the same bowl. After that he asked them to sip Amrit from the same bowl to signify their initiation into **the casteless fraternity of the Khalsa.** All the five faithfuls were baptized in this way by the Guru who then called them **'PANJ PYARE' or Five Beloved Ones.** He gave them the appellation of **SINGHS or lions** and they were named from Daya Ram to Daya Singh, Dharam Das to Dharam Singh, Mohkam Chand to Mohkam Singh, Himmat Chand to Himmat Singh, and Sahib Chand to Sahib Singh. The Guru then addressed them **as the supreme, the liberated ones, pure ones and he called them THE KHALSA.**

He then ordained them to do the following:

I.   First they must wear the following articles whose names begin with 'K':
1. Kes- unshorn hair. This represents the natural appearance of saintlihood. This is the first token of Sikh faith.
2. Kanga- A comb to clean the hair.
3. Kachha- An underwear to denote chastity.
4. Kara- A steel bracelet on the wrist, a symbol of dedication to the Divine Bridegroom.
5. Kirpan- A sword for self-defence and a symbol of dignity, power and unconquerable spirit.

II. They must observe the following guidelines:

1. Not to remove hair from the body.
2. Not to use Tobacco or other intoxicants.
3. Not to eat 'Kutha', a meat of an animal slaughtered by slow degrees as done by the Muslims.
4. Not to commit adultery- 'Par nari ki sej, bhul supne hun na jayo' (never enjoy, even in dream, the bed of a woman other than your own wife)
(A supplementary ordinance was issued that any one who did not observe any of the four directives, must be re-baptized, pay a fine, and promise not to offend any more; or he must be excommunicated from the Khalsa).

III. They must rise at dawn, bathe, meditate on Gurmantar-'Waheguru', Moolmantar- the preamble of Japji, and recite five banis- Japji, Jap Sahib and Swayas in the morning; Rehras in the evening; and Kirtan Sohela at bed time at night.

IV. They must not have matrimonial relations with smokers, with persons who killed their daughters, with the descendants or followers of Prithi Chand, Dhir Mal, Ram Rai, or masands who had strayed away from the tenets and principles of Guru Nanak.

V. They must not worship idols, cemeteries, or cremation grounds, and must believe only in One Immortal God.
The Guru further spelled out that they should practise arms, and never show their backs to the foe in the battlefield. They should always be ready to help the poor and protect those who sought their protection. They were to consider their previous castes erased, and deem themselves all brothers of one family. Sikhs were to intermarry among themselves.

THE MASTER BECOMES THE DISCIPLE:

After the Guru had administered Amrit to his Five Beloved

Ones, he stood up in supplication and with folded hands, begged them to baptize him in the same way as he had baptized them. **This was the height of this remarkable episode setting up unparallel example in the world that first as Guru, he created the Khalsa blessing them with power, supremacy and glory, and then he himself became their disciple- Wonderful is Guru Gobind Singh, himself the Master and himself the disciple.** In the annals of human history a disciple could become a Guru but never a Guru became a disciple. The Five Beloved Ones were astonished at such a proposal, and represented their own unworthiness, and the greatness of the Guru, whom they deemed God's Vicar upon earth. They asked him why he made such a request and why he stood in a supplicant posture before them. He replied," I am the son of the Immortal God. It is by His order I have been born and have established this form of baptism. They who accept it shall henceforth be known as the KHALSA. The Khalsa is the Guru and the Guru is the Khalsa. There is no difference between you and me. As Guru Nanak seated Guru Angad on the throne, so have I made you also a Guru. Wherefore administer the baptismal nectar to me without any hesitation."   Accordingly the Five Beloved Ones baptized the Guru with the same ceremonies and injunctions he himself had employed. The Guru was then named Gobind Singh instead of Gobind Rai.

Guru Gobind Singh was the first one to take Amrit from the Khalsa, the Five Beloved Ones. About 80,000 men and women were baptized within a few days at Anandpur.

By creating the Khalsa, the Guru embedded two qualities in one person. A Khalsa is a Saint-Soldier. A Sikh is a saint because he worships the All-Pervading Divine Spirit and in whom that Spirit shines day and night like a full moon. A Sikh is a soldier because he is ever ready to take up the arms to uphold righteousness.

The Guru promised the Five Beloved Ones (The Khalsa) that whenever they called upon him, he would agree to their proposal. This was the establishment of democratic Khalsa. The Guru fulfilled this promise by submitting to the demand of the Five Beloved Ones at the battle of Chamkaur and left the Garhi.

The Guru himself gives the definition of his beloved Khalsa:

"He who constantly keeps in mind
Intent upon Ever Awake Living Light of Consciousness
And never swerves from the thought of One God;
And he who is adorned with full faith in Him
And is wholly steeped in the Love of the Lord,
And even by mistake never puts his faith in fasting
Or in worship of tombs, sepulchre or crematoriums,
Caring not for pilgrimages, alms, charities,
Penances or austerities;
Or anything else but devotion to One God;
And in whose heart and soul the Divine Light
Shines forth as the full moon
He is known as Khalsa, the purest of the pure."
(Guru Gobind Singh-Swayas)

The Persian historian Gulam-ul-din, the newswriter of that period, sent Emperor Aurangzeb a copy of the Guru's address to his Sikhs on the first of Baisakh, Sambat 1756 (1699 A.D.) which reads as follows:

"Let all embrace one creed and obliterate differences of religion. Let the four Hindu castes who have different rules for their guidance abandon them all, adopt the one form of adoration, and become brothers. Let no one deem himself superior to another. Let none pay heed to the Ganges, and other places of pilgrimage which are spoken of with reverence in the Shastras, or adore incarnations such as Rama, Krishna, Brahma, and Durga, but believe in Guru Nanak and the other Sikh Gurus. Let men of the four castes receive my baptism, eat out of one dish, and feel no disgust or contempt for one another."

When the Guru addressed the gathering, several Brahmans and Khatris stood up and accepted the religion of Guru Nanak while others insisted that they would never accept any religion which was opposed to the teachings of the Vedas and Shastras.

So far the leadership had remained in the hands of non-militant urban Khatris from whom the majority of the masands were drawn, but now the situation had completely changed. Peasantry and other classes of rural areas formed the bulk of the converts. Even those people who had been considered the dregs of humanity were changed like a magic into something rich and super. The sweepers, the barbers and confectioners who had never touched a sword and whose whole generations had lived as slaves of the higher castes, became doughty warriors under the stimulating leadership of the Guru.

Ideologically, the Khalsa was created to be aimed at a balanced combination of the ideals of Bhakti and Shakti, of moral and spiritual excellence and militant valor or heroism of the highest order; or in other words the Khalsa was to be a brotherhood in faith and brotherhood in arms at one and the same time. The Khalsa symbolized in itself the determination to complete the social and religious revolution inaugurated by Guru Nanak. The code of conduct prescribed for the newly created Khalsa was so devised as to impose a strict discipline on the Sikhs to ensure firm coherence and commitment on their part to the holy and lofty ideals of Sikhism.

With the creation of the Khalsa, some new doctrines were also established. The first doctrine of the Khalsa was the doctrine of the theocratic democracy by his selected, not elected, five representatives of the people from amongst the thousands of the devotees from all over the country while second was the doctrine of collective responsibility by authorizing the Five Beloved Ones only, in the presence of the holy Guru Granth Sahib to assume authority implicitly to be obeyed by the whole nation.

The Guru set the souls of the Khalsa free and filled their hearts with a lofty longing for religious and social freedom and national ascendancy. The Khalsa, therefore, accepted the challenge to combat terror inspired by tyranny of the powerful Mughal empire and embarked upon a national struggle of liberation.

BHAI NAND LAL:

Bhai Nand Lal Goya, born at Ghazni in Afghanistan in 1643, was an accomplished persian scholar who composed verses in praise of God and Guru Gobind Singh. He was hardly nineteen when his parents passed away and after that he moved to the city of Multan. The Nawab of Multan being impressed with his scholastic talents and personality, appointed him as his 'Mir Munshi' (Revenue officer). At the age of 45 Nand Lal left the service and set out in pursuit of peace. At last he reached Anandpur. Nand Lal wanted to test the Guru before he could accept him. He took a small house and started living quietly in that and made up his mind that he would go to the Guru only when the Guru beckoned him. The Guru did not call for sometimes. During this period Nand Lal became very restless which he recorded:

> "How long shall I patiently wait?
> My heart is restless for a vision of thee,
> My tearful eyes, says Goya,
> Have become flooding streams of love
> Flowing in a passionate affection towards thee."
>
> (Nand Lal- Translated)

At last the Guru called Nand Lal. When he reached there for his holy sight, the Guru was sitting in a trance with his eyes closed. As Nand Lal saw the Master, he was wonder-stuck and he recorded:

> "My life and faith are held in bondage,
> By His sweet and angelic face;
> The glory of Heaven and earth,
> Is hardly worth,
> A hair of His golden looks.
> O! How can I bear the light,
> Shed by the piercing glance of His love,
> To ennoble and enlighten life,
> A glimpse of the Beloved is enough."
>
> (Bhai Nand Lal)

After a short while the Master opened his eyes and smiled as he looked towards Nand Lal. By mere opening of his eyes, he enabled Nand Lal to see the Divine. His one glance of Grace opened the spiritual eyes of Nand Lal. He bowed down saying,"Lord, my doubts are dispelled. I have known the Truth. The doors of my heart are opened and I have attained peace."

Nand Lal, thus, continued to live at Anandpur in the

service and love of the Master. One day the Guru commanded him," You left the home and renounced the world; such a renunciation is not acceptable to me. Go back and live in the world, work for your living and serve the humanity; but remain unattached to Maya (materialism), keeping God alive in thy mind." Nand Lal asked," Whither should I go, O Master?" The Guru replied," To whichever direction your feet carry thee."

Bhai Nand Lal bowed and left Anandpur and after sometimes he reached Agra, the city of Taj Mahal where Prince Bahadur Shah was holding his court. There were some poets, scholars and artists patronized by the prince. Nand Lal was soon recognized at Agra as a great scholar which earned him a high office and emoluments from the prince. It is said that Emperor Aurangzeb had to send a letter to the King of Persia and Nand Lal's draft of that letter was deemed as the most suitable. Upon this Aurangzeb sent for Nand Lal, and after an interview he remarked to his courtiers that it was a pity that such a learned man should remain a Hindu. Aurangzeb told Prince Bahadur Shah to convert Nand Lal to Islam by persuasion if possible, and by force otherwise. This news leaked out and Bhai Nand Lal with the help of Ghiasuddin, a Muslim admirer and follower of him, escaped from Agra one night, and fled to Anandpur, the only place where such refugees could find safe asylum.

Enjoying the blissful life at the Master's feet at Anandpur, Bhai Nand Lal then settled down to a routine of a devoted disciple. He presented to the Guru a Persian work called Bandagi Nama in praise of God, a title which the Guru changed to Zindagi Nama, or 'Bestower of Eternal life'. The following few extracts are from that work:

"Both worlds, here and hereafter, are filled with God's light;
The sun and moon are merely servants who hold His torches.
....
They who search for God are ever civil
(Bhai Nand Lal- Translated)

BHAI JOGA SINGH:

From the early youth Joga Singh was living at the Guru's

Darbar and was a great devotee. One day Guru's eye caught him and he asked what his name was. He replied," O true king, my name is Joga Singh." The Guru asked," Whose Joga you are?" (Joga means for whose service he is fit or simply for whom he is?) "I am Guru Joga (I am in the service of the Guru)," replied Joga Singh. Upon this the Guru promised," If you are Guru Joga, then Guru is tere Joga (then the Guru is for you)."

After sometimes Joga Singh went to his home in Peshawar for his marriage. When the marriage ceremony was half-way through, a man arrived with an urgent message from the Guru to him to proceed to Anandpur without delay. Joga Singh read the command and instantly left for Anandpur without completing the marriage ceremony. He obeyed Guru's order over everything else. Indeed the path of the devotees is sharper than the edge of a razor blade, and it is even narrower than the hair-breadth on which they have to tread.

Joga Singh continued his journey to Anandpur as fast as he could. After passing through Lahore and Amritsar, he reached a resting spot at Hoshiarpur. On his way his ego got inflated and he thought," Who could have acted like me? Certainly very few Sikhs would carry out the Guru's order like me." This sense of pride brought his fall. At night he was overwhelmed by evil-passion and he started towards the house of a prostitute. Joga Singh was wearing Guru's uniform- a turban and beard. On his way to the prostitute, Joga Singh talked to himself," If some one sees me going into the house of a prostitute, it will bring disgrace to the Guru. Outwardly I am in Guru's attire. So nobody should see me entering the prostitute's house."

As soon as he reached near the house of the prostitute, a watchman appeared saying aloud," Be aware fellows!" Joga Singh could not enter the house and he walked on to the next street. Looking around and thinking that the watchman might have left, he hurried towards the house of the prostitute again. To his amazement the watchman reappeared shouting," Be aware fellows!" Joga Singh could not afford to be seen by anybody going into the house of the prostitute, knowing in his heart that it would bring slur to Guru's name since he was in Guru's uniform. Finally he quit his evil act after trying a few times without success.

Next morning he started his journey and reached Anandpur. Joga Singh stood mute before the Guru with his head
down. The Guru asked him about the well-being of himself and his
family but Joga Singh stood mute. The divine Guru then addressed
him," Joga Singh, do you remember when you said that you were
Guru Joga, and the Guru had promised, if you were Guru Joga,
then Guru tere Joga." Upon this the Guru further explained,"In the
garb of a watchman I guarded you in the streets of Hoshiarpur last
night, against the sinful deeds and thus saved you from disgrace."
Joga Singh fell on Guru's feet and asked for forgiveness.

Such are the ways of the Master. Once we put our complete
faith in him, he does not abandon us. The Guru confirms:

"As long as the Khalsa remain distinct and intact,
I shall bless them in every way;
When they detract from the prescribed path,
I detest them for ever."
(Guru Gobind Singh)

POST-KHALSA PERIOD ACTIVITIES:

The hill Rajas including the Raja of Kahlur came to visit the
Guru and had a good deal of discussion about the pros and cons of
the Khalsa. The Guru advised them to embrace the Khalsa religion
in order to elevate the fallen condition of their country. The hill
Rajas took their departure without accepting the Guru's proposal
to accept Khalsa creed.

The immediate effect of the creation of the Khalsa was the
anxiety of the hill Rajas who considered the Guru's activities as a
potent threat to their own religion and state power. The Guru
asked his Sikhs, wherever they resided, to come to Anandpur and
accept baptism, thus, become members of the Khalsa. They started
coming in large numbers to pay homage to the Guru and get
baptized. This growing number of the baptized Sikhs, surcharged
with their spirit of equality, and disengaged from the orthodox
way of living, who seemed to be always ready to combat evil,
alarmed the hill Rajas who considered it a direct challenge to their
feudal order and their orthodox way of living.

One day the Guru went on a hunting excursion in the Dun

when Balia Chand and Alim Chand, two hill chiefs made a surprise attack on the Guru's party. There were only a few Sikhs with the Guru. Both sides fought desperately. Alim Chand aimed a blow of his sword at Alim Singh, who received it on his shield and then with his return blow struck off Alim Chand's right arm. He managed to escape and left Balia Chand in sole command of the troops. However Balia Chand was soon shot dead by Ude Singh. The hill troops, having found one of their chiefs dead and the other having fled, abandoned the battle field leaving the Guru's party victorious.

FIRST BATTLE OF ANANDPUR:

After this defeat, the hill Rajas thought it highly dangerous to allow the Sikhs to increase in power and number. They therefore, decided collectively to complain to the Delhi government against the Sikhs. Aurangzeb was still busy in the south. The viceroy of Delhi sent General Din Beg and General Painde Khan each with five thousand men to resist the Guru's encroachments on the rights of the hill Rajas. When the imperial forces reached Rupar, they were joined by hill Rajas.

The Guru appointed the Five Beloved Ones as generals of his army. The Sikh chronicler states that, when the engagement began at Anandpur, the Turks were roasted by the continuous and deadly fire of the Sikhs. General Painde Khan seeing determined resistance of the Sikhs, shouted to his men to fight to the death against the infidels. He came forward to engage in a single combat with the Guru and invited the Guru to strike the first blow. The Guru refused the role of an aggressor and claimed that he had vowed never to strike except in self-defence. Upon this Painde Khan discharged an arrow which whizzed past Guru's ear. He charged another arrow which also missed the mark. The whole of Painde Khan's body except his ears was encased in armour. Knowing this the Guru then discharged an arrow at his ear with such an unerring aim that he fell off his horse on the ground and never rose again. This, however, did not end the battle. Din Beg assumed sole command of the troops. Maddened by Painde Khan's death they fought with great desperation but could not make any impression on the firm hold of the Sikhs. On the other hand, however, the

Sikhs caused a great havoc upon the enemy. The hill chiefs left the field. In the meantime Din Beg was wounded and he beat a retreat but was pursued by the Sikhs as far as Rupar (upto the village of Khidrabad near Chandigarh where there is a Gurdwara in that memory). This battle was fought in the beginning of 1701.

SECOND BATTLE OF ANANDPUR:

The Rajas of Jammu, Nurpur, Mandi, Bhutan, Kullu, Kionthal, Guler, Chamba, Srinagar, Dadhwal, Handur and others, assembled at Bilaspur to discuss the newly created situation. Raja Ajmer Chand of Kahlur (son of late Raja Bhim Chand) addressed them that if they overlooked the growing power of the Guru, he would one day drive them out from their territories. On the other hand if they were to seek assistance from Delhi again and again, they might be taken over by the Mughal empire for ever. It was, therefore, decided that they must defend themselves. If all the hill Rajas contributed reasonable contingents, they could muster a large army which would be sufficient to annihilate the Guru and his Sikhs. Thus a simple and feasible measure was thought out to invest the Guru's capital, Anandpur, and starve its occupants into submission.

Accordingly all the Rajas brought their contingents and marched towards Anandpur. On arriving near the city they dispatched a letter to the Guru in which they wrote," The land of Anandpur is ours, we allowed your father to dwell on it and he never paid any rent. Now you have originated a new religion which is opposed to our religious system. We have endured all this up to the present, we can no longer overlook it. You should pay the arrears of rent for the occupation of our land and promise to pay it regularly for the future. If you fail to accept these terms, then prepare your departure from Anandpur or be ready for the consequences." The Guru replied," My father had purchased this land and he paid for it. If you deprive me of Anandpur, you shall have it with bullets added thereto. Seek my protection, and you will be happy in both worlds. Also seek the protection of the Khalsa and abandon pride. Now is the time for a settlement. I shall act as a mediator between the Khalsa and you. You may then rule your states without apprehension."

It was now clear to the Rajas that the Guru would not surrender. Next morning they beat the drum of war. As anticipated a large number of Ranghars and Gujars under the command of Jagatullah flocked to the side of the hill Rajas. Five hundred men from the Majha area arrived under the command of Duni Chand to join the Guru's forces, and other reinforcements from other quarters also arrived at that juncture. There were two main forts[5], Lohgarh and Fatehgarh. The Guru ordered his forces not to advance beyond the city but remain as far as possible on the defensive. Sher Singh and Nahar Singh were appointed as chiefs to guard Lohgarh, and Fatehgarh was entrusted to Ude Singh. Sahibzada Ajit Singh, Guru's eldest son, asked his father's permission to join hands with Ude Singh.

The hill Rajas opened fire with large guns on the Guru's fortress. Several brave Sikhs made a determined stand against the enemy and forced them to retreat. The allied chiefs then held a brief council of war in which it was decided to despatch Raja Kesari Chand, the haughty chief of Jaswal, to attack the right flank and Jagatullah the left flank of the Guru's position while Ajmer Chand himself and his troops made a front attack on Anandpur. Jagatullah was shot dead by Sahib Singh and the Sikhs did not retreat to allow the enemy to remove his body. Raja Ghumand Chand of Kangra rallied his troops but failed to cause the Sikhs to retreat. The hill chiefs were in great dismay at the result of the battle and held a council of war during the night. Raja Ajmer Chand advised the council for peace with the Guru saying that the Guru occupied Guru Nanak's spiritual throne and there would be no indignity in appealing to him as supplicants. Many Rajas agreed to the proposal but Kesari Chand of Jaswal opposed the reconciliation and promised to fight with more determination the next day in order to oust the Guru from Anandpur.

Next morning the allied forces contented themselves with concentrating their attack on one particular part of the city but the Sikhs again offered valiant resistance. The allied forces rallied many times but could not overcome the brave Sikhs and so they decided to siege the city which lasted for a few weeks. As the

---

5:*As a matter of fact there were five forts built at Anandpur in 1689. They were Anandgarh, Lohgarh, Fatehgarh, Kesgarh and Holgarh.*

blockade prolonged successfully, Raja Kesari Chand prepared to intoxicate an elephant and direct him against the city. Whole body of the elephant was encased in steel. A strong spear projected from his forehead for the purpose of assault. The intoxicated elephant was directed towards the gate of Lohgarh fort and the allied army followed him. The Guru blessed his Sikh, Vichitar Singh to combat the elephant. Vichitar Singh took a lance to meet the furious animal. He raised his lance[6] and drove it through the elephant's head armor. On this the animal turned around on the hill soldiers, and killed several of them. Meanwhile Ude Singh continued to advance against Kesari Chand, challenged him, and then with one blow cut off his head. Mohkam Singh, one of the Five Beloved Ones, cut off the mad elephant's trunk with one blow of his sword. What remained of the hill army now fled. In the retreat the Raja of Handur was severely wounded by Sahib Singh.

On the following day Ghumand Chand of Kangra directed the efforts of his troops against the city. Ghumand Chand's horse was killed by a bullet from the musket of Alim Singh. The battle lasted with varying success until evening, when Ghumand Chand, as he was proceeding to his tent in the evening, was mortally wounded by a chance bullet. All the hill chiefs now became disheartened and demoralized. Raja Ajmer Chand was the last to leave Anandpur and marched home in the dead of night. This battle was fought in 1701.

BATTLE OF NIRMOH:

Ajmer Chand in spite of the defeat of the allied forces, determined to oust the Guru. He sent an envoy to the Emperor's viceroy in Sirhind and another envoy to the viceroy of Delhi to complain against the Sikhs and sought their help to assist the hill chiefs in destroying the Guru's power and expelling him from Anandpur. Accordingly the imperial forces were directed to assist the hill chiefs.

At the same time to save their faces, the hill chiefs proposed to the Guru through Pamma Brahman, that they would be friends

---

6:*Vichitar Singh was not a very big person and this lance was weighing about 40 pounds and it is still present inside the fort Anandgarh at Anandpur.*

with him for ever only if he left Anandpur for a while and come back later. The Guru agreed to the proposal and left for Nirmoh, a village situated about a mile from Kiratpur. After the Guru reached Nirmoh, Raja Ajmer Chand and Raja of Kangra both thought that since the Guru was now in the open and he had no fort around him for protection, it would be better to launch an attack. They attacked the Guru's army without even waiting for the arrival of the imperial army. A fierce battle ensued in which the Sikhs were ultimately victorious. One afternoon as the Guru was sitting in his open court, the hill chiefs engaged a Mohammadan gunner to kill him for an adequate remuneration. The gunner fired a cannon ball which missed the Guru but took away the life of Sikh who was fanning him. The Guru picked up his bow and shot an arrow which killed the gunner and with another arrow killed his brother who was assisting him. On seeing this the hill men quit fighting. The two Mohammadans were buried on the spot called Siyah Tibbi or the black hill and a Gurdwara was erected by the Sikhs to commemorate Guru's escape from the bullet.

The army of Wazir Khan, the viceroy of Sirhind, arrived in due time. The Guru found himself in a very dangerous position between the hill Rajas on one hand, and the imperial army on the other. But he resolved to defend himself in whatever way it was and his Sikhs stood faithfully and valiantly by him. Wazir Khan gave an order to his troops to make a sudden rush and seize the Guru. The Guru was successfully protected by his son Ajit Singh and his other brave warriors. They stopped the advance of the imperial forces and cut them down in rows. The carnage continued until night. Next day the imperial army and the hill chiefs made a furious assault when the Guru decided on retiring to Basoli whose Raja had frequently invited him to his capital. Until the Guru's army reached the river Satluj, fierce fighting continued in which brave Sahib Singh was slain. Bitting his thumb Wazir Khan admitted that he had never before witnessed such desperate fighting. The Guru with his troops crossed over the river and reached Basoli. The hill chiefs were overjoyed and presented elephants to Wazir Khan and departed to their homes. Wazir Khan returned to Sirhind. This battle was fought at the end of 1701.

Daya Singh and Ude Singh requested the Guru to return to Anandpur. After staying a few days at Basoli, he marched back to

Anandpur and the inhabitants of the city were delighted to see him again among them. Finding the Guru again firmly established at Anandpur, Raja Ajmer Chand thought it most wise to pursue for peace. The Guru told Ajmer Chand that he was willing to come to terms with him, but he would punish him if he were again found guilty of treachery. Ajmer Chand was glad to find peace with the Guru and he sent his family priest with presents to him. The other hill Rajas also followed Ajmer Chand's example and made good relations with the Guru.

After this the Guru went to Malwa for the propagation of his mission. In January 1703 he went to a fair held at Kurukshetra on the occasion of a solar eclipse in order to purchase horses to replace those which were killed or stolen in previous warfare. The custom of sale and barter of horses and other animals at religious fairs was prevalent even during the time of the Guru.

Two Mohammadan generals, Saiyad Beg and Alif Khan, were on their way from Lahore to Delhi. Raja Ajmer Chand who also went to Kurukshetra along with other hill chiefs, thought to secure their assistance. He promised the generals large remuneration if they attacked the Guru. Instead on hearing favorable accounts of the Guru, Saiyad Beg withdrew his army, and when the battle ensued at Chamkaur between the Guru's and Alif Khan's troops, he joined the Guru's forces. Upon this Alif Khan retired from the contest thinking that he had no chance for victory. The Guru returned to Anandpur. Saiyad Beg threw his lot with the Guru and accompanied him to Anandpur, and remained with him as a trustworthy and powerful ally.

After two years of peace, the old hostilities reappeared. The reasons being, the increasing prestige of the Guru and the clashes as a result between the hill Rajas and the Sikhs.

THIRD BATTLE OF ANANDPUR:

At that time there were only 800 Sikhs in the Guru's army at Anandpur. Raja Ajmer Chand summoned his allies, Rajas of Handur, Chamba and Fatehpur with the object of chastising the Guru. They all expressed themselves in favor of immediate measures and attacked the Guru's forces at Anandpur. In the previous battles of Anandpur the Sikhs had mostly remained behind their battlements but they met the enemy this time in the open field outside Anandpur. The Sikhs fought with their usual courage and determination. The hill chiefs could not achieve any success and retired from the battle in despair. This battle was fought in 1703.

FOURTH BATTLE OF ANANDPUR

Owing to the repeated representations of the hill chiefs, the Emperor sent a large army under the command of General Saiyad Khan to subdue the Guru. Saiyad Khan was a brother-in-law of Pir Budhu Shah of Sadhaura who fought on the side of the Guru at the battle of Bhangani. On his way to Anandpur Saiyad Khan met Pir Budhu Shah and heard all favorable accounts of the Guru and, thus, had a wish to behold him.

It was the end of March, 1704 and was a crop-cutting time of the year, so the majority of the Guru's Sikhs had dispersed to their homes. There were only five hundred strong troops left at Anandpur at that time. The Guru had to make best defence with the present force. Maimun Khan, a faithful Mohammadan who had attached himself to the Guru, asked his permission to show his bravery. The brave and faithful Saiyad Beg also came forward to render his services to the Guru. Both Musalmans fought like tigers in the battle, and were followed by the Sikhs.

The Sikhs advanced boldly against the enemy. Saiyad Beg entered into a single combat with Raja Hari Chand. After they had repeatedly missed each other, Saiyad Beg at last struck off the hill chief's head. On seeing this Din Beg of the imperial army rushed at Saiyad Beg and mortally wounded him. Maimun Khan from horseback charged in every direction and committed great havoc among the imperial troops. The Guru knew what was passing in General Saiyad Khan's mind, and advanced ostensibly to challenge him. Saiyad Khan on obtaining the wish of his heart to behold the Guru, dismounted and fell at the feet of the Guru. The Guru conferred on him the true Name. After Saiyad Khan's defection, Ramzan Khan took command and fought with great bravery against the Sikhs. The Guru shot an arrow which killed Ramzan Khan's horse. The Sikhs rallied and presented a bold front to the enemy but being too few in number were overpowered by them. When the Guru saw that there was no chance of retrieving his position, he decided to evacuate Anandpur. The Mohammadan army plundered the city. After obtaining this booty they proceeded back to Sirhind. When the imperial army was resting at night, the Sikhs made a sudden attack, which created great confusion in the enemy camp. The Turks who turned to oppose the Sikhs, were killed and only those who fled, escaped the vengeance of the Guru's pursuing army. The Sikhs also deprived them of all the booty they had captured at Anandpur. After this the Guru returned and took possession of Anandpur.

FIFTH BATTLE OF ANANDPUR:

The Emperor called on his troops to account for their cowardice. They pleaded that the Sikhs had taken an unfair advantage of their position in the battle field. At one point the Emperor asked what sort of person the Guru was and what force he possessed. A Mohammadan soldier gave highly colored accounts of the Guru's beauty, sanctity and prowess. He described the Guru as a young handsome man, a living saint, the father of his people and in war equal to one hundred twenty-five thousand men. The Emperor was much displeased on hearing this elaborate praise of the Guru and ordered that he should be brought to his presence. In the meantime Raja Ajmer Chand made a strong representation to the Emperor for assistance to bring the Guru to submission. Accordingly the viceroys of Sirhind, Lahore and Kashmir were ordered to proceed against the Guru.

Some faithful Sikhs informed the Guru of war preparations as a result of Raja Ajmer Chand's representation to the Emperor. The Guru made arrangements accordingly and sent for his followers. The Sikhs of Majha, Malwa and Doaba and other places thronged to Anandpur. They were delighted at the prospect of battle, and congratulated themselves on their good fortune in being allowed to die for their Guru and their faith. The Guru affirmed that the death in the battle-field in the name of religion was equal to the fruits of many years' devotion, and ensured honor and glory in the next world.

The noteworthy point in this whole episode is that the Guru having won battle after battle, never captured an inch of territory, never nurtured enmity, and never attacked anybody as an aggressor. By the creation of the Khalsa he established equality and brotherhood of mankind. The down-trodden segments of the society which were ever ridiculed by the so called high caste Brahmans and Khatris, had now become undaunted saint-soldiers after being baptized by the Guru and joining the brotherhood of the Khalsa. The Brahmans and the hill chiefs considered all this a threat to their very existence. They were, therefore, waging a constant war against the Guru and his Sikhs.

The hill chiefs who arrayed themselves against the Guru were Raja Ajmer Chand of Kahlur, Rajas of Kangra, Kullu, Kionthal, Mandi, Jammu, Nurpur, Chamba, Guler, Garhwal, Bijharwal, Darauli and Dadhwal. They were joined by the Gujars and the Ranghars of the area, and all of them formed a formidable force. The imperial army of the viceroys' of Sirhind, Lahore and Kashmir came in large number. The chronicler judiciously remarks that the Khalsa must be congratulated because, though few in number, having the blessings of their Guru they had confidence in themselves to fight for their religion, and delighted in anticipation of the approaching conflict. It is recorded that there were ten thousand Sikhs at Anandpur while the opposing army came as strong as fifteen to twenty times in number than the Sikhs.

The allied forces fell on Anandpur like locust. On seeing this the Guru ordered his artillery men to discharge their cannon into the hostile army at the thickest spot. The enemy made a charge to seize the artillery, but were quickly restrained by the fatal accuracy with which the Sikhs served their guns. They were supported by the infantry. The city of Anandpur was on a little higher elevation and the allied forces were in the open and had no protection, and consequently fell in heaps. A fierce battle was fought for a few days.

The Mohammadan gunners were promised large reward if they killed the Guru but they were unsuccessful in their mission because their gun fire was either high or too low and could not hit the target. The allied army finding their guns useless tried hand to hand fight. On seeing this the Guru began to discharge his arrows with marvelous effect. The fearful carnage continued, horses fell on horses, men on men. The allied forces rallied a strong effort to conquer, but was so vigorously and successfully repulsed that they were obliged to suspend hostilities at the end of each day of warfare. The Mohammadans and the hill chiefs had different opinions as to the cause of the success of the Sikhs. Some thought that the Guru had supreme miraculous power and the supernatural forces fought on his side. Others maintained that the Guru's success was owing to the fact that his men were protected behind their ramparts. While this discussion was going on, the Mohammadan viceroys decided to storm the fortress where the Guru was stationed. On seeing this the Sikhs put their two guns called Baghan (tigress) and Bijai-ghosh (sound of victory) in position. The aims were taken at the enemy. The tents were blown away and great havoc was caused. On seeing this the Mohammadan viceroys retreated and the hill armies fled. That evening the Guru offered thanksgiving, and beat the drum of victory.

Having failed through direct assault, the allied army planned a siege of the city of Anandpur in such a way that all entrances and exits for both goods and persons were completely closed. They completely besieged the city, and the Guru's supplies were failing. Food position became extremely serious and the Sikhs were driven to undertake some dangerous expeditions. They went out at night to snatch provisions from the besiegers. After some time the allies collected their stores at one place and guarded them day and night.

When the enemy learnt about the distressful situation of the Sikhs, they planned a different strategy to induce the Guru to leave Anandpur. Raja Ajmer Chand sent his envoy to the Guru saying that if he left Anandpur, their armies would withdraw and the Guru could afterwards return whenever he pleased. The Guru did not pay any heed to this proposal. The offer was repeated several times, but the Guru did not accept it. Having suffered extreme hardships, the Sikhs besought the Guru to evacuate the fort, but the Guru counselled them patience for some time more. The Sikhs who heard enemy's proposal, went to the Guru's mother to use her influence on him. She pleaded with him but in vain. The Guru told her that the enemy's proposal was hypocritical since they planned to draw out the Sikhs from within the shelter of the city and attack them. Some of the Masands and the Sikhs who were influenced by the hill chiefs, insisted that the proposal of the enemy be accepted and the city be abandoned. Some Sikhs became impatient and disheartened. The Guru asked them to declare their allegiance. Forty of them signed a disclaimer saying that he was not their Guru and they were not his Sikhs. After they signed the disclaimer, they were allowed by the Guru to go away. The Guru then brought out a scheme to expose the hypocrisy of the enemy.

The Guru sent for Raja Ajmer Chand's envoy and told him that he would evacuate Anandpur if the allied armies would first allow the removal of his treasure and property. The Hindus swore on the Salgram (their idol) and the Mohammadans on the holy Quran, that they would not deceive or molest his servants departing with his property. The Guru then immediately ordered a number of cartloads of useless articles. To the bullocks' horns were attached torches and at the dead of night, the caravan of bullocks with their loads, started along with some Sikhs accompanying them. When the caravan reached the enemy lines they forgot all their pledges and fell upon the small company of the Sikhs to loot the treasure. Their disappointment was great when they found out that the treasure was made up of rubbish articles. In this way the Guru exposed the treachery of the enemy and told his Sikhs that everything they had endured had been by the Will of God, and he quoted Guru Nanak- "Happiness is a disease, the remedy for which is unhappiness".

At last came an autographed letter from the Emperor to the Guru- "I have sworn on the Quran not to harm you. If I do, may I not find a place in God's court hereafter! Cease warfare and come to me. If you do not desire to come hither, then go whithersoever you please." The Emperor's envoy added that the Emperor promised that he would not harm the Guru. The hill Rajas also swore by the cow and called their idols to witness, that they would allow safe passage to the Guru. The Guru told the enemy," You are all liars, and therefore all your empire and your glory shall depart. You all took oaths before and then perjured yourselves."

The Sikhs went again to the Guru's mother to complain of his refusal to listen to reason. He, however, felt that their pleading was reasonable but it was not appropriate to accept the terms of the enemy and leave the fort. The Sikhs stricken with hunger, supported the envoy's representation. The Guru comforted them," My brethren, waver not, I only desire your welfare. You know not that these people are deceivers and design to do us evil. If you hold a little longer, you shall have food to your heart's content." When the Sikhs refused to wait any longer, the Guru asked them to wait only a few days more when the great God would send them relief[7]. The Sikhs, however, refused to wait even for a day. The Guru repeated his request saying that the enemy would then retire and they would all be happy. He also warned the Sikhs," O dear Khalsa, you are rushing to your destruction, while I am endeavoring to save you."

The Sikhs were so much hunger stricken that they refused to stay even for a day. The Guru's mother was also in favor of evacuating the fort. The allied armies sent a Saiyid (a Mohammadan priest) and a Brahman, both of whom were to swear, on behalf of the allied armies, solemn oaths of safe conduct for the Guru should he evacuate Anandpur. On seeing this the Sikhs began to waver in their allegiance to the Guru, and in the end only forty Sikhs decided to remain with him and share his fortunes. The Guru told them that they too might desert him. They refused and said that they would either remain within the fort or force their way out as the Guru directed. The Guru then knew that the seed of his religion would flourish. He then finally decided to leave Anandpur and gave orders to his men that they all were to march at night. Anandpur was finally evacuated on 6-7 Poh, Sambat 1762 (20-21 December, 1705).

Bhai Daya Singh and Ude Singh walked in front of the Guru, Mohkam Singh and Sahib Singh on his right, the second batch of baptized Sikhs on his left. His sons Ajit Singh and Jujhar Singh followed with bows and arrows. Then came Bhai Himmat Singh carrying ammunition and matchlocks. Gulab Rai, Sham Singh and other Sikhs and relations accompanied him. The rest of the followers brought up the rear, about five hundred in all[8].

The moment the enemy got the news of Guru's departure, they again forgot all about their pledges and set out in hot pursuit immediately. Skirmishes started from Kiratpur onwards. Realizing the impending danger the Guru charged Ude Singh with the responsibility to check the advance of the enemy. Bhai Ude Singh fought a bloody battle at Shahi Tibbi. The enemy surrounded and killed the dauntless and the bravest of the Guru's brave warriors,

---

7:*The Guru was then expecting reinforcements of the Malwa Sikhs and that was the reason he was asking for delay. In fact the reinforcements did come, but arrived too late for the defence of Anandpur.*

8:*Some writers say that there were 1500 Sikhs who followed the Guru.*

Ude Singh. When the battle of Shahi Tibbi was in progress, the Guru had reached the bank of Sarsa river. At that time a news came that a contingent of enemy troops was fast approaching. Bhai Jiwan Singh[9], a Rangretta Sikh, was given a band of one hundred warriors to encounter the pursuers. With the rest of his people the Guru plunged into the flooded waters of the Sarsa river. The flood was so strong that many were drowned and many were scattered in different directions including the Guru's mother with two younger sons, Zorawar Singh and Fateh Singh. Besides, there was a heavy loss of valuable literature and property. The Guru accompanying his two eldest sons and some veteran Sikhs reached the village Ghanaula on the other side of Sarsa river. Apprehending that the route ahead might be beset with danger, the Guru gave Bhai Bachitar Singh a band of one hundred Sikhs and instructed him to march by the direct route to Rupar, whereas he with some veteran Sikhs preferred to take a longer route and reached Kotla Nihang near Rupar to stay with Pathan Nihang Khan who was an old and sincere devotee of the Sikh Gurus. Bhai Bachitar Singh and his men had to fight their way through a cordon of the Ranghars of Malikpur, a village near Rupar, and the Pathans of Rupar. During the fierce fighting that took place on this occasion, majority of the Sikhs fell dead and Bachitar Singh was mortally wounded.

The Guru did not stay long at Kotla Nihang. It seems that he was to proceed to Machhiwara and Rai Kot. Accompanied by his two eldest sons and forty Sikhs, the Guru halted at Bur Majra after Kotla Nihang. A news was received that a large body of Sirhind troops was chasing them. Immediately the Guru decided to face the enemy from within the Garhi of Chamkaur and he hurried towards it. He was well aware of the importance of this Garhi (mud fortress) as he had, on a previous occasion, fought a battle at this place.

BATTLE OF CHAMKAUR:[10]

The imperial army which was in hot pursuit, besieged the fortress. They were joined by the hill chiefs and the Ranghars and

---

9:Bhai Jaita's name after baptism. Bhai Jaita had brought Guru Tegh Bahadur's head from Delhi to Anandpur.
10:A place about ten miles from Rupar.

the Gujars. The Guru appointed eight men to guard each of the four walls. Two Sikhs held the door and other two were appointed sentinels. The Guru himself, his two sons; and Daya Singh and Sant Singh went on the top storey. The Sikhs held the fortress for a long time against the heavy odds. Nahar Khan and Ghairat Khan, the two imperial officers, attempted to scale the little fort, but were shot down by the Guru. After that none of the Mohammadan officers dared to attempt the fatal ascent. Five Sikhs went forth to contend with the enemy. After fighting with great bravery, they were killed. They continued in batches of five. Guru's eldest son, Ajit Singh (about 18 years old) asked permission to go forth and fight the enemy. The Guru approved the proposal and Ajit Singh went with five Sikh heroes. He performed prodigies of valor and ultimately fell, fighting bravely along with his companions. On seeing his brother's fate, Jujhar Singh (14 years old) could not restrain himself and asked his father's permission. Like his elder brother, Jujhar Singh went in the battle field, but after a little while he turned back and asked for water. The Guru shouted," Go back, there is no more water left for you on this earth. See yonder, Ajit Singh is holding the cup of nectar for you." Jujhar Singh went back and created havoc upon the enemy and fell fighting valiantly. **Upon this the Guru's face was jubilant. His expression of mental composure showed glow of divinity upon the glorious end of his sons.** After the sons had achieved their splendid mission, the Guru then got ready to go out and fight. The remaining few Sikhs fell on their knees before the Guru and entreated him not to go. At that moment their victory lay in saving the Guru. If the Guru lived, they argued, he would create millions like them. They therefore, persuaded the Guru to leave the place but he would not listen to them. At that point Bhai Daya Singh who was the first of the Five Beloved Ones, recalled that at the time of creation of the Khalsa, the Guru had promised that the mandate of the Five Beloved Sikhs would be binding even upon the Guru. Upon this Bhai Daya Singh took four other Sikhs and formed an assembly which passed a 'Gurmata' (resolution) and said," **O true king, the Khalsa now orders you to leave this place.**" As promised at the time of administering Amrit to the Five Beloved Ones, the wonderful supreme lord **Guru Gobind Singh submitted before the Khalsa and accepted their verdict to leave the Garhi (fortress).**

Sant Singh and Sangat Singh offered to remain in the fort while Daya Singh, Dharam Singh, and Man Singh were determined to accompany the Guru[11]. It is said that Sant Singh very much resembled the Guru. Therefore he gave his plume to Sant Singh, clothed him in his armor and seated him in the upper room where Guru was stationed. He and three of his companions escaped during the night. He told them that if per chance they were separated from him, they were to go in the direction of a particular star which he showed to them. It was a cold night of December and the allied armies were resting in their tents. The Guru decided to awaken the enemy, lest they should think that he absconded. He discharged two arrows on the Turkish sentries. The arrows first struck torches which they held in their hands and then they passed through their bodies. In the darkness which followed the extinction of the torches, the Guru and his three companions escaped. A little far outside, he clapped his hands and shouted aloud that he was leaving if any one wanted to capture him, should try[12].

When he was escaping, he bade his men to stand firm. The Sikhs who were left behind, inflicted great loss on the enemy. The Mohammadans at last were able to scale the building and they believed that they were going to capture the Guru. They were greatly disappointed to subsequently learn that the person who was wearing plume and armor, was not the Guru but he was Sant Singh, and that the Guru had escaped. The allied armies retreated to their respectable places. Wazir Khan sent orders in all directions of his areas that any one who offered aid to the Guru, would be severely punished, and the one who captured the Guru or gave his whereabouts would be greatly rewarded.

After leaving the Garhi, the Guru proceeded barefooted on his journey alone and after passing through Jandsar and Behlolpur, he reached the thorny wilds of Machhiwara, a place between Rupar and Ludhiana. Thirst, hunger and fatigue overtook him. His feet were blistered. When he reached a garden he rested his head on a heap of earth and slept. While he was resting in the garden, his

---

11:Some writers say that there were eleven Sikhs left inside the Garhi at that time.

12:There is a Gurdwara called Tari Sahib on this spot where he clapped his hands. At Chamkaur Sahib there are four Gurdwaras. The first one is called Damdama Sahib where he rested before entering the Garhi; then Garhi Sahib which was the fortress; then Katalgarh Sahib where the bodies of Guru's sons were cremated, and the last one is the Tari Sahib.

three companions, Daya Singh, Dharam Singh and Man Singh reached and rejoined him. The situation was very grave because the enemy was in hot pursuit of the Guru. Gulaba, an old Masand of Machhiwara, took the Guru and his three companions to his home, but soon he got frightened and feared for his own safety if the Guru stayed with him. At this juncture two Pathan horse merchants, Nabi Khan and Ghani Khan, who were old acquaintances of the Guru, came and chose to risk their lives for the service of the Guru. There lived a Sikh woman in the village who had spun and weaved a cloth for the Guru and had vowed to keep it until his arrival in the village. The Guru had the cloth dyed blue and a robe was made from it in imitation of the attire of Mohammadan pilgrims. He wore the blue robe and then departed from Gulaba's village. The Guru was carried in a litter by Nabi Khan and Ghani Khan in front, and Dharam Singh and Man Singh in rear, while Daya Singh waved a chauri[13] over him. They told all inquirers that they were escorting Uch da Pir[14] or a high priest. Since Nabi Khan and Ghani Khan were very famous horse merchants in the area, people believed them.

From there they reached Ghangharali village and then Lal. At the village Lal which is about five miles from Doraha in Ludhiana district, a military officer had some doubts and he made searching inquiries. Pir Mohammad of Nurpur who was known to the Guru, was asked to identify the occupant of the litter. He confirmed that he was really Uch da Pir, upon which the officer let the Guru go. From Lal he visited Katana and then Kanoch where masand Fateh put him off with excuses and did not let him stay. From there he reached Alam Gir. Here Nand Lal, a Zamindar presented a horse to the Guru[15], thereby enabling him to change from litter to horse. The situation became easier and the Guru asked Nabi Khan and Ghani Khan to return home, after giving them a letter of appreciation (Hukam Nama) recommending them for the consideration of the faithful. Pir Mohammad was also

---

13: *Chauri- it was a bunch of peacock's wings which were waved over him as mark of respect.*

14:*Uch da Pir meant priest (Muslim faqir) of Uch, a town in the south western Punjab. The expression also meant high priest.*

15:*It is also said that Guru met the elder brother of Bhai Mani Singh called Nagahia Singh. He and his son were horse merchants and they offered the horse to the Guru*

honored with such a letter of appreciation. From Alam Gir he advanced on horse back in the direction of Rai Kot. At Silaoni the chief of Rai Kot, Rai Kalla who was Guru's devotee and a close relative of Nihang Khan of Kotla Nihang, waited upon him and took him to Rai Kot. Here Nura Mahi brought the news from Sirhind about Guru's younger sons.

INNOCENT CHILDREN MARTYRED:

During the catastrophe that befell in crossing the flooded Sarsa river, the companions of the Guru and his family were scattered in different directions. Mata Jit Kaur, Mata Sahib Kaur and their two female attendants, Bhai Mani Singh, Dhana Singh and Jawahar Singh, were all together in one group. Jawahar Singh who was an inhabitant of Delhi, took this whole group to his house in Delhi. Guru's old mother and his two younger sons, went with Gangu Brahman to his village Saheri near Morinda. Gangu worked in Guru's kitchen for twenty-one years. Guru's mother, Mata Gujri was carrying money in a bag. Seeing Mata's money, Gangu got tempted forgetting that he ate Guru's salt for twenty-one years. As Mata Gujri was half-asleep, Gangu stole the money and shouted,"Thief, thief," to create the impression that some thief stole the money. Mataji encountered Gangu and told him that she did not see anybody else entering the house. Upon this he tried to defend himself by saying that he was being blamed because he had given shelter to the homeless and the outlawed. Instead of admitting his guilt, he ordered them to leave his house. Gangu finally handed them over to the police officer of Morinda who in turn took them to Wazir Khan, the viceroy of Sirhind. They were imprisoned in a tower.

Next morning the two children, Zorawar Singh and Fateh Singh, were presented in the court of the viceroy. Wazir Khan reflected that if the children became Mohammadans, it would be a glory to his faith- Islam. He, therefore, told them that if they accepted Islam, he would grant them an estate, would marry them to the princesses and they would be happy and be honored by the Emperor. The nine years old Zorawar Singh replied," Our grandfather, Guru Tegh Bahadur, parted with his head but not with his religion and he ordered us to follow his example. It is best that we should give our lives to save the Sikh religion and bring down God's vengeance on the Turks," continued Zorawar Singh,"O viceroy, I spurn your religion and will not part with my own. It has become the custom of our family to forfeit life rather than faith. Why do you seek to tempt us with worldly ambitions? We shall not be led astray by the false advantages of your offer."

Wazir Khan could not endure such an outspokenness and got very angry. He decided that he must put these children to death. Sucha Nand, a Hindu minister supported Wazir Khan by implying that their arrogant words were uncalled for. He ignited Wazir Khan's anger by saying that when these children grew up, they would follow their father's foot steps and would destroy enemies. Therefore, this progeny of a cobra must be smothered in time. At that time, outspoke Nawab Sher Mohammad Khan of Maler Kotla," O viceroy, these children are still drinking milk in the nursery, and are too young to commit an offence and know not good from evil. The holy Quran does not allow the slaughter of innocent and helpless children. Therefore be pleased to release them." In spite of his appeal, the Qazi confirmed that the holy law would give the infidels the choice between Islam and death.

It is said that in order to bring the children to submission to Islam, they were made to enter, next day, through a very small door while the Quran was displayed on the other side. The idea was that as the children would enter the door with their heads down, they would then be told that they had bowed to the holy Quran and thereby to Islam. When the children saw that trap, the seven years old Sahibzada Fateh Singh threw his feet first instead of his head while entering through the small door. Throwing the feet towards the Quran meant an insult to Islam. Wazir Khan, therefore, could not conquer the nine and seven years old children of Guru Gobind Singh. When every effort failed to convert the children to Islam, it was finally ordered that they should be bricked alive in the wall. A wall was, therefore, built step by step on their tender limbs until it came up to the shoulders of Sahibzada Fateh Singh. The executioner advanced with his sword, and asked whose head he should chop off first? Upon this Sahibzada Fateh Singh said," Listen O executioner, since the wall has reached my shoulders first, therefore cut off my head first." Sahibzada Zorawar Singh exhorted,"No, you cannot cut off his head till you do mine, because I am the eldest and therefore, I have the right to go first. Cut off my head first." Hearing such a strange debate, the whole assembly of Wazir Khan's court was stunned. The small children were ridiculing the angel of death. The chronicler states that Sahibzada Fateh Singh's head was cut off first. Therefore, that place is called Fatehgarh Sahib to commemorate the memory of the young children. When this news was delivered to Mata Gujri in the tower, where she was waiting for them, she breathed her last on the spot. This treacherous event took place on the 13th Poh, Sambat 1762 (27th of December, 1705). A rich Sikh called Todar Mal cremated[16] the bodies of the Guru's mother and her grandsons. A Gurdwara stands to symbolize their memory.

As Nura Mahi narrated the tale of woes, Rai Kalla and other listeners were torn with grief and wept bitterly. The Guru was unruffled and remained as composed as ever. When Mahi finished his distressing story, the Guru thanked God for the glorious and triumphant end of his sons. He then addressed to the Almighty," O God, Thou gavest me father, mother, and four sons. They were all Thy trust to me. Today I have been successful and happy in restoring that entire trust back to Thee." While the Guru was listening to Mahi's story, he was digging up a shrub. He then pronounced,"As I dig up this shrub by the roots, so shall the Turks be extirpated."[17] The Guru also remarked," No, my sons are not dead. They have returned to their Eternal Home. It is Sirhind that shall die."[18]

The Guru resumed his march to Hehar where he spent two days with Mahant Kirpal Das, a hero of the battle of Bhangani. The next stop was Lamma Jatpura. It was here that Rai Kalla who was accompanying him, took leave. Realizing that the territory around Rai Kot was not suitable place for meeting the enemy's challenge, the Guru directed his Sikhs towards the Jungle Desh, the land of Brars. On the way he passed through the villages of Manuke,

---

16:It is stated in 'Suraj Parkash' that Tilok Singh and Ram Singh who were the sons of Baba Phul of Mehraj, cremated their bodies. They happened to be at Sirhind at that time.

17:Guru Nanak had granted a boon to Mughal Emperor Babar for a long rule of his dynasty. Since the Mughal Monarchs resolved to injustice, falsehood, deceit, tyranny and oppression, their rule needed end. By digging up a shrub the Guru actually dug up the roots of the Mughal rule and it did end after that.

18:Three years after this atrocity, Banda Singh Bahadur razed the whole of Sirhind to the ground and destroyed the enemy root and branch.

Mehdiana Chakkar, Takhatpur and Madhen and reached Dina, in Ferozepur district.

At Dina a devoted Sikh, Rama presented the Guru with an excellent horse which he accepted for himself and gave his former horse to Bhai Daya Singh. The Guru's arrival soon became known to the people of the area and they began to rally around him. Some of the influential people who met the Guru at Dina were Shamira, Lakhmira and Takhat Mal, grandsons of Jodha Rai who had rendered material assistance to Guru Har Gobind in the battle of Gurusar. Param Singh and Dharam Singh, grandsons of Bhai Rup Chand, also came to the Guru. The viceroy of Sirhind heard that the Guru was entertained by Shamira and his brothers. He wrote to Shamira on the subject and ordered him to arrest and surrender the Guru. Shamira replied that he was only entertaining his priest, who was merely visiting his Sikhs and harming none. Shamira however, feared that the viceroy would send his troops and arrest the Guru, so he sent a spy to obtain information of the viceroy's movements and proceedings.

The Guru stayed at Dina for some days. It was here that he **wrote his celebrated 'Zafarnama',**[19] or Persian epistle to Emperor Aurangzeb. It was in fact an exquisite reply to the letters of the invitation to the Guru which he had received from the Emperor. The letter is characteristic of the sublimity of the Guru and each line is pregnant with stimulating truths and righteous indignation. The Guru wrote to the Emperor that he had no faith in his solemn promises in the name of God and oaths on the Quran. The fact remained that he, the Emperor, on all occasions violated his sacred promises and proved false, mean and treacherous. The Guru wrote,"......What though my four sons were killed, I remain behind like a coiled snake. What bravery is it to quench a few sparks of life? Thou art merely exciting a raging fire the more...........As thou didst forget thy word on that day, so will God forget thee. God will grant thee the fruit of the evil deed thou didst design......Thou art proud of thine empire, While I am proud of the kingdom of the Immortal God........When God is a friend, what can an enemy do even though he multiply himself a hundred times? If an enemy practice enmity a thousand times, he cannot, as long as God is a

19:Zafarnama- *Zafar means victory. It was a letter to the Emperor written in Persian verse. It is also famous as being a masterpiece of Persian language.*

friend, injure even a hair of one's head."

The letter was sent through Bhai Daya Singh and Dharam Singh to the Emperor and they delivered it to him in Daccan. This letter awakened the Emperor's dormant conscience and evoked in him a sense of true repentance. It cast such a miracle effect on him that he began to pine and soon confined to bed. Aurangzeb dictated this letter to his son when death was at hand, in which he acknowledged his defeat in the life that he led:

"......Whatever good or bad I have done, I am taking it as a load upon my head to the Great Unseen............I am totally in the dark about the destiny that awaits me. But what I know is that I have committed enormous sins. Canst tell what grim punishment is in the store for me........."

While staying at Dina, the Guru visited a few places in the neighborhood. In the meantime he came to know that his whereabouts became known to the viceroy of Sirhind and he was, therefore, anxious to find a suitable place where he could best meet the challenge of the enemy. So he left Dina and visited many places such as Bander, Bargarh, Baihbal and Saravan etc. At Saravan the Guru gave his people a little practice in arrow shooting. Next he proceeded to Jaito, Kotla Maluk Das, Lambhawali and then reached Kot Kapura. Realizing that the pursuing enemy had come too near, the Guru asked Chaudhri Kapura, a Brar Jat, to lend the use of his fort to him for a few days. Fearing the wrath of the Mughals, he refused to oblige the Guru. From there the Guru reached Dhilwan Sodhian where one of his relatives received him with great warmth and cordiality. It was here, as the tradition goes, that one of the Prithi Chand's descendants, Kaul visited the Guru and presented him clothes. The Guru took off his blue robe which he had been wearing since he left Machhiwara, and tearing it piece by piece burned it in fire. The historic words that he is said to have uttered on his occasion are memorable:

"I have torn the blue clothes which I wore, and with that the rule of the Turks and Pathans is at an end."

Chaudhry Kapura being repentant of his disgraceful act,

came to see the Guru and asked for his forgiveness which the Guru did. Then he provided him with a good guide, Chaudhry Khana with whom the Guru marched westward in the direction of Dhab Khidrana. On the way he passed through Ramina, Mallan, Gauri Sanghar and Kaoni.

Meanwhile a large number of followers had rallied around him. The forty Sikhs who had deserted him at Anandpur and had given a disclaimer to him, were taunted by their wives who would not let them enter into their own homes. They came back to reinforce the Guru's small army. One brave lady, Mai Bhago brought them to the aid of the Guru along with a large contingent of other Majha Sikhs. The Guru had taken up his position on a sandy hillock at Khidrana in the district of Ferozepur. The Mughal army advanced towards his camp, but before they could attack him, they had to encounter a contingent under Mai Bhago and Jathedar Mahan Singh. A fierce fighting ensued. They were all overpowered but not before they had shown their mettle as the toughest fighters whom the experienced Mughal commander had ever known in his life. The Guru from his position of high altitude about two miles from the place of the battle, discharged arrows with fatal effect against the Mohammadans who could not see from what quarter destruction was raining on them. As the tank at Khidrana was dry, Mohammadan army was in great state of distress for want of drinking water, thus, Wazir Khan decided to return without striking a blow on the main body of the Khalsa with Guru Gobind Singh. The Guru became victorious.

After the departure of the Mohammadan army, the Guru decided to see the battle field and went about wiping the faces of both dead and wounded, and praising their unsurpassed valor. He found out that forty Sikhs including their leader Mahan Singh, who had given him disclaimer at Anandpur, all but Mahan Singh, died fighting bravely. Mahan Singh was still alive but was on his last breath when the Guru told him to open his eyes and said," Mahan Singh, ask for any boon you desire from an empire to salvation." After opening his eyes, Mahan Singh was delighted to see the Guru and replied," O true king! We are sinners because we disclaimed you at the time of need at Anandpur. The doors of Heaven are closed for those of us who had departed ahead of me. O Lord, grant us your Grace and disregard that disclaimer." It is recorded that the gracious Master took out that disclaiming document, which he carried on his vest during all these times, tore it up as a sign of forgiveness and reconciliation. Mahan Singh saw this with his own eyes and then breathed his last as happy, forgiven and emancipated soul. The souls of forty were also emancipated. Those forty Sikhs are called **Forty Mukte**-the Saved Ones or Emancipated Ones and are remembered in our daily prayers as Forty Muktas. Khidrana has since that time been called Mukatsar or the tank of salvation. The Guru then found Mai Bhago who inspired these forty Sikhs. A little aid revived her and she was blessed by the Master.

From Mukatsar the Guru moved to Rupana, Bhander, Gurusar, Thehri Bambiha, Rohila, Jangiana and Bhai ka Kot. Then he proceeded to Sahib Chand and to Chatiana where Brars who had fought for him demanded the arrears of their pay under threat of blocking his onwards march. By the grace of God it so happened that a Sikh from the neighborhood brought enough money about the same time which enabled the Guru to pay off all the arrears. However the leader of the Brars, Chaudhri Dana was extremely sorry for the arrogant behavior of his people and refused to accept any payment for himself. On the request of Chaudhri Dana, the Guru then went to his native place Mehma Swai. Reaching there he encamped at a place which is now called Lakhisar. From there he visited other places in the vicinity. On the request of Chaudhry Dalla, the Guru then decided to move to Talwandi Sabo. On his way he passed through Chatiana, Kot Sahib Chand, Kot Bhai, Giddarbaha, Rohila, Jangirana, Bambiha, Bajak, Kaljhirani, Jassi Bagwali, Pakka Kalan and Chak Hira Singh, and reached Talwandi Sabo now called Damdama Sahib or Takhat Damdama Sahib. This place appealed to the Guru so much that he assumed a permanent residence there and lived at this place for nine months and nine days.

GURU AT DAMDAMA SAHIB:

By this time all restrictions against the Guru by the Mughal government had been removed. On receipt of Zafarnama, the governors had been ordered by Aurangzeb to cease all molesting activities against the Guru.

It was here that the Guru's wife joined him. When she arrived, the Guru was seated in a big gathering of his disciples.

Addressing the Master, she asked,

"Where are my four sons?"

The Master replied,

**"What then if thy four are gone?
They yet live, and shall ever live- the Khalsa,
Millions of our dear brave sons."**

The peaceful period at Damdama Sahib was put to best possible use by the Guru. He laid abiding foundations of Sikhism in the Malwa tract. Large crowds came from far and near and presented a spectacle of New Anandpur. The Guru extensively visited the neighboring areas. Many old and hereditary Sikhs were baptized and brought more thoroughly into the Khalsa. Dalla, the chief of Talwandi; Tiloka, the ancestor of Nabha State; and Rama, the ancestor of Patiala State, are outstanding examples. Besides new converts were also made in large numbers.

The Master sent for the Adi Granth from Kartarpur, near Beas, in order to incorporate Guru Tegh Bahadur's hymns in it. The original copy was with the Dhirmalias and they refused to part with it and rather remarked that if Guru Gobind Singh was the Guru, he should make one himself. **It was, therefore, here that Guru Gobind Singh dictated the whole of Granth Sahib as it stands today, to Bhai Mani Singh.** The sacred volume concludes with 'Rag Mala' (1430 pages). It appears that 'Rag Mala' does not form an essential part of Guru Granth Sahib. Macauliffe writes,

"A Mohammadan poet called Alim in A.H. 991 (1583 A.D.) wrote a work in 353 stanzas generally from four to six lines each, called 'Madhava Nal Sangit', which purports to be an account of the love of Madhava Nal and a lady called Kam Kandala. The Rag Mala, which forms the conclusion of Guru Granth Sahib and contains a list of rags and raginis and their subdivisions, is a portion of Alim's work extending from sixty-third to seventy-second stanzas. It is not understood how it was included in the sacred volume. The rags mentioned in it do not correspond with the rags of the Granth Sahib."

This sacred volume is called 'Damdama Sahib di Bir'[20]. This Bir was installed at Hari Mandar Sahib but it is not available NOW. It is not known whether it has been destroyed or taken away by Ahmed Shah Abdali when he plundered the town of Amritsar during one of his raids.

The order of the Nirmala Sikhs was also created here with a view of giving the Sikhs a band of the Sikhs exclusively devoted to the study and preaching of the Sikh faith. The Guru's Darbar here was as splendid as it used to be at Anandpur. Quite a large number of poets and scholars gathered around in the court of the Guru. Due to all of this, Damdama Sahib became a famous educational center. The Guru also reorganized his forces. His strength had increased considerably. Besides regular followers, he had also taken some Dogras and Brars into his service[21].

GURU PROCEEDS TO THE SOUTH TO SEE AURANGZEB:

In response to the Guru's letter called 'Zafarnama', it was here that he received imperial messengers who had come to convey to him the Emperor's wish for a personal meeting. In the Ahkam-i-Alamgiri (Aurangzeb's writing), the receipt of a letter from Guru Gobind Singh is acknowledged by the Emperor and it contains the orders which he issued to Munim Khan of Lahore to reconcile with the Guru and also to make satisfactory arrangements for his travel towards the south. It is also evident from Ahkam-i-Alamgiri that Aurangzeb was anxious to meet the Guru. May be the Emperor wanted to secure peace in the Punjab so that he could concentrate on his schemes to bring the Marahtas to their knees in the south. It was, therefore, on the 30th of October, 1706 (some say it was 20th of October) that the Guru decided to proceed to the south to see

---

20:Copies were prepared of this Bir later on.

21:Koer Singh- Gur Bilas Patshahi 10: 'Everyday would the Guru distribute gold and silver coins, countless soldiers were thus attractedKoer Singh- Gur Bilas Patshahi 10: 'Everyday would the Guru distribute gold and silver coins, countless soldiers were thus attracted to the place.'

Aurangzeb.

The Guru set out in the direction of Rajasthan enroute to Ahmednagar where the Emperor was encamped. From Damdama passing through Kewal, Jhora, he reached Sarsa. Thence he proceeded to Nohar, Bhadra, Sahewa, Madhu Singhana and then to Pushkar, a place of pilgrimage sacred to Brahma. From there he moved to Narainpur, generally known as Dadudwara where saint Dadu had lived and his sect flourished. The Guru paid a visit to the shrine and held a discussion with Mahant Jait Ram. Here the Guru was censured by his Sikhs for lowering his arrow in salutation to Dadu's cemetery. Man Singh quoted the Guru's own written instruction, "Worship not even by mistake Mohammadan or Hindu cemeteries or places of cremation." The Guru explained that he saluted the shrine to test his Sikhs' devotion and their recollection of his instructions. The Guru, however, admitted that he had technically rendered himself to a fine and he cheerfully paid one hundred and twenty-five rupees. Here he met Bhai Daya Singh and Dharam Singh who returned from their official mission with Aurangzeb. Then he reached Baghaur where he received the news of Aurangzeb's death and that the war of succession had broken out among his sons. There was no point now in proceeding any further and he remained there for some time.

Bahadur Shah who was the eldest son of Aurangzeb, hurried back from Peshawar to oppose his younger brother, Azim, who had proclaimed himself as Emperor. Bhai Nand Lal had served prince Bahadur Shah before he permanently moved to the Guru's court. Bahadur Shah, therefore, sought the Guru's help through the good offices of Bhai Nand Lal[22] and in doing so he promised the Guru that he would be fair and just to the Hindus and Muslims alike and undo all the wrongs that his father had done to them. So the Guru helped him with a detachment of his men in the battle of Jaju in which Bahadur Shah became victorious. In grateful regards for the Guru's timely help, Bahadur Shah invited him to Agra where he was being crowned. A royal robe of honor was conferred upon the Guru on July 24, 1707.

During his stay in Agra, the Guru made Dholpur, a place about 25 to 30 miles from Agra, a center of his missionary activities.

22:*Some writers say that Bahadur Shah sent other persons to the Guru.*

He carried his missionary tours in the areas of Mathura, Aligarh, Agra, and also in the states of Bharatpur and Alwar for many months before proceeding to Daccan. Many people became Guru's followers. It is said that the Guru had talks with Emperor Bahadur Shah, but these talks were still inconclusive when the Emperor had to leave for Rajasthan to suppress the revolts of some Rajput chiefs. He requested the Guru to accompany him. By now the news reached Bahadur Shah that his younger brother, Kam Bakhsh, in the Daccan had proclaimed himself the Emperor of India. Bahadur Shah proceeded towards Daccan via Chittorgarh. From there he left for Burhanpur and the Guru accompanied him enroute to Hyderabad. The Guru stayed there for many days and met Jogi Jiwan Das. He also met Mahant Jait Ram of Dadudwara who happened to be there. Both of them told the Guru about one Bairagi Madho Das and his great occult power. He decided to meet with Bairagi Madho Das. In the meantime the Guru was not satisfied with Bahadur Shah's evasive replies in making clear decision against Wazir Khan, the viceroy of Sirhind, and other officers about their atrocities in the Punjab. The Emperor avoided to give a firm reply under one pretext or the other. Accordingly the Guru parted company with the Emperor at Hingoli and moved to Nader where he reached July, 1708.

Some writers like Bute Shah and Malcolm, say that the Guru went to the Daccan because he despaired at the terrible reverses and bereavement which had been his lot and wanted a change. Others say that he joined the Mughal service. Cunningham says that the Guru received a military command in the valley of Godavari.

All these accounts are untrue and irresponsible and show gross irreverence to Sikh faith. It seems that majority of these writers are ignorant of the Sikh fundamentals. It should be pointed out to all these writers that the whole ideology of the Guru (all of Sikh Gurus) is based on:

"Tera kia meetha lagai, Har Nam padarath Nanak Mangai."
(Asa Mohalla 5, p-394)

'Sweet be Thy Will, my Lord
Nanak beseecheth the gift of Nam.'

(Translation of the above)

At the age of nine, Guru Gobind Singh sacrificed his father to save Hinduism and stood face to face with formidable Mughal Empire at its zenith. When his wife asked him where her four sons had gone, he replied,

"What then if thy four are gone?
They yet live, and shall ever live- the Khalsa,
Millions of our brave sons."

In Zafarnama he openly threatened the Emperor when he wrote,

"What though my four sons have been killed, when lives the Khalsa, all my sons! What bravery is it to quench a few sparks of life? Thou art merely exciting a raging fire the more..."

There is no trace of grief or despair in these lines. Therefore, in the presence of such unimpeachable evidence, it is absurd to put faith in the dejection theory.

'Service Theory' can also be rejected in the light of the ideology and the ideals of the Guru. What for he had to have a service under the Mughal government? He was called a 'true king' by his followers and he was actually a true king sitting on the throne of Guru Nanak. As a true king he had vast wealth and true following. Even if for a moment, we listen to these writers- the memory of the wrongs that had been inflicted on him and his followers was too fresh in him to reconcile joining the army of oppression. Nor can this service theory be adjusted with the Guru's commission of Banda Bahadur to the leadership of the Punjab Khalsa. The whole argument is baseless and it rather seems a mud-slinging on the part of these writers to say that the Guru joined the Mughal service.

GURU AT NADER:

At Nader the Guru selected a lovely spot on the bank of the river Godavri. Two reasons are generally given for his choice of this place. Firstly he wanted to see Banda Bairagi and secondly there were eight Ashrams of different religious sects. The Guru wanted to enter into a dialogue with the leaders of the holy camps to show them the true path and to convert them to his own viewpoint. It was perhaps because of this that he immediately started addressing congregations. Crowds of people seeking spiritual light flocked to him. Soon it was indeed a model of 'Anandpur' reproduced in the Daccan.

A news reached here that the Emperor's army had ransacked Sadhaura and treated Pir Budhu Shah as a rebel, for having faith in Guru Gobind Singh whom they considered as a 'Kafir' or infidel.

One day the Guru went to the place of Bairagi Madho Das, a hermit. Finding the Bairagi absent, and on hearing that he possessed supernatural powers who could overthrow anyone who sat on his couch, the Guru took comfort in sitting on it. The Guru's followers killed a goat and had cooked it in the forbidden square of the Bairagi. A disciple went to inform the Bairagi of the Guru's actions. It was a sacrilege to kill an animal at the Bairagi's place and another sacrilege to take possession of the couch which served him as a throne. Bairagi was mad with anger and violently moved headlong towards the Guru. He tried all his powers to hurt the Guru but in vain. When he found himself helpless, he asked the Guru who he was. The Guru replied that he was Gobind Singh. Bairagi was pacified and his anger suddenly transformed into worship. The Divine Light from the Guru's eyes dispelled all darkness from the mind of the Bairagi who immediately knelt before the Master and in total submission admitted that he was his (Guru's) Banda- a slave.

The Master then instructed him on the tenets of Sikh religion and baptized him. He was named Gurbakhsh Singh but continued to be known as Banda or Banda Singh. He had heard from the Sikhs the atrocities of the Muslim rulers in the Punjab

including the massacre of Guru's innocent children, thus, became
ready for any service he could perform for the Master. Upon this
the Guru instructed him to proceed to the Punjab and fight oppression of the rulers upon the Khalsa. Saying this the Guru presented
him with his bow and five arrows and addressed," As long as thou
remainest continent, thy glory shall increase. He who is content,
turneth not away from the combat, his opponents cannot withstand him. Once thou forsakest the Khalsa principles and associate
unlawfully with woman, thy courage shall depart." The Guru
despatched some Sikhs to assist him in this enterprise. Banda took
the oath, bowed and departed. This was an outstanding example of
Guru Gobind Singh's power to make sparrow to hunt the hawk
and make one Sikh fight with one hundred twenty-thousand.
Banda Bahadur who was a hermit wedded to the creed of non-
violence, was made into the greatest general of the time by the
Guru's power.

(Banda Bahadur planted the Guru's flag in a village about
thirty-five miles of Delhi. The Sikhs from all over the Punjab gathered under his banner and made such powerful and devastating
attacks that within a few months they razed Samana, Shahbad,
Sadhaura and Chhat Banur to the ground. Next came Sirhind.
Banda Bahadur made so strong and sweeping attack that the
enemy could not stand against his army. Wazir Khan and his
minister Suchnand were both put to sword. Emperor Bahadur
Shah failed to crush him and died in delusion of victory over the
Sikhs.)

After Banda's departure the Guru lived at various places in
the neighborhood called Shikar Ghat where he used to go hunting,
at Nagina Ghat where a Sikh presented him with a valuable signet
ring which he threw into the river. At the Hira Ghat where he
disposed of a similar valuable diamond ring, and also at a spot now
called Sangat Sahib where he used to give religious instructions to
his followers.

The close connections between the Guru and Emperor Bahadur Shah had alarmed Wazir Khan, the viceroy of Sirhind. He
had ordered the infant sons of the Guru to be bricked alive in the
wall and beheaded. It was he, who was responsible for inflicting
most of the atrocities upon the Sikhs in the Punjab. He feared that
his life would be in danger if the new Emperor and the Guru came

to a compromise. He, therefore, conspired a plot to kill the Guru and he sent two Pathans, Gul Khan alias Jamshed Khan and Ataullah, to assassinate him.

All kinds of people started attending the congregations of the Guru at Nader. Soon the two Pathans also started coming to the assembly which was addressed by the Guru. On the third or fourth day, Jamshed Khan found an opportunity and as Guru Gobind Singh retired to his personal apartment after the evening prayer, he entered the apartment and, wounded him with a dagger. The Guru put him to death immediately, though he himself was wounded seriously. His fleeing companion was stabbed to death by a Sikh who rushed to the Guru's place hearing the noise.

Various views and stories have been expressed with regard to the circumstances of the assassination of the Guru. Cunningham writes that a Pathan merchant who had sold horses to the Guru, came one day and asked for immediate payment. The Guru who was short of funds, asked him to come some other day. The Pathan used an angry gesture, and his uttering of violence provoked the Guru to strike him dead. The body of the Pathan was removed and buried, and his family seemed reconciled to the fate. His sons nursed their revenge, and availed an opportunity of fulfilling it. They succeeded in stealing upon the Guru's retirement, and stabbed him mortally when asleep and unguarded. (Cunningham- History of Sikhs, p-82)

Other writers such as McGregor (History of Sikhs, vol.1 p-99-100) states that the Guru shortly after, realized his mistake and as a recompense for the fate of the victim, the Guru showed special favor to the widow and brought up her son as a father would do. When the boy grew to manhood, he is said to have been incited by the Guru himself to strike him. The boy did it with fatal results for the Guru. Trumpp also believes in this version and to give a rationale to it, states that the Guru had been disgusted with life and wanted to end it.

These stories are absolutely baseless. These writers should understand who the Guru was. Guru Gobind Singh was sitting on the divine throne of Guru Nanak, therefore, he was the embodiment of Divine Light; the Divine never feels disgusted or dejected. The Guru never uttered any word of grief nor did he show any sign of despair during the unparallel sufferings he went through. It is not recorded any place in Guru's sermons or writings that he had ever expressed a sigh of grief. When Nura Mahi brought the news of the brutal massacre of his younger children, the Guru thanked God,"Father, mother and four sons, all were Thy trust to me. Today I have been successful and happy in restoring that entire trust back to Thee." One can hardly find such an example in the annals of human history.

In recent years fresh light is thrown by a Hukamnama according to which no demand for immediate payment was put before the Guru. The Pathan actually refused to make any demand when reminded of it by the Guru. This is shown by Hukamnana (letter of appreciation issued by the Guru) which the Guru granted to the Pathan for his good and friendly behavior and which is still preserved by the descendants of that Pathan. (Kartar Singh: Life of Guru Gobind Singh, p-263)

A probe into the historical circumstances leads to the Emperor's involvement. The Emperor was enraged with the Guru for deputing Banda to Punjab to renew the struggle and kill Wazir Khan. It seems that the Emperor was also afraid that the Guru might join the Marahattas in their battle against the Mughals during the time of his struggle with his brother at Hyderabad. It was perhaps for this reason, he was not leaving the Guru alone. Bahadur Shah had the mistaken belief that the Guru's death would be a fatal blow to his scheme of renewing the revolution in Punjab, he, therefore, entered into conspiracy with two Pathans deputed by Wazir Khan to put an end to Guru's life. The following historical facts testify this view:

On October 28, 1708, the Emperor ordered that a dress of mourning be presented to the son of Jamshed Khan Afghan who had been killed by Guru Gobind Singh. The imperial newsletter of Bahadur Shah's court records reads:

"Keh Guru Gobind Singh Rai Jamshed Khan Afghan ra bajan Kushtah bud khilat-e-Matami bapisar-i-Khan Mazkur Mrahmat shud." (Akhbarat-i-Darbar-i-Mualla, dated 24 Shaba, second year of Bahadur Shah (Oct. 28, 1708) quoted by Dr. Ganda Singh in Makhiz-i-Twarikh-i-Sikhan, p-83)

Jamshed Khan was not a high dignitary upon whom the Emperor had to bestow high honors. He was only a spy of Wazir Khan.

Two days later on October 30, 1708, the Emperor ordered for the grant of a robe of mourning to Guru Gobind Singh's family.

It means that the Emperor treated Jamshed Khan and Guru Gobind Singh on equal footing, thereby confirming that Jamshed Khan enjoyed the patronage of the Emperor.

"On November 11, 1708 it was represented that the deceased Guru left huge property." The courtiers asked how should it be disposed? It was ordered that such chattels would not replete the imperial treasury. "This was the property of a darvesh (saint). There should be no interference with it," ordered the Emperor.

The Emperor's refusal to attach the property of the Guru against the will of his courtiers shows his diplomacy and cunningness. It was purely an eye-wash of his complicity, a pious fraud, writes H.R. Gupta in his 'A history of Sikh Gurus', p-240.

The Guru's wound was immediately stitched by the Emperor's European surgeon and within a few days it appeared to have been healed. Soon after when the Guru tugged at a hard strong bow, the imperfectly healed wound burst opened and caused profuse bleeding. It was now clear to the Guru that the call of the Father from Heaven had come and he, therefore, gave his last and enduring message of his mission to the assembly of the Khalsa. He then **opened the Granth Sahib, placed five paise and a coco-nut before it and solemnly bowed to it as his SUCCESSOR, GURU GRANTH SAHIB.** Saying 'Waheguru ji ka Khalsa, Waheguru ji ki Fateh', he circumambulated the sacred volume and proclaimed," O beloved Khalsa, let him who desireth to behold me, behold the Guru Granth. Obey the Granth Sahib. It is the visible body of the Gurus. And let him who desireth to meet me, diligently search its hymns." He then sang his self-composed hymn:[23]

> "Agya bhai Akal ki tabhi chalayo Panth
> Sabh Sikhan ko hukam hai Guru manyo Granth
> Guru Granth Ji manyo pargat Guran ki deh
> Jo Prabhu ko milbo chahe khoj shabad mein le
> Raj karega Khalsa aqi rahei na koe
> Khwar hoe sabh milange bache sharan jo hoe."

Translation of the above:

> "Under orders of the Immortal Being, the Panth was created. All the Sikhs are enjoined to accept the Granth as their Guru.

> Consider the Guru Granth as embodiment of the Gurus. Those who want to meet God, can find Him in its hymns. The Khalsa shall rule, and its opponents will be no more, Those separated will unite and all the devotees shall be saved."

He, in grateful acknowledgement of the spiritual benefactions of the founder of his religion, uttered a Persian distich, the translation of which is:
> "Gobind Singh obtained from Guru Nanak
> Hospitality, the sword, victory, and prompt assistance."

(These lines were impressed on a seal made by the Sikhs after the Guru left for his heavenly abode, and were adopted by

23: *Surjeet Singh Gandhi-History of the Sikh Gurus, p-466.*

Ranjit Singh for his coinage after he had assumed the title of Maharaja in the Punjab)

The Guru then left for his heavenly abode. The Sikhs made preparations for his final rites as he had instructed them, the Sohila was chanted and Parsahd (sacred food) was distributed.

While all were mourning the loss of the Guru, a Sikh arrived and said," You suppose that the Guru is dead. I met him this very morning riding his bay horse. After bowing to him when I asked whither he was going, he smiled and replied that he was going to the forest on a hunting excursion."

The Sikhs who heard this statement arrived at the conclusion that **it was all the Guru's play, that he dwelt in uninterrupted bliss, that he showed himself wherever he was remembered. He who treasures even a grain of the Lord's love in his heart, is the blessed one and the Guru reveals himself to such a devotee in mysterious ways.** Wherefore for such a Guru who had departed bodily to Heaven, there ought to be no mourning.

The Master returned to his Eternal Home on the 5th of the bright half of Katik, Sambat 1765 (7th October, 1708 A.D.). He was 42 years of age.

Before leaving this world, the Guru had ordained," If any one erects a shrine in my honor, his offspring shall perish."

The Sikh temple at Nader is called Abchalnagar. It was built by Maharaja Ranjit Singh in 1832 in defiance of the Guru's interdiction. After Maharaja Ranjit Singh, the rule of his dynasty, therefore, came to an end. Guru's prophecy was fulfilled.

GURU GRANTH SAHIB
(1708 - For Ever)

CONCEPT OF GURU IN SIKHISM:

In Sikh religion the word 'Guru' is not denoted to its usual meaning such as a teacher or an expert or a guide or a human body, but this is composed of two words- GU and RU.

GU means darkness and RU means Light i.e.
Light that dispels all darkness is called

JOT OR DIVINE LIGHT.

When Impersonal God manifested His attributes in person, that person was called Guru Nanak:

'Jot rup har aap gur nanak kahayo.'
(Swayas Bhattan- p.1408)

Guru Nanak was thus the embodiment of Divine Light.

'In the true Guru (Nanak), He installed His Own Spirit, Through him, God revealed Himself.'
(Asa di Var, pauri 6, page 466)

Guru Nanak seated Bhai Lehna (later called Guru Angad) on his throne, placed five paise and a coco-nut before him, and then bowed to him declaring him as GURU ANGAD. When Guruship was conferred on Guru Angad, he too became the embodiment of Divine Light.

'Jot uha jugat sai, seh kaya pher paltiae.'
(Sata Balwand, p-966)
'The Divine Light was the same,
The Way and Mode were the same,
The Master had merely changed the body.'

The most important point to remember here is that the people bowed to Guru Angad ONLY when JOT was installed in him. Nobody bowed to him before the Guruship, which means the Sikhs did not bow to the human body (of Guru Angad) because human body was not Guru, but to the Divine Light which was passed on to that body by Guru Nanak.

The same process of conferring the Guruship continued till the tenth Guru. Then the tenth Master, Guru Gobind Singh seated the Adi Granth (the Holy Scripture- the Divine Word) on the throne of Guru Nanak, placed five paise and a coco-nut before it and then bowed declaring it as the Last Guru forever. When the Guruship was passed on, Guru Granth Sahib too became the embodiment of Divine Light. It should, therefore, be remembered very clearly that bowing before Guru Granth Sahib as Sikhs do, **is not a bowing before a book, but it is a bowing before the Divine Light or JOT (Guru) which was passed on when the Guruship was conferred upon it.**

In Sikh religion the word 'Guru' has been used in three inter-related aspects:

Firstly it is used for God, the All-Pervading Divine Spirit, the Divine Light:

'The Guru is Beneficent, the Sanctuary of peace,
The Guru is the Light of three worlds[1],
He is the Eternal Being,
O Nanak, he who believeth in Him, attaineth peace.'
(Slok Mohalla 1, p-137)

'The Guru is All-Powerful,
The Guru is the Formless Lord,
The Guru is the Highest, Fathomless and Limitless,
Ineffable is His praise; what can a sayer say?'
(Sri Rag Mohalla 5, p-52)

1: *Three worlds- one world is whatever is on our plane, second one is whatever is above us, and the third one is whatever is below us.*

The Guru is Infinite God Himself
Nanak, meditate upon such a Guru day and night.'
(Asa Mohalla 5, p-387)
Secondly the word 'Guru' is also used for Guru Nanak as he was
the Embodiment of God's Light:

'Guru Nanak is the perfect Guru,
With the true Guru I meditateth upon God.'
(Ramkali Mohalla 4, p-882)

'Guru Nanak is the true Guru,
The true Guru taketh me to God.'
(Kanra Mohalla 4, p-1310)

'The Guru and God are one,
Divine Master pervadeth everywhere.'
(Sri Rag Mohalla 5, p-53)

Thirdly the word 'Guru' is used for Gurbani, the Divine Word.
Since Gurbani came direct from God, and **as there is no difference
between God and His order (Divine Word), Gurbani is Guru too:**

'The Word is the Guru,
And the Guru is the Word,
The Guru's Word is full of life-giving Elixir,
Whosoever shall obey, what the Word commandeth,
Verily he shall get salvation.'
(Nat Mohalla 4, p-982)

'The Word is the True Guru and True Guru is the Word,
And the Word revealeth the path of salvation.'
(Kanra Mohalla 4, p-1310)

DIVINE WORD CAME DIRECT FROM GOD:

Guru Granth Sahib does not narrate the life story of Guru
Nanak, but each and every word is dedicated to the Glory of the
Almighty God only. It is not a reproduction of earlier religions, but
the Divine Word (Gurbani) came   to the Gurus direct from God.

Guru Nanak stated that it was not his philosophy, it was not his understanding and it was not his thinking, but the Word was coming to him direct from God and he was simply delivering His message to the world. As he confirms:

'O Lalo[2], as comes the Divine Word from Lord to me,
So do I narrate it.'
(Tilang Mohalla 1, p-722)

'I have said what Thou commandeth me to say.'
(Wadhans Mohalla 1,p-566)

This was repeatedly confirmed and emphasized by all the Gurus in their Bani such as:

'From God springs ambrosial Gurbani
The exalted Guru narrates and preaches the same to world.'
(Majh Mohalla 3, p-125)

'This Word comes from Him, Who hath created the World.'
(Mohalla 4, p-306)

'This Word that hath come from God, It dispelleth all woes
and worries.'
(Sorath Mohalla 5, p-628)

'I speak but the Will of the Lord,
For, the Lord's devotee narrateth the Word of the Lord.'
(Sorath Mohalla 5, p-629)

'Whatever the Lord hath instructed me,
Hear, O my brother.'
(Tilang Mohalla 9, p-727)

The tenth Master, Guru Gobind Singh established the same truth that it was God's Word that was being revealed through the Gurus:

2: *Lalo was Guru's disciple.*

'Whatever the Lord sayeth to me
I say the same to the world.'
                    (Guru Gobind Singh)

The Janamsakhi (biography) reveals that Guru Nanak many times said to his minstrel Mardana, "Mardana, start playing the rebec, Gurbani (Divine Word) is coming." And the Divine Word was then recorded. **That Divine Word is GURBANI- Guru Granth Sahib.**

AUTHENTICITY:

Guru Granth Sahib was not written by the devotees after the Gurus had gone, but it was dictated and compiled by the Gurus themselves. Thus it is the **Authentic Divine Scripture.** Nobody is allowed to change even a comma or a period out of 1430 pages. The seventh Guru's son, Ram Rai, changed the meaning of only one verse to please the Emperor, Aurangzeb, upon which he was excommunicated forever by his father (the seventh Guru), thereby establishing the fact that no one could ever change the God's Word, the Gurbani.

Max Arthur Macauliffe, an English writer, delivered a speech in Punjabi language at Akal Bunga, Amritsar in 1899, the translation of which is:

"There is another point to the merit of the Sikh religion that the founders of other religions in this world never wrote even one line with their own hands. You might have heard that there was a very famous Greek philosopher called Pythagoras who had many followers, but he never left behind anything written by him from which we could have known about the principles of his sect. After him came the second Greek philosopher named Socrates who was born in 500 B.C. He became a very famous religious leader who claimed that he was receiving Divine instructions from God within himself, which persuaded him to do good and prohibited from doing any evil deeds. But he too never left anything behind written by him which could have shed light on his philosophy and its principles. Whatever we know about him, has only come through the writings of his follower, Plato. Besides there came Mahatma Buddh in India and he never wrote anything with his hands. After that came Christ who did not write anything himself. His teachings are only known through Bible. However the Sikh Gurus acted quite opposite to all these religious leaders that they   them selves dictated their message of Truth and compiled Guru Granth Sahib. In that respect the Sikh religion is far ahead than others."

(Translation Sri Guru Granth Sahib- pothi 1,p-gaga, by Bhai Vir Singh)

GURU GRANTH SAHIB BEGINS UNIQUELY:

In Hindu mythology the word 'OM' always meant for God as monotheistic. Then they started interpreting it as more than one God. Guru Nanak put an integer '1' before it and a kar (a semi-circle) after it. Thus it becomes 'EK-OM-KAR' and by doing so, he sealed the position for ever meaning **'There is One and only One God'**. Therefore Guru Granth Sahib uniquely begins with integer One ('1').

Guru Granth Sahib begins with Mool-Mantar or the Preamble of Japji which is the Essence of the whole Guru Granth Sahib:

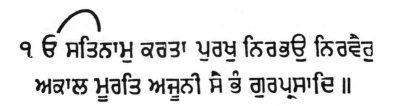

੧ ੴ ਸਤਿਨਾਮੁ ਕਰਤਾ ਪੁਰਖੁ ਨਿਰਭਉ ਨਿਰਵੈਰੁ ਅਕਾਲ ਮੂਰਤਿ ਅਜੂਨੀ ਸੈ ਭੰ ਗੁਰਪ੍ਸਾਦਿ ॥

Ek-Onm-Kar	There is But One God
Sat-Nam	He is the Eternal Truth
Karta-Purkh	The Creator, All-Pervading Divine Spirit
Nirbhao-Nirvair	Unfearful, Without hate and enmity
Akal-Murat	Immortal Entity
Ajuni, Saibhang	Unborn, Self-Existent
Gurparsad	Realized by His Own Grace (the Guru)

The next verse is generally called Sach (True) Mantar:

Jap	Meditate upon
Aad Sach	Who was True before the Creation
Jugad Sach	Who was True in the beginning of Creation
Haibhi Sach	Who is True now, and
Nanak Hosibhi Sach	O Nanak, Who shall be True for ever.

Guru Arjan Dev had accomplished a task by authenticating the diverse compositions and prepared the Adi Granth for the benefit of his followers. Since the work had remained where it was left, Guru Gobind Singh included in it the Bani of Guru Tegh Bahadur and put the seal of Finality on it. Subsequently this finalized version of the Adi Granth was invested with the Guruship by Guru Gobind Singh.

Guru Granth Sahib is the only refuge for a man tossed about in the furious ocean of worldly existence. It helps a person to live by certain directives or moral codes which are necessary for the achievement of salvation.

Man is the epitome of God's creation. This human body is attained after transmigrating through various lower species. Guru Granth Sahib advocates the excellence and utility of human life because it is through human form that a person can attain final emancipation. Man has great capacity for conscious awareness which helps him reach the desired spiritual goal. Therefore, all teachings and exhortations for spiritual enhancement are addressed to man in Guru Granth Sahib. Man's material values are listed as false, 'koor':

> "False are kings, false their subjects, false the whole world;
> False are mansions, false palaces, false those who dwell
> therein;
> False is gold, false sliver, false he who weareth them;
> False husbands, false wives, they pine away and become dust.
> Man who is false, loveth what is false, and forgetteth the
> Creator.
> With whom contact friendship? The whole world passeth
> away.
> False is sweetness, false honey, in falsehood shiploads are
> drowned-
> Nanak humbly asserteth- Except Thee, O God, everything
> is thoroughly false."
> (Slok Mohalla 1, p-468)

Guru Granth Sahib signifies the importance of Nam by identifying it with the Guru. Nam releases man from all his previous sins, sorrows, sufferings and cycle of birth and death. **No rituals, no alms, no sacrifices, no fasts and no penances equal Nam.**

Guru Granth Sahib initiates a disciple on the path of spiritual progress and guides him at the various stages of his journey to God. It is a ship that steers clear a devotee through the ocean of Maya (Materialism), thus, leading the human soul to its ultimate destination which is the Absolute Bliss.

> "The fearful ocean of the world is dangerous and
> formidable; it hath no shore or limit,
> No boat, no raft, no pole, and no boatman;
> But the true Guru hath a vessel for the terrible ocean,
> and ferrieth over him on whom he looketh with favor."
> (Sri Rag Mohalla 1, p-59)

Guru Granth Sahib is completely authentic and is preserved in its original form. It is a highly valuable possession which Sikhs have received from God through Guru Nanak and is held in supreme reverence by them.

A BRIEF OUTLINE OF FUNDAMENTALS OF SIKHISM

The seed for the reformation of humanity which was sown by Guru Nanak and watered by his successors, ripened in the time of Guru Gobind Singh and culminated in the creation of the Khalsa. The sword that carved the Khalsa's way to sublime glory was undoubtedly forged by Guru Gobind Singh but its steel was provided by Guru Nanak. **The whole program of Guru Nanak's initiation reached its exalted state of finality when the tenth Nanak (Guru Gobind Singh) passed on 'Gur Nanak Jot' to the Adi Granth, Holy Scripture- par excellence, and proclaimed it as Guru Granth Sahib, the last Guru for ever.**

From the moment of its initiation by Guru Nanak to its consecration by the tenth Master, Guru Gobind Singh, a period of 239 years, Sikhism acquired its holy scripture, signs and symbols, and unmistakable form or stance. Transformation from one Guru to the other happened in the same way as one lamp were to lit from another. The holy transformation of ten Gurus is recognized as ONE, since all of them came from the same Divine Flame in continuity of the same Divine Mission. The establishment of Guruship, the line of succession, the founding of Amritsar and other seats of Sikhism, the compilation of the Adi Granth, the institution of Sangat (holy congregation) and Pangat (Guru's free kitchen), the martyrdom of the Gurus, the panoply and plumage of power, the investiture of the Khalsa, all these and many other events which make the Sikh chronicle, give Sikh religion a color of the highest distinction.

In Sikhism, Guruship does not stand for mere order of mystics, since the Guru attached no values to renunciation of worldly life. Those who practiced renunciation such as Yogis and Sidhas were condemned as shirkers of responsibilities- they were considered as escapists and runaways from social responsibilities and obligations. In Sikhism a man is called upon to accept the Will of God and thus sublimate his suffering and loss. Sikhism believing in the conquest of sorrow and suffering, stipulates ceaseless endeavor.

PURPOSE OF LIFE:

According to the Guru, moral life is not a matter of a few commandments or a code or a ritual, but the fruit of a life directed towards spiritual quest involving incredibly hard discipline. Most people generally believe in enjoying materialistic life to the brim. Thus, the life goes on till a person ultimately finds oneself physically spent up and spiritually bankrupt. Lured by the charm of success in this materialistic world, one gives little or no thought to the Eternal values of life.

According to the eastern religions, there are eighty-four lakhs (8.4 million) of lives in the world, half of which are in the water and the other half are on the land and air. All life is transient. It moves on and on through the wheel of transmigration in accordance with its 'karmas' or actions good or bad. The human soul is achieved after transmigrating through various lower species as Gurbani (the Divine Word) confirms it:

"In how many births wert thou a worm or a moth!
In how many births an elephant, a fish, or a deer!
In how many births a bird or a serpent!
In how many births wert thou yoked as a horse or an ox!
Meet the Lord of the world, this is the time to meet Him
After long period of time hast thou attained human body."
                    (Gauri Guareri Mohalla 5, p-176)

The Gurmat (Guru's teaching) defines the purpose of life as:

"This time having born as human being
This is thy turn to meet the Supreme Lord.
Thy other activities will be of no avail at the end,
Seek the company of the holy men
And only contemplate on God.
Set thy mind on crossing the sea of life,
For life is being wasted away
In pursuits of pleasures of the world."
                    (Asa Mohalla 5, p-12)

Human soul is the door for liberation, but enchanted by the mate-

rialistic world, one loses highly precious chance of life:
"O man, thou comest to earn merit (spiritual)
But how vainly art thou engaged
While the night of life passeth away."
(Sri Rag Mohalla 5, p-43)

"Sleeping through, man wasteth the night,
Eating, he wasteth the day away
And lo, the Jewel of life is bartered away for a trite."
(Gauri Bairagan Mohalla 1, p-156)

"Having wandered through eighty-four lakhs of species
Thou hast obtained the very precious human life,
Nanak, remember thou then the Nam
For thy days are numbered."
(Sri Rag Mohalla 5, p-50)

"Without the Name of God, birth into this world is fruitless,
Without Nam one eats poison, speaks evil, dies without
merit and transmigrates."
(Bhairo Mohalla 1, p-1127)
"O God, the mothers of those who keep not God's Name in
their hearts ought to have been barren,
For they who wander without the Name, pine away and die
in agony."
(Jaitsari Mohalla 4, p-697)

The purpose of human life in Sikhism is not to attain paradise or Swarga of the popular Hindu conception, but to seek God, and be united with Him. The ultimate goal of Sikh religion is to merge with the Supreme Soul and then enjoy the Uninterrupted Bliss for ever. A Sikh aspires for spiritual union with the Lord- a state of Bliss. Human life is an opportunity to attain that goal, if it is missed, a person falls back in the cycle of birth and rebirth.

CONCEPT OF GOD IN SIKHISM:

The definition of God is given in the very opening sentence of Guru Granth Sahib, which is called Mool-Mantar (Preamble of

Japji):

> There is but One God
> He is the Eternal Truth
> The Creator, All-Pervading Divine Spirit
> Unfearful, Without hate and enmity
> Immortal Entity, Unborn, Self-Existent, and
> He is realized by His Own Grace.
>
> Meditate upon
> Who was True before the Creation
> Who was True in the beginning of the Creation
> Who is True now, and
> O Nanak, Who shall be True for Ever.

As a matter of fact the whole of Guru Granth Sahib is the explanation of the above definition. The Guru elaborates the concept of God in Rag Sorath:

> The Unseen, Infinite, Inaccessible, Inapprehensible God is
>   not subject to death or destiny.
> He is of no caste, unborn, self-existent, without fear or doubt.
> I am a sacrifice to the Truest of the true.
> He hath no form, or color, or outline;
> He becometh manifest by the true Word.
> He hath no mother, father, son, or kinsman;
> He feeleth not lust, and hath no wife
> Or family; He is pure, endless, and infinite; all light is
>   Thine, O Lord.
> God is concealed in every heart; His light is in every heart.
> He whose understanding's adamantine doors are opened by
> the Guru's instruction, fixeth his gaze on the Fearless One.
> God having created animals made them subject to death, and
>   retained all contrivances in His Own power.
> He who serveth the True Guru obtaineth the real boon, and is
>   delivered by repeating the Word.
> Truth is contained in pure vessels; few there are whose acts
>   are pure.
> By seeking Thy protection, saith Nanak, the soul blendeth
>   with the Supreme Soul.

(Sorath Mohalla 1, p-597)

God is both Impersonal (Nirgun) and Personal (Sargun). Impersonal God is Formless and beyond the human reach. When He reveals Himself through His Creation, He becomes related and personal. It is just like the rays coming out of the sun. The source is Formless, and the whole universe is His Personal form. No form howsoever unique it may be, is independent of Him. Infinite can manifest into unlimited number of finites, but any number of finites, alone or together, cannot be equal to the Infinite. **So any finite form cannot be worshipped as God, Who is Infinite and Formless:**

> "God is Formless, colorless, markless,
> He is casteless, classless, creedless;
> His form, hue, shape and garb
> Cannot be described by any one,
> He is the Spirit of Eternity,
> Self-Radiant, He shineth in His Splendor."
>
> (Guru Gobind Singh)

God neither takes birth nor does He die:

> "Burnt be the tongue that says
> The Lord takes birth and undergoes death."
>
> (Bhairon Mohalla 5, p-1136)

The Guru warned that he was not God, and those who called him God, should fall into hell:

> "Whosoever calleth me God
> May fall into hell."
>
> (Guru Gobind Singh)

i) God protects His saints and devotees from dangers, unless He wills that their sufferings and martyrdom should serve a higher purpose. To protect the righteous is His Sovereign Characteristic (Birdh). In the face of some acute dangers, saints have prayed for aid and intervention of God to help them in distress.

God came to their help and protected them in a miraculous way. The stories of Prahlad, Dhru and others, and the autobiographic statements of Namdev and Kabir in Guru Granth Sahib, show His Sovereign Power to protect the righteous. Such miracles are part of the doctrine of divine Providence and Preservation. These supernatural miracles of God should be distinguished from the miracles of human beings performed by their occult powers, which in Sikhism are considered dangerous and unbecoming.

ii) 'As you sow, so shall you reap', leads to the theory of 'Karma', actions, good or bad, where a person is rewarded for his good actions and punished for his bad deeds. Therefore, according to the theory of Karma, a worst sinner will always suffer for his deeds and can never attain salvation. Guru Nanak has rejected this stating that pardoning even the worst sinner is the Sovereign Characteristic (Birdh) of God:

> "Patat pavan prabh birdh tumaro."
> (Bilawal Mohalla 5, p-829)
> 'Redeeming the repentant sinner, is Thy Characteristic.'
> (Translation of the above)

The Guru emphasizes that the sinner whom no body affords protection in the whole world, if he surrenders before the Almighty, becomes pure, that is he is blessed by His Grace:

> "Jis papi kau milai na dhoee Saran aawai ta nirmal hoee."
> (Bhairon Mohalla 5, p-1141)]

> 'The sinner who is patronless in the world When surrenders before God, gets deliverance.'
> (Translation of the above)

The Guru reiterates that to save the saints, to protect the righteous, and even to redeem the repentant sinners is Paramount Characteristic of God.

CONCEPT OF NAM (DIVINE NAME):

According to Gurmat (Guru's teaching), before the creation, God lived Absolutely by Himself, Formless. When He made
Himself manifest, He first formed Himself into NAM (Divine
Name) and then created Nature. After creating Nature, He did not
go away from it, rather He sustained His creation with His Own
presence into it, and felt delighted.

"Aapinai aap sajio aapinai rachio Nao
Dui kudrat sajiai kar asan ditho chao."
(Asa Mohalla 1- pauri 1, p-463)

"God created Himself and assumed Name
Second besides Himself He created Nature
Seated in Nature He watches with delight what He creates."
(Translation of the above)

1) NAM (Divine Name) and God are not two different entities. Nam is just another aspect of the Almighty, still Formless.
Nam is the total expression of all that God is. Nam sustains everything:

"Nam sustains and controls all beings
Nam supports the universe and its regions."
(Gauri Sukhmani Mohalla 5, 16-5, p-284)

2) Nam is not expressed as mere noun and it does not mean
that there is a special name of God and by enchanting of which, one
will meet Him. He is Infinite and can be called with infinite names,
but who can count His infinite names? The enlightened and the
blessed ones remember Him through His Attributes:

"Tav sarb nam kathai kavan
Karm nam barnat sumat."
(Guru Gobind Singh- Jap Sahib)

3) God may be called by countless names by the devotees,
who create these names according to the attributes of their God-

head, but the first and the foremost name of God is clearly depicted as 'SAT' (Eternal Truth) which shows the ever-existence of God:

"Kirtam nam kathai terei jihba
Satnam tera pra purbla."

(Maru Mohalla 5, p-1083)

4) The word NAM is a mystic Word used in practical religious life and in discipline of meditation. God is remembered by His attributive names. There is another aspect of it called true Name which emanates from a prophet's personal experience. It emerges from a vision that the Prophet has of the Divine Being. Such a mystic Word in Sikh religion is called **'Waheguru'** or Wonderful God or 'Thou art Wonderful'. True Name is not the word by which we describe an object, but the total power, quality and character of **Reality**. Through the word 'Waheguru' the prophet has tried to sum up mystic power and experience of His presence all around. Prophets have given us Divine Names of the nameless God, which reflect His presence in our consciousness. Contemplation or meditation on true Name (Waheguru) is called practicing the presence of God in one's conscious.

5) Gurbani (Divine Word) itself is NAM.

a) Gurbani itself is Nam:

"Gurmukh bani nam hai, nam ridai vasaie."
(Sarang ki Var-pauri, p-1239)

b) The term 'Nam Japo' means to remember God and to invoke His presence in one's conscious. All modes of meditation take the devotee into the presence of God, but according to Gurbani, Hari Kirtan, the musical recitation of Gurbani, is the super form of meditation. It invokes one's consciousness to the maximum level, into the presence of God:

"Har kirat utam Nam hai vich kaljug karni sar."
(Kanre ki Var Mohalla 4, p-1314)

c) The Gurmat explains that the recitation of the word 'Har Har..' is Nam Japna:

"Har har har har nam hai gurmukh pavai koei."
(Kanre ki Var Mohalla 4, p-1313)

d) Salvation cannot be attained without Nam. In other words anything that delivers salvation is Nam. Since Gurbani delivers salvation, therefore, Gurbani is Nam:

"Sachi bani mithi amritdhar
Jinh piti tis mokhdwar."
(Malar Mohalla 1, p-1275)

'The True Bani is sweet-nectar
Whosoever is devoted to it, attaineth salvation."
(Translation of the above)

"Sachi bani sion dhare piyar
Tako pavai mokhdwar."
(Dhanasari Mohalla 1, p-661)

'Whosoever devoted to Eternal Bani
Will get deliverance."
(Translation of the above)

It is therefore, very clear and evident that any form of recitation of Gurbani, may be simple reading with attention and devotion or meditation on any Sabad of Gurbani or Kirtan of Gurbani, **is fully deemed as Nam Japna (meditation on Nam)**, that is to invoke the presence of God in one's conscious.

It may be mentioned here that there are small sects who mislead the innocent Sikhs on the subject of Gurbani and Nam. These sect leaders very emphatically say to the innocent Sikhs," Gurbani says that one must meditate on Nam, but Gurbani is not Nam. Come on, we will give you Nam." Then they whisper in their ears some broken sentence of Gurbani which they call Nam, and warn them not to tell any one; if ever they disclose this Nam to any one, some curse will fall on them. In this way they run their cults (shops). Thus, innocent Sikhs and others are lured and misled into their fold. The Sikhs should, therefore, be very careful from such sects. Those who try to say that Gurbani is not Nam, they are either misguided or are deceitful. According to Gurmat (Guru's teaching), Gurbani is everything:

Gurbani is Nam: "Gurmukh bani Nam hai.."
                      (Sarang ki Var-pauri, p-1239)

Gurbani is Guru: "Bani Guru, Guru hai Bani..."
                      (Nat Mohalla 4, p-982)

Gurbani is Nirankar: "Wauh wauh bani nirankar hai
                          Tis jiwad avar na koi."
                          (Slok Mohalla 3, p-515)

                      'Wauh wauh Bani is the Formless One
                      There is none as great as He."
                      (Translation of the above)

Gurbani is every Nad and Ved:

                "Sabh nad beid gurbani Man rata sarang pani."
                (Ramkli Mohalla 1, p-879)

It is, therefore, Nam that ultimately leads a person to Eternal Bliss. For God consciousness, one must come in contact with Nam, but without Guru one cannot attain Nam and would wander away in the darkness.

"Were a hundred moons to appear
Were a thousand suns to arise
There would still be utter darkness
If there were no Guru."
                (Asa di Var, Mohalla 2, p-463)

"Let no one in the world remain in doubt

That it could ever be possible to be saved without the Guru."
(Gaund Mohalla 5, p-864)
"In this age of falsehood, Nam lieth hidden
Though the Lord filleth all hearts,
The Jewel of Nam becomes manifest in the hearts of only
those Who resort to the Guru's refuge."
(Parbhati Mohalla 3, p-1334)

"All repeat God's Name, yet He is not attained
But when through the Grace of the Guru
God comes to reside in the mind
It is only then one's life becomes fruitful."
(Gujri Mohalla 3, p-491)

CONCEPT OF GURU:

The concept of Guru has been explained in the previous chapters. A yogi asked Guru Nanak who his Guru was? He replied,"The Word[1] is Guru." God anointed Guru Nanak with His Word, His Wisdom (Logos), and the Guru's whole personality was Word-personified. The Guru made it very clear that his human body was not the Guru, and the mere outward glimpse of the Guru, or the outward profession of faith in him, could not bring the disciple close to the Guru. The light of the Word within his heart was the real Guru and the disciple should approach him with a receptive mind to receive His Light.

BAPTISM IN SIKHISM:

Nam is the whole source which takes a person back into the Unmanifest One. Guru is the sole Channel to Nam. The Gurmat tells us that the Jewel of Nam becomes manifest in the hearts of only those who resort to Guru's refuge.

How do we resort to Guru's refuge?

When we go to the Guru, he gives us Nam and then we meditate

1:*Sidh Gosht page 938.*

upon the Guru given Nam which in turn takes us back to our destination, the Almighty. **How do we go to the Guru?**
In Sikhism the one and the only one way to go to the Guru is through Baptism. A Sikh has to take Pauhal or Amrit, from the Five Beloved Ones (Panj Pyare), then he becomes of the Guru or Guruwala. Without baptism a Sikh remains without Guru or Nigura.

> "Nigure ka hai nau bura."
>
> (Rag Asa Mohalla 3 Pati, p-435)

Everybody repeats God's Name, but simply repeating it He is not attained. When through the Grace of the Guru, Nam enshrines the mind, only then one's efforts of meditation become fruitful. Without the Grace of the Guru, a Sikh cannot attain his objective of salvation. In order to seek the Guru's Grace, we have to go to the Guru and that is only done through baptism.

> "Ram Ram sabh ko kahai kahiai ram na hoi
> Gurparsadi Ram man vasai ta fal pavai koi."
>
> (Gujri Mohalla 3, p-491)

> 'All repeat God's Name, yet He is not attained
> But when through the Grace of the Guru
> God comes to reside in the mind
> It is only then one's life becomes fruitful.'
>
> (Translation of the above)

The question arises, is there any other way for a Sikh to attain his objective of salvation?

No, says Gurmat, there is no other way. This world is a vast and formidable ocean of Maya (materialism). A Sikh has to cross this ocean to meet his Beloved God. The ocean seems endless and there are countless obstructions in the way. In order to get through this dangerous and formidable sea, one needs a strong ship and that ship is only the Guru, the Divine Light. In order to get into the Guru's ship, a Sikh needs a passport, and that passport is baptism.

"Bhavjal bikham dravno na kandhi na par
Na beri na tulha na tis vanj malar
Satgur bhai ka boihtha nadri par utar."
(Sri Rag Mohalla 1, p-59)

'The fearful ocean of the world is dangerous and formidable;
it hath no shore or limit,
No boat, no raft, no pole, and no boatman;
But the true Guru hath a vessel for the terrible ocean, and
ferrieth over him on whom he looketh with favor.'
(Translation of the above)

The ceremony of baptism was started by the very first
Guru. Those persons who became Guru's Sikhs, were baptized by
the Guru. By mere attending the assembly of the Guru, one did not
automatically become a Sikh of the Guru. From the first to the tenth
Guru, baptism ceremony consisted of taking Charanpauhal i.e.
Guru's toe (or feet) was dipped in the water which was then given
to the devotee to drink and also Gurmantar (Word) was given by
the Guru. After the creation of the Khalsa, the tenth Guru changed
this tradition and entrusted this ceremony to the Five Beloved
Ones. After that those who accepted the Guru's religion (Sikh
religion), were baptized and they were called the Khalsa (the word
Sikh and Khalsa became synonymous). The Guru issued instructions to all to get baptized and join the order of the Khalsa. **Guru
Gobind Singh was the first one to get baptized by the Five
Beloved Ones.** Let it, therefore, be very clear to every Sikh that in
order to get into Guru's fold and seek Guru's grace, one will have
to get baptized by the Five Beloved Ones. Only then one's efforts
towards spiritualism become fruitful. From Guru Nanak to Guru
Gobind Singh, those who called themselves Guru's Sikhs, were
always baptized by the Gurus. It is the Guru's order for every Sikh
to get baptized and therefore after obeying his order one can get
accepted by the Guru:

"Hukam maniai howai parvan ta khasmai ka mahal paisi."
(Asa di Var pauri 15, p-471)

'By obeying His order, one is acceptable

And shall then reach his Master's court."
Translation of the above)
Baptism is only the starting point towards the attainment of spiritual goal. Virtuous and religious living according to the Guru Rahit Maryada (Code of Conduct) is to be cultivated in daily practical life. The codes of conduct include spiritual awakening, conscientious performance of one's duty, humility, temperance and charity. Mere outward faith without practical adherence to the codes of conduct, will not lead the disciple towards the spiritual goal. After baptism, through constant devotion and heartfelt love to the order of the Guru in every walk of life, the disciple seeks the Guru's grace. Through submission and unconditional surrender before the Guru, the devotee is reborn in the spirit of the Guru; and only at that stage a disciple is truly called a Sikh:

> 'Guru sikh, sikh guru hai eko gur updes chalai
> Ram nam mant hirdai devai Nanak milan subhai.'
(Asa Mohalla 4, p-444)

> "The Guru is a Sikh, the Sikh is a Guru; they are both one,
> but it is the Guru who giveth instruction
> He putteth the spell of God's Name in the heart, O Nanak,
> and then God is easily obtained."
(Translation of the above)

HAUMAI (EGOISM - I-AM-NESS):

God is everywhere and within us too, but a veil of ego separates us from Him, it hides the Truth from us:

> "God, the Incomprehensible, is within us but not perceived
> For the screen the 'ego' hangs in between."
(Rag Sorath Mohalla 5, p-624)

All the five vices- lust, anger, greed, attachment and ego; are the obstructions in the way of spiritual path, but egoism is the paramount of all. In the Guru's words one of the most recurring key terms is Haumai (I-am-ness) which is regraded as synonymous with the most insidious evil. Egoism is the moral evil which is the root cause of all ill doings. This egoism is the consequence of illusion, of looking upon the individual- self as of paramount importance. All his activities are exclusively directed towards himself. "In ego he takes birth and in ego he dies," (Asa Mohalla 1, p-466). It spoils the fruit of great penances. The veil of ego when descends on a great Yogi makes him loose in a moment, whatever he had gained through self-mortification practised for years. This egoism is a disease and an obstacle in the way of spiritual uplift of an individual. **Purpose of life centers on the spiritual salvation of a man through the glorification of the Divine and imbibing Divine qualities in the process.** Blinded by the ego man cannot perceive the glory of the Divine. Therefore, Nam will not reside in the mind as long as ego is there. Nam and ego are two opposing elements:

"Haumai nawai nal virodh hai doai na vasai ek thai."
(Wadhans Mohalla 3, p-560)

Egoistic mind cannot realize the 'morals' as laid down by the Guru, thus leaving the depressed soul groping in the dark, never realizing its goal. Egoism stands in the way of the desired spiritual attainment. Guru calls egoistic man as 'Manmukh'. By the grace of the Guru, ego is burnt only through the Sabad:

"Gur kai Sabad parjaliai ta eh vicho jai."
(Bilawal ki var, Mohalla 3, p-853)

SALVATION - THE WAY TO GOD:

A body is dead without life and life itself is dead without Nam. Nam is the Elixir of life without which life would be meaningless and an accumulative waste. Forgetting Nam torments the soul. There is no spiritual awakening, no peace of mind, no joy and no bliss without Nam. Realization of Nam is the essential condition for a true and fruitful life.

"The tongue that repeateth not His Name
Better it be cut out bit by bit."
(Funhe Mohalla 5, p-1363)

Gurmat rejects all fasts, rites and rituals as a means to attain salvation. Gurmat rejects claims of yoga, mortification of body, self-torture and penances or renunciation. Gurmat does not believe in the worship of gods and goddesses, stones, statues, tombs, crematoriums, Samadhies, idols and pictures. Gurmat forbids the worship of anything of the Creation as a means to attain salvation. Only one God, the Formless, the Creator of the world is to be Glorified.

The road that leads to God is the most difficult and complex. Guru Nanak has made this road simple and as clear as crystal by showing us a technical approach. The Guru explains that since the human life is attained after passing through numerous lives, so it has gathered along the way impurities of every life it has passed through. Human mind has become black smeared with these impurities:

"The impurity of many births hath attached to man's mind, and it hath become quite black."

(Slok Mohalla 3, p-651)

As long as the human mind remains impure, it will not merge with the One Who is Absolute Pure. As the mind becomes pure, the soul will merge with the Supreme Soul. How does the mind become pure?

"Maen te dhokha ta lahai ja sifat kari ardas."

(Rag Wadhans Mohalla 1, p-557)

'Praise and prayer (to God) maketh the mind pure."

(Translation of the above)

Those who have done it, have crossed the ocean of Maya and merged with Him:

"Tu sacha sahib sifat sualio jin kiti so par piya."

(Slok Mohalla 1, p-469)

'Thou art the True Lord, Beautiful is Thy Praise;
He who utters it, is saved.'

(Translation of the above)

Explanation: If a glass is full of dirty water, pour constantly pure water into it. The constant pouring of pure water into the glass, will throw the dirty water out of the glass and ultimately the glass itself will be full of pure water.

In the same way the constant prayer and praise of God, will clean the impure mind. Human mind is in chaotic state. It is full of five vices- lust, anger, greed, attachment and pride or ego. These are the obstacles in the realization of Nam. Purity of mind is needed for spiritual uplift. No man or monk can achieve salvation without disciplining the world of inner chaos. This discipline of inner chaos by banishing these five vices from the mind, is a pre-requisite for spiritual excellence which is commanded by the Guru. Singing the Glory of the Lord, the Mighty King, will help purge the mind of its impurities. By glorifying the Divine, the human mind imbibes divine qualities in the process. As a result when all the impurities are gone, Nam will enshrine the pure mind. This will lead to exalted mental state from chaotic state. Spiritual evolution will occur resulting in Heavenly Bliss:

"Prayer and praise of God, shall give rise to Nam inside."
(Ramkali Mohalla 3-Anand, p-917)

Gurmat further states that when hands are smeared with ordinary dirt, simple water will wash it away. If urine makes the cloth dirty, ordinary water cannot wash it, only soap will clean it. Similarly when our mind is full of impurities (sins), it needs some strong detergent and that detergent is Nam:

"As hands or feet besmirched with slime,
Water washes white; As garments dark with grime,
Rinsed with soap are made light; So when sin foils the soul,
Prayer alone shall make it whole."
(Japji- pauri 20, p-4)

The effect of Prayer and Praise is, firstly all the impurities of the mind are washed away and it becomes pure; secondly as a result when the mind becomes pure, then the nectar of Nam enshrines the mind:

> "Prayer and praise of Almighty removeth the impurity of
> mind
> And the Ambrosial Nam then filleth the mind."
> (Gauri Sukhmani Mohalla 5, 1-4, p-263)

That is the stage a true devotee yearns for. By prayer and praise, one's mind comes in touch with Nam and becomes illuminated. An enlightened mind emerges and a person is reborn in the spirit of the Guru and he begins to make spiritual progress slowly. Nam is registered by the consciousness and penetrates into the human soul and mind. This glorious transformation or metamorphosis helps transcend human soul to a state of Absolute Bliss. It is a change in a person which occurs within the self from one form to another. The aspect of realization of God changes within and lifts the devotee from the Personal to the Impersonal. All boundaries, limitations and barriers are broken and the individual soul starts merging with the Supreme Soul, as water blends with water, the light blends with the Divine Light:

> "His soul and body dyed with the Name of One God
> Shall ever abide with the Supreme Soul.
> As water blendeth with water,
> So light is blended with Light.
> Transmigration is ended and rest obtained-
> Nanak is ever a sacrifice to the Lord."
> (Gauri Sukhmani Mohalla 5, 11-8, p-278)

WHAT TO MEDITATE UPON OR HOW TO DO PRAISE AND PRAYER:

A Sikh is to worship only One God and None else. But God is Formless, then what to meditate upon? During the dialogue with the Sidhas, one Yogi called Charpat asked the Guru," O Guru, you say that one should not renounce the world rather live in it but the element of Maya (materialism) is so powerful, how can one overcome it and become one with God while living in Maya itself? Please explain your logic behind it."

"The great sea of life is hard to cross, pray tell us how to
get safely across it."
(Sidh Gosht- Charpat, p-938)

Guru Nanak gave two example:

A lotus flower always floats above the surface of the water.
It cannot exist without water, yet it remains unaffected by the
waves, always rising above the water level. A duck swims in the
water but never lets its wings get wet. If its wings get wet, it will
drown and the duck knows it. Although the duck cannot live
without water, yet it disregards the waves.

In the same way a person cannot live without Maya (materialism) in the world, yet while living in it, we are to live above
Maya. Material needs are desired and are necessary to sustain the
very vital functions of life. Therefore, as a lotus flower and duck do
not drown in the water while living in it, a person should remain
detached and disinterested with Maya, not forgetting God. That is
possible through praise and prayer. Communion with Sabad (Divine
Word) will suppress the element of Maya and would enshrine
Nam within oneself which in turn would lead a person back into
the Unmanifest One:

"As a lotus flower remains unaffected in water
As also a duck swims in it and is not drenched by water
So with fixed intent on Sabad realizing Nam
O Nanak, the dreadful world ocean is crossed safely."
(Ramkali Mohalla 1, Sidh Gosht.5, p-938)

To achieve an objective in life, a complete attention and
dedication is required. The purity of mind and the sincerity of
purpose are the requisites to obtain such an object. This task
becomes more and more difficult when the object is Formless God.
When we recite Gurbani, and if we do not know the meaning of the
Sabad which is being recited, our meditation becomes mechanical,
formalistic and hence futile. The result cannot be positive. Secondly, even if we know the meaning of the Sabad, but our mind is
not in the Sabad and it keeps wandering away while we are reciting

the Sabad, the outcome will not be significant. One must, therefore, remember that Prayer with absent mindedness will not be fruitful and thereby not acceptable to the Lord ('Ardas hazuri di manzoor hundi hai'). Attentive, alert and completely untainted mind is required for meditation. **Thus whenever we read, hear or sing Gurbani (Sabad), we must put our whole ATTENTION IN THE MEANING OF THE SABAD, which is being read, heard or sung. As our attention of mind and Sabad become one, our mind starts taking the impact of the spirit of the Sabad and the result of this COMMUNION IS BLISS, PEACE AND EVERLASTING JOY.** In this communion one experiences a taste which cannot be described and is called Heavenly Elixir (Hari Ras):

> "O man, all other 'Rasas' (things of relish) thou tasteth
> Satiate not thy thirst even for a moment.
> But if thou ever tasteth the Heavenly Elixir (Hari Ras)
> Thou shalt be simply wonder-stuck."
> (Gauri Guareri Mohalla 5, p-180)

When the communion of mind with Sabad is established, the disciple is **reborn in the Spirit of the Guru.** He then blends with the Word (Sabad), and never faces death after this spiritual rebirth:

> "He who dies in the Word, never dies again
> And his devotion becometh fruitful."
> (Rag Sorath, Slok Mohalla 3, p-649)

Those who establish communion with Sabad (Gurbani - Divine Word), shall certainly experience uninterrupted Bliss:

> **"He will become holy, holy, holy, shalt undoubtedly be holy
> O Nanak, who uttereth Nam with heartfelt love."**
> **(Gauri Sukhmani Mohalla 5, 12-8, p-279)**

A FEW SABADS OF PRAISE AND PRAYER:

"Thou art the Lord, I make this supplication unto Thee;

Soul and body are all Thy gifts.
Thou art mother and father, we are Thy children;
By Thy favor we obtain many comforts.
Nobody knows Thy limit;
O God, Thou art the most Exalted of the exalted.
The whole creation is strung on Thy Will;
And must obey the orders Thou issuest.
Only Thou knowest Thine Own condition and limit;
Nanak, Thy servant, is ever a sacrifice unto Thee."

(Gauri Sukhmani Mohalla 5, IV-8, p-268)

"O Eternal, O Infinite, Imperishable, Destroyer of sins;
O Competent, O All-Pervading, Destroyer of sufferings,
Ocean of Virtues.
O Companion, O Formless, O Bodiless, Prop of all;
O World-Creator, O Treasure of attributes, in Thy court there
is always justice.
O Incomprehensible, Destroyer of sins, most remote Thou
art, wast, and shalt be;
O Constant Companion of saints, Support of supportless.
O Lord! I am Thy servant, I am virtueless, I have no merit;
Saith Nanak, grant me the gift of Thy Nam that I may engrave
it in my heart."

(Gauri Bavan Akhri Mohalla 5, 55, p-261)

"Thou art my father, Thou art my mother,
Thou art my relation, Thou art my brother,
Thou art my protector everywhere; then why should I fear O
my mind.
By Thy favor I recognize Thee;
Thou art my shelter, Thou art my honor.
Besides Thee there is none other, the whole world is the
arena of Thy play.
Men and lower animals all hast Thou created;
Thou didst appoint them to whatever duties pleaseth Thee.
Everything happens according to Thy Will, there is nothing
ours.

I have obtained great comfort by meditating on Thy Name;
And my mind is refreshed by singing Thy praises.
The perfect Guru hath congratulated me; Nanak hath over
come his difficulties."
(Majh Mohalla 5, p-103)

"Ocean of mercy, dwell for ever in my heart;
So enlighten my understanding that I may love Thee, O God.
May I obtain the dust of Thy saints' feet and apply to my
forehead;
From being a great sinner may I be purified by singing Thy
praises.
May Thine order be sweet to me, and what Thou doest please
me;
May what Thou givest, satiate me, and I may run after no one
else.
O Lord, may I ever know Thee near me, and may I remain the
dust of all men's feet;
May I meet the company of saints so that I may obtain my
God.
We are ever ever Thy children; Thou, O God, art our Master;
Nanak is Thy child, Thou art mother father: put Thy Nam in
my mouth."
(Todi Mohalla 5, p-712)

"O Lord, the Pardoner, O compassionate to the poor,
O Kinder to the saints and ever Merciful.
O Patron of the patronless, world Protector, world Sustainer,
Thou cherisheth all creatures.
O Primal Being, the Creator of the world,
Thou art the support of the souls of the devotees.
He shall become pure, whosoever repeateth Thy Name,
With devotion, affection and heartfelt love.
We are devoid of virtue, low and ignorant,
Nanak seeketh Thy protection O Supreme Power."
(Gauri Sukhmani Mohalla 5, 20-7, p-290)

PILGRIMAGES- Bathing at Holy Places:

A great deal of emphasis on rituals had been the way of Indian religious life for the millions before Guru Nanak appeared on the scene. Wherever Guru Nanak went, he tried to emancipate the masses from the shackles of superstition and ignorance, and instil faith in One All-Pervading and Formless God. At that time people believed that bathing in the river Ganges and other holy places would absolve them of their sins. The Guru asserted that mere bathing at these sacred places, would not cleanse the mind riddled with the impurity of egoism.

"Tirath bharmas biadh na jawai
Nam bina kaise sukh pawai."
(Ramkali Mohalla 1, p-906)
'Wandering through the pilgrim places,
One is not rid of one's maladies.
There can be no peace without Nam.'
(Translation of the above)

The Guru stressed that no abiding peace could be achieved without meditating on Divine Name. Meditation on Nam is the only true pilgrimage:

"Tirath nahvan jao tirath nam hai
Tirath sabad vichar unter gian hai."
(Dhanasri Mohalla 1, p-687)

'Shall we go to bathe at the pilgrim places?
No. Nam is the only true pilgrimage.
Pilgrimage is the contemplation on the Word
That gives inner spiritual light.'
(Translation of the above)

The Guru emphasizes the futility of rushing to the sacred bathing places for the expiation of sins. Guru Nanak states in Japji that he would bathe at the spots considered sacred, if it could please the Lord. The implication is that such ceremonies by themselves would not win God's approbation, without cultivating the moral life:

"If it pleaseth the Lord
I would bathe at the sacred places.
If it pleaseth Him not Worthless is that pilgrimage.
I see in the whole world around
That nothing can be gained without right action."

(Japji, pauri-6)

In another place, the Guru has compared those who bathe at the sacred places to attain merit, with jars full of poison, which are washed only from outside. It means that the evil inside a man, cannot be removed despite outward ritual performances.

CASTE SYSTEM AND SOCIAL EQUALITY:

In an age when class distinction was very rigid and when the bonds of caste system in India had strictly divided the people, Guru Nanak taught equality and brotherhood. The Guru rose above rites and rituals, above creeds and conventions, above all national-cults and all race-cults, to a vision of the deeds of love. He preached a religion of love, sacrifice and service. Complete equality among men was declared by the Sikh Gurus to be the fundamental moral principle required to regulate the social relations and communication.

The Guru points out that there is no fundamental difference among men of different castes in terms of physical constitution. In a polemical discussion with the Brahmans, Kabir inquires:

"How are you a Brahman and I am a low caste?
Is it that I have blood in my veins and you have milk?"

(Gauri Kabir p-324)

This exposes the absurdity of any contention or a claim by the higher caste men that there are physical differences among men of the different castes.

The Guru points out that the laws of nature do no react differently in respect to the higher caste men. Since the nature makes no discrimination in favor of the higher caste men by recognizing their superiority in any manner, the myth of caste superiority is clearly seen as man-made. The Guru states:

> "What merit is in caste?
> The real truth is that he who tastes the poison will die."
> (Var Majh, Mohalla 1, p-142)

The Guru vehemently regards caste as an abnormality and social perversity when he says:

> "Every one says there are four castes, but it is from God that
> every one comes;
> The same is the clay which fashions the whole world;
> The five elements make up the body's form, and who can say
> who has less of these or who has more?"
> (Rag Bhairon Mohalla 3, p-1128)

The Guru denies that caste was prevalent from the beginning. In the primordial state:

> "No man of caste or birth could be seen ....
> There was no distinction of color or coat or of the Brahman
> or Kashatriya......."
> (Maru Mohalla 1, p-1035-36)

The claim that the different caste men had emanated from the different parts of the Primeval Man is also repudiated by the Guru:

> "His caste is castelessness. He is incarnated not, He is Self-
> Existent.......
> All hearts are illuminated by the Light of the Lord...."
> (Sorath Mohalla 1, 1-2 of 6, p-597)

The Guru, thus, refuses to accredit the caste institution in social ethics and further denies God having favored a few by bringing them out from the higher parts of His body. (These were some of the arguments of the Brahmans to have superiority from birth over low castes).

Finally it is held by the Guru that the caste is of no consideration in the spiritual realization, that men of lower caste need not wait to be born again in the next higher class for the attainment of deliverance:

"Tumra jan jat avijata har japio patat pavichhe."
(Basant Mohalla 4, p-1178)

'Whosoever contemplates on God, caste or no caste,
he becomes a blessed devotee of God."
(Translation of the above)

The tenth Master, Guru Gobind Singh, declared caste a taboo in the order of the Khalsa. In Akal Ustat, he states," There is no consideration of caste or membership of varnas." He further writes,"I shall not adopt the habits of any creed, but shall sow the seeds of the pure love of God." (Vachitar Natak, chap. 6, verse 34). The first of the Sikhs baptized into the order of the Khalsa belonged to different castes. The theory of separate duties for different castes was replaced by the same ethical and religious duties for all men. Therefore, the fundamental equality of all men was ensured by free and voluntary admission into the order of the Khalsa.

Social Equality:

Wealth also provides a determinant of social classes as against birth in the case of caste system. In Sikhism the relation among classes based on economic resources is envisaged in terms of equality. It rejects the notion of superiority of the economically better placed class over others. The Guru says:

"The man who knoweth God looketh on all men as equal,
As the wind bloweth on the commoner and the king alike."
(Gauri Sukhmani Mohalla 5, 8-1, p-272)

Thus in Sikhism the higher classes are not governed by any separate code of ethics, but all men, rich or poor, are entitled to equal judgement, value and social equality. Since the death is the leveller, the Guru highlights this notion:

"One lives not for ever in the world;
Neither king nor beggar would remain, they all come and
go."
(Ramkali Mohalla 1, 11, p-931)

Therefore improper consideration of the superiority of rank are
based on a wrong conception of the nature of the world. The need
for the recognition of human dignity, irrespective of economic
classes, is also stressed in an anecdote from the biography of Guru
Nanak called the story of Bhai Lalo and Malik Bhago. In that
incident Guru Nanak refused a rather sumptuous dinner of Malik
Bhago for the ordinary bread of the coarse grain of Bhai Lalo. The
moral is drawn that the poor ought not to be treated as low, all
must be treated as equal irrespective of their material resources.

STATUS OF WOMEN:

The position of a woman in the society in India, has not
been always the same. While at times she had been accorded a very
high status, there are also historical and scriptural instances when
under some influences, she has been relegated to an inferior
position. At the start of Sikhism the status of women was very low
in Indian society.

In Sikhism it is considered preposterous to regard woman
a 'temptress' or 'seductress' or 'unclean'. The Guru does not regard
'woman' as an obstruction on the way to ultimate goal of Eternal
Bliss. This being so, the Guru rejects asceticism or renunciation as
the requisite pathway, and regards the house-holder's life if it is led
in a righteous manner, superior to that of an ascetic. By emphasizing this type of vision to the people, the Guru stresses that women
should be given honorable status in every social segment of the
society. Guru Nanak asserted that women were not at all inferior
to men:

"From the woman is our birth, in the woman's womb are we
shaped;
To the woman we are engaged, to the woman we are wedded;
The woman is our friend and from the woman is the family;

If one woman dies, we seek another, through the woman are
the bonds of the world;
Why call woman evil who gives birth to kings?
From the woman comes the woman, without woman there is
none;
O Nanak, God alone is the one Who is independent of the
woman (because He is unborn)."
(Var Asa Mohalla 1, 2-19, p-473)

This declaration shows unequivocally the high esteem in which a woman's status is held in Sikhism. Woman 'the mother of mighty heroes' is elevated to the highest position in the hierarchy of beings.

In the moral codes of the Sikhs a large number of injunctions deal with the rejection of unethical practices like-(i) female infanticide; (ii) immolation of the widow (Sati) with the deceased husband, and (iii) wearing of veils by women. In the ancient period in India, it was stated according to spiritual authority that self-immolation on the funeral pyre of her husband was the only meritorious course that a virtuous woman could follow; not only would such a woman enjoy eternal bliss in heaven along with her husband, but her action would expiate the sins of three generations of her husband's family both on his father's and mother's side[2].

Guru Amar Das, the third Master, carried out a vigorous campaign against this practice of Sati, and thereby he emancipated the women from this social oppression and religious cruelty. The Guru declared that "the Sati is one who lives contented and embellishes herself with good conduct, and cherishes the Lord ever and calls on Him." (Rag Suhi, Slok Mohalla 3, 2-6, p-787)

One of the most notable social improvement was the emancipation of women. Many women found salvation through the Guru's teachings. In Sikhism widow remarriage is also permitted whereby the widow can be rehabilitated if she so desires.

2:R.C. Majumdar- *British Paramountcy and Indian Renaissance, p-823._*

INSTITUTIONS OF SANGAT AND PANGAT:

SANGAT- Society of the Holy:

Sangat means assembly or congregation, but in Sikhism Sangat is usually called Sat Sangat (holy congregation) which may be defined as the Home of Truth where people love God and learn to live in Him:

"Sat Sangat kaisi janiai jithai eko nam vakhaniai."
(Sri Rag Mohalla 1, p-72)

'How should we know of Sat Sangat?
Where the lovers of Truth hold communion with One Lord
alone.'
(Translation of the above)

Again the fourth Guru gives definition of Sangat:

"Sat Sangat is the school of the True Guru,
There we learn to love God and appreciate His greatness."
(Var Kanra Mohalla 4, p-1313)

Guru Nanak attached great importance to the setting up of Sangats, the holy assemblies, and wherever he went, he tried to establish them. The Divine Word (Gurbani) and the Sat Sangat were the only two means that the Guru employed to rid the people of their selfishness and evil passions; and finally for their salvation and for uniting them with God:

"Sat Sangat is the treasury of Divine Name;
There we meet God;
Through the Grace of Guru,
One receives there Light and all darkness is dispelled."
(Sarang ki Var, Mohalla 1, p-1244)

It is well recognized fact that spiritual progress cannot be achieved without the company of the Holy. The society of the holy is the means of destroying egoism and helps one in freeing oneself from evil passions:

"The dirt of egoism of ages which has soiled the soul,
Will be removed only in the Society of the Holy.
Just as iron floats when tied to timber
So will one cross the ocean of life by following
The Guru's Word in the company of the saints."
(Kanra Mohalla 4, p-1309)

"O friend, tell me how I might cross
Through the difficult ocean of Maya;
If God in His mercy gives the fellowship of the Truthful
Nanak, Maya cannot come even near."
(Bavan Akhri Mohalla 5,(7), p-251)

Wherever Guru Nanak went, the Sikhs built Gurdwara (house of the Guru) and met there every day and formed into a regular Sangat. From the time of the third Master, Guru Amar Das, it was felt that the Sikhs should have their own seats of religion. He founded the town of Chak Ram Das which subsequently got its present name, Amritsar; and he got a Bawli (a well with staircase reaching down to the water surface) constructed at Goindwal. The fourth and fifth Masters also evinced great interest in building up new religious centers for their followers such as Amritsar, Kartarpur etc. These religious centers formed a great cementing force for the rising Sikh community. The Sikh Sangats from far and near used to visit these centers and had the opportunity not only meeting the Holy Guru and having his blessings, but also coming into close contact with one another. During their visit they were provided with free accommodation and free food. Simron (participation in daily religious service) and seva (participation in the community projects and Guru ka Langar, kitchen) were the two major constituents of the daily routine of the visiting Sikhs. These close contacts formed the bases of a well-integrated Sikh organization.

The process of integration of Sikhism went hand in hand with the enlargement of its ranks. During the time of the third Guru, there were twenty-two manjis and fifty-two piris, which were all big and small centers for the spread of Sikh religion in the country. Guru Ram Das, the fourth Master, established a new order of missionaries called Masands. This new order was reorganized and elaborated by the fifth Guru. As the number of new Sikh Sangats grew larger in the country, the mode of initiation of prospective Sikhs through the ceremony of Charanpauhal (Charanamrit) was allowed to all authorized missionaries. Although the ideal Charanamrit was the one administered by the Guru himself, since it was not possible for the Guru to be present physically everywhere, the authority of initiation was delegated to local missionaries. The bulk of the people who came to the fold of Sikhism as a result of the above efforts, were drawn from the commercial classes mostly dwelling in the towns. During the period of the fifth Guru, the movement became popular in the country side also, with the result that a large number of Majha Jats embraced Sikhism.

Finances are most necessary for the success of any movement. In the beginning, the voluntary offerings of the devotees were sufficient. When big projects were undertaken, the existing practice was found inadequate. In order to meet the situation, the masands were required not merely to concentrate on the dissemination of Sikh teachings, but also to collect voluntary offerings from the faithful and to bring them to the headquarters of the Guru.

In the very beginning Sikh sangat was merely a religious gathering of devotees, functioning more or less in isolation. Gradually there was an increase in its functions. Preparation of copies of holy scripture, the building up of certain religious centers, institutions of Manjis and Masands as the agencies of the central leadership and the assertion of the principle of the supremacy of the Guru, all these factors were common links in uniting one to another. Therefore, the isolation of one from another was lessened. The movement continued till it culminated in the creation of the Khalsa aimed at a well-balanced combination of the ideals of Bhakti and Shakti, of moral and spiritual excellence and militant valour or heroism of the highest order. A day before he left this world, Guru Gobind Singh made the historic announcement abolishing the line of personal Guruship and conferring the powers of deliberation upon the Khalsa. With the foundation of the Khalsa, the network of semi-integrated Sangats was fully integrated. The investing of Khalsa with supreme power, marked the completion of this long process of about two and a half centuries.

Any one irrespective of caste, creed and cline can become a

member of the Sangat. All services can be performed by the Sikh and non-Sikh devotees except the functions of baptism which can only be performed by the ordained Khalsa who has lived up to the ideals. Sangat is not merely a gathering of worshippers nor is it just a forum for seeking personal salvation and blessedness, but it has stood for the total re-orientation of life of the individuals and society towards a creative purposeful existence. Sangat was considered to be so important that even the Gurus used to submit to the decisions of it. Guru Arjan did not marry his son to Chandu's daughter because Sangat had decided against it. Sangat can be a small unit but in its Totality, it is called Panth- The Holy Way of Life.

PANGAT- Guru's Free Kitchen known as Langar:

Another institution, that of Pangat or Langar (free common messing), organized almost simultaneously with that of Sangat. It was initiated by Guru Nanak and its consolidation and extension was affected by the third Guru. The rules of the Langar require that all should sit in the same row and partake of the same food without any distinction of high or low, rich or poor, and prince or the peasant. It was the injunction of Guru Amar Das that none could have his audience unless he had eaten in the Langar. When the Raja of Haripur or even Emperor Akbar, came to see the Guru, they had to sit with other common people and dine together with them before the Master gave consent to see them. In this way the people were made to renounce their social prejudices. Common kitchen also served as a medium of social integration.

The institution of Pangat imparted a secular dimension to the Sangat. Most importantly it translated the principle of equality into practice, and it also served as a cementing force among the followers of Sikhism. This institution provides safeguard against the immoral social practice of untouchability which is a by-product of the caste system.

This institution is run with the help and contributions of all and not by any one particular person or class of persons. The free kitchen where prince and peasant could mess together, fostered a spirit of charity on a large scale and also became a powerful binding force.

UNIVERSAL BROTHERHOOD:

The ideal of social equality is not the ultimate aim of the ethics of Sikhism. This equality may be maintained without feeling any affection or regard for each other, but such bare equality would not be enough because it does not conform to the ideal of humanistic morality. Hence in order to make it whole, it should be saturated with the idea of spiritual unity of mankind. The Guru stated:

"As out of a single fire, millions of sparks arise; arise in separation but come together again when they fall back in the fire. As from a heap of dust, grains of dust sweep up and fill the air, and filling it fall in a heap of dust. As out   of single stream, countless waves rise up and being water,   fall back in water again. So from God's form emerge alive and inanimate things and since they arise from Him, they shall fall in Him again."

(Guru Gobind Singh- Akal Ustat)

This means that every human being deserves to be treated as a member of the same human brotherhood. The fellow human being is not an 'other'. The Guru says:

"Meeting with the Guru, I have abandoned the sense of the otherness."

(Bhiro Mohalla 5, 1-29-42, p-1148)

The other is in fact not an 'other' but a co-sharer of the same source of emanation and a part of the same spiritual order. This sense of brotherhood of humanity is, thus, linked together by bonds deeper than family, social or national affinities. This brotherhood of mankind in terms of God being the common father is stressed by the Guru:

"Thou art the father of us all.......all are the partners, Thou art alien to none."

(Majh Mohalla 5, p-97)

The Guru is pointing to the common bonds of existence in the world:

"Air is the Guru, water is father, great earth the mother;
In the lap of two nurses, night and day, the whole world is
brought up."
(Japji, Slok, p-8)

According to the Guru, the brotherhood is the reality but it is hidden from us by the veil of houmai (I-am-ness or individuation). Houmai is the dirt over our mind which it has gathered during the process of transmigration. Once this dirt over our mind is removed and the veil of houmai (I-am-ness) is felled, the relationship across the human lines becomes a clear reality. As long as our minds remain under veil of I-am-ness, our understanding will continue to be hollow and away from reality. How do we clean our mind?

As mentioned before the Guru gives direction how to clean the mind:

"Only through praise and prayer to God
Mind will become pure."
(Wadhans Mohalla 1, p-557)

Once mind becomes pure, it attains a spiritual height in which reality opens up and all delusion is gone and then sense of universal brotherhood prevails:

"There is One father of us all
And we are children of the same father."
(Sorath Mohalla 5, p-611)

"I am neither a Hindu nor a Muslim;
The soul and body belong to God whether He be called
Allhah or Ram."
(Bhairo Mohalla 5, p-1136)

"O eyes of mine, God infused light unto you, look at none but

God;
Look at none but God; look on Him intently.
All this world which you behold is God's image; God's
                        image appeareth in it.
When by the Guru's grace I received understanding,
I saw that God was One, and that there was none besides.
Saith Nanak, these eyes were blind, but on meeting the true
                Guru they obtained divine light."
                    (Ramkali Mohalla 3, Anand-36, p-922)

Once by the grace of the Guru, our heart is filled with divine light, then there is no 'other', there is no enmity, no hatred, but it is all altruism and service for the brotherhood of mankind. In the practical experience we find an example of Bhai Ghanaya. In the battlefield Bhai Ghanaya was on duty to serve water to the thirsty. He was found serving water to the Sikhs as well as to the Hindus and Muslims alike. The Sikhs complained to the Guru that Bhai Ghanaya was serving water to the enemy soldiers who after getting water, became afresh and fought against them. The Guru sent for him and asked him what the Sikhs had complained. Bhai Ghanaya replied," O true king, I do not see who is a friend and who is a foe. I see your image in every one of them alike. I saw that they were all your Sikhs and none else and so I served water to every one of them."

This is the desired mental stage commanded by the Guru when a person's mind is lifted above the lines of religion, color, race or national entity; and the sense of real universal brotherhood is born:

"There is no enemy, none is 'other',
A sense of universal brotherhood has come to me."
                        (Kanra Mohalla 5, p-1299)

Sikhism believes in it, stands for it and takes practical measures to realize it. There are numerous examples in the Sikh history to emphasize this fact.

Guru Nanak travelled for fourteen years on foot and he covered the area from Assam Hills in the east of India to as far as Iran and Iraq in the west; from Tibet in the north to Ceylon in the south. During this long journey he went to various famous Hindu temples and their learning centers, Maths of Sidhas, and the various centers of Mohammadans including Mecca, and delivered the Divine Message (brotherhood of mankind and Fatherhood of God) for which he came to this world. Never he asked any one to become his disciple in order to go to heaven. He rather held guarantee to the entire humanity that if a person, irrespective of race, color, caste, creed, sex, religion or nationality, meditated on God, the Formless One, would get deliverance:

> "Jo jo japai so hoai punit
> Bhagat bhai lavai manhit."
> (Gauri Sukhmani Mohalla 5, 20-7, p-290)

> 'He shall become pure, whosoever repeateth His Name
> With devotion, affection and heartfelt love."
> (Translation of the above)

Sikhism fully stands for universal brotherhood in word and in spirit. Every Sikh living in every corner of the world when he prays in the morning and in the evening, ends his prayer by saying:

"By Thy Grace, may every one be blessed in the world."

PICTURES OF THE GURUS:

Some artists have painted imaginary pictures of all the ten Gurus. Have these artists ever seen the Gurus? One can find these pictures hanging in almost all the Gurdwaras and in the majority of the Sikh homes. The irony of fate is that many of the Sikhs place garlands of flowers upon these pictures and also burn incense in front of them. Is it not idol (picture) worship? How can we call this Gurmat? In Zafarnama which Guru Gobind Singh wrote to Emperor Aurangzeb, he mentioned about hill Rajas, "They worshipped idols, and I was an idol-breaker.." While the Guru was an idol-breaker, his so called Sikhs have now become idol (picture) worshippers!

From Guru Nanak to Guru Gobind Singh, emphasis was

laid to worship only one God, the Formless, and they strongly forbade the worship of idols, crematoriums, Samadhies, tombs etc. etc. These picture worshippers quote the following verses of Gurbani in support of their action:

> 'Gur ki murat man meh dhyan.'
>
> (Gaund Mohalla 5, p-864)

> 'Worship Guru's picture in mind.'
>
> (Translation of the above)

> 'Satgur ki murat hirdai vasai.'
>
> (Dhanasri Mohalla 1, p-661)

What is GURU and what is Guru's MURAT (picture)?

As explained earlier in this book, according to Gurbani Guru is not body (deh), Guru is Jot (Divine Light) and Guru's murat (picture) is the Divine Word (Gurbani):

> 'Jot roop har aap gur nanak kahaio.'
>
> (Swayas Bhattan p-1408)

The Gurmat (Guru's teaching) explains that true Guru is not a physical body and therefore the body is not considered to be worthy of any kind of worship:

> 'Satgur niranjan soi
> Manukh ka kar roop na jan.'
>
> (Ramkali Mohalla 5, p-895)

Therefore, the meaning of "Gur ki murat man meh dhayan" is clearly not the worship of Guru's picture but to put attention in the meaning of the Sabad (Word). Gurbani confirms that by seeing Guru's physical body, salvation cannot be attained:

> 'Satgur no sabh ko vekhda jeta jagat sansar
> Didhai mukat na hovai jichar sabad na kare vichar.'
>
> (Slok Mohalla 3, p-594)

If by seeing Guru's body one can get salvation, then Mehta Kaluji would not have slapped his son, Guru Nanak. Since the father had seen the Guru, he should have attained salvation. Instead history has recorded that Mehta Kaluji could not see the Divine Light in his son and continued slapping him. If by seeing Guru's body one can get salvation, both sons, Sri Chand and Lakhmi Das, would not have disobeyed the Guru, their father. The executioner who was pouring hot sand over the naked body of Guru Arjan, would not have done that, because he had seen the Guru and should have gotten salvation. The executioner would not have severed the head of Guru Tegh Bahadur, because he had seen the Guru. **Therefore, when the Guru Jot was in human body even then the mere sight of the Guru's physical body did not give salvation to any one, how can these Fake Pictures salvage us?** They can only derail us from the true prescribed path of Gurmat.

In Tavparsad Swayas the Guru describes that those who worship the idols are 'Pas' (animal like):

"Kou butan ko pujat hai 'pas' kou butan ko pujan dhayo."

Translation:

'Some worshipping stones put them on their heads,
        some hang lingams from their necks;
Some see God in the south,
        some bow their heads to the west;
Some fools worship idols, others busy themselves with
        worshipping the dead;
The whole world entangled in false ceremonies hath
        not found God's secret.'
                    (Guru Gobind Singh- Tavparsad Swayas)

Some Sikhs are also wearing necklaces with Guru's picture around their necks. Is it Gurmat? This is totally manmat,this is perverseness. Guru is not an idol. Guru is not a picture. Guru is not a human body. After he breathed his last, none could find Guru Nanak's body. Therefore Guru is JOT. Guru is Divine Light. Guru is All-pervading Divine Spirit. Guru is Divine Word (Gurbani). To garland the fake and imaginary pictures of the Gurus is totally anti-Gurmat. How can we have Guru's blessings when we act against the very dictum of the Guru?

The Impersonal Absolute cannot be installed as an image. He has no form and, thus, cannot be described through symbols. Such actions in themselves would not win Guru's approbation. Without total allegiance to the Guru's order, Sikh faith would be burried deep under a heap of senseless dogmas, meaningless rituals and ceremonial acts.

Sikhism is not a dogma but a way of life lived according to Guru Rahit Maryada (code of conduct). A Sikh has to hold his Guru's word as paramount in his daily existence. Without glorifying His presence in one's existence, life will be contaminated and polluted and will be in deplorable state which will lead to spiritual degeneration. Deep and continuous contemplation on Nam is needed and is indispensable for the exalted state of Sikh character. Nam is neither a philosophy nor knowledge to be gained from books. It dwells within and is realized from within through the grace of the true Guru (Gurbani-Divine Word). Let the following be our daily supplication:

> "O my friend, the Divine Guru!
> Illuminate my mind with the Name Divine!
> Let the Name revealed to me by the Guru be my
> life-companion;
> And singing Thy Glory be my daily routine."
> (Rag Gujri Mohalla 4, p-10)

BIBLIOGRAPHY

PUNJABI

1. Guru Granth Sahib
2. Bhai Gurdas- Varan
3. Bhai Vir Singh-Santhia Sri Guru Granth Sahib
4. Dr. Kartar Singh-Sikh Fundamentals
5. Prof. Sahib Singh-Jiwan Britant of the Gurus

ENGLISH

6. Archer, John Clark-The Sikhs
7. Avtar SIngh-Ethics of the Sikhs
8. Gandhi, Surjeet Singh-History of the Sikh Gurus
9. Harbans Singh-Perspectives on Guru Nanak
10. Kohli S.S.-Outline of Sikh Thought
11. Macauliffe., M.A.-The Sikh Religion Vol. 1-6
12. Ranbir Singh-Glimpses of the Divine Masters
13. Ranbir Singh-The Sikh Way of Life
14. Sikhism-Fauja Singh, Trilochan Singh,
           Gurbachan Singh Talib, J.P.Singh Oberoi
           Sohan Singh